HATE CRIMES

Other Books in the Current Controversies Series:

HATE CRIMES

David Bender, *Publisher*
Bruno Leone, *Executive Editor*

Scott Barbour, *Managing Editor*
Brenda Stalcup, *Senior Editor*

Paul A. Winters, *Book Editor*

CURRENT CONTROVERSIES

Cover Photo: Andrew Lichtenstein/Impact Visuals

Library of Congress Cataloging-in-Publication Data

Hate crimes / Paul A. Winters, book editor.
    p. cm. — (Current controversies)
    Includes bibliographical references and index.
    ISBN 1-56510-373-4 (lib. bdg. : alk. paper). — ISBN 1-56510-372-6
    (pbk. : alk. paper)
    1. Hate crimes—United States. 2. Hate crimes—Government
policy—United States. 3. Hate speech—United States. I. Winters, Paul
A., 1965-   . II. Series.
HV6250.4.E75H37 1996
364.1—dc20
                                    95-23817
                                      CIP

Contents

Chapter 2: Should Racist Hate Speech Be Limited?

Yes: Hate Speech Should Be Limited

No: Special Penalties Should Not Apply to Hate Crimes

Chapter 4: Are Certain Groups Responsible for Promoting Hate and Violence?

founded on the right to bear arms and the tradition of local self-defense, are conscientiously weeding out extremists and hatemongers.

Foreword

By definition, controversies are "discussions of questions in which opposing opinions clash" (Webster's Twentieth Century Dictionary Unabridged). Few would deny that controversies are a pervasive part of the human condition and exist on virtually every level of human enterprise. Controversies transpire between individuals and among groups, within nations and between nations. Controversies supply the grist necessary for progress by providing challenges and challengers to the status quo. They also create atmospheres where strife and warfare can flourish. A world without controversies would be a peaceful world; but it also would be, by and large, static and prosaic.

The Series' Purpose

The purpose of the Current Controversies series is to explore many of the social, political, and economic controversies dominating the national and international scenes today. Titles selected for inclusion in the series are highly focused and specific. For example, from the larger category of criminal justice, Current Controversies deals with specific topics such as police brutality, gun control, white collar crime, and others. The debates in Current Controversies also are presented in a useful, timeless fashion. Articles and book excerpts included in each title are selected if they contribute valuable, long-range ideas to the overall debate. And wherever possible, current information is enhanced with historical documents and other relevant materials. Thus, while individual titles are current in focus, every effort is made to ensure that they will not become quickly outdated. Books in the Current Controversies series will remain important resources for librarians, teachers, and students for many years.

In addition to keeping the titles focused and specific, great care is taken in the editorial format of each book in the series. Book introductions and chapter prefaces are offered to provide background material for readers. Chapters are organized around several key questions that are answered with diverse opinions representing all points on the political spectrum. Materials in each chapter include opinions in which authors clearly disagree as well as alternative opinions in which authors may agree on a broader issue but disagree on the possible solutions. In this way, the content of each volume in Current Controversies mirrors the mosaic of opinions encountered in society. Readers will quickly realize that there are many viable answers to these complex issues. By questioning each author's conclusions, students and casual readers can begin to develop the critical thinking skills so important to evaluating opinionated material.

Current Controversies is also ideal for controlled research. Each anthology in the series is composed of primary sources taken from a wide gamut of informational categories including periodicals, newspapers, books, United States and foreign government documents, and the publications of private and public organizations. Readers will find factual support for reports, debates, and research papers covering all areas of important issues. In addition, an annotated table of contents, an index, a book and periodical bibliography, and a list of organizations to contact are included in each book to expedite further research.

Perhaps more than ever before in history, people are confronted with diverse and contradictory information. During the Persian Gulf War, for example, the public was not only treated to minute-to-minute coverage of the war, it was also inundated with critiques of the coverage and countless analyses of the factors motivating U.S. involvement. Being able to sort through the plethora of opinions accompanying today's major issues, and to draw one's own conclusions, can be a complicated and frustrating struggle. It is the editors' hope that Current Controversies will help readers with this struggle.

"The [Anti-Defamation League] has promoted a model hate-crime statute that increases punishment for criminals who victimize others 'by reason of . . . race, religion, national origin or sexual orientation.'"

Introduction

On June 21, 1990, a group of white teenage skinheads broke into the fenced yard of the sole black family living in their St. Paul, Minnesota, neighborhood and burned a crudely made cross. This incendiary act of vandalism became the focus of a fiery debate on the constitutionality of hate-crime laws—laws that target for special punishment violent acts motivated by bigotry. On one side of the debate are civil rights groups such as the Anti-Defamation League (ADL), which feels that hate crimes are especially harmful because they intimidate whole communities, "causing them to feel isolated, vulnerable, and unprotected by the law." Since 1981, the ADL has promoted a model hate-crime statute that increases punishment for criminals who victimize others "by reason of . . . race, religion, national origin or sexual orientation" or who vandalize religious buildings, schools, or cemeteries. On the other side of the debate are civil libertarians—among them Nat Hentoff, a columnist for several liberal publications—who believe that punishing bigotry violates the First Amendment's protection of free speech. Hentoff maintains that adding extra penalties for bigoted motives to crimes of violence or vandalism punishes thoughts, beliefs, and speech. Over the three years that followed the St. Paul cross-burning incident, the battle over hate-crime laws was waged first in a number of state supreme courts and eventually in the U.S. Supreme Court.

R.A.V. v. City of St. Paul

Among the teenagers arrested for the June 1990 cross burning was seventeen-year-old Robert A. Viktora, who was charged with and convicted of violating St. Paul's Bias-Motivated Crime Ordinance. The ordinance banned the display of any symbol, "including but not limited to a burning cross or Nazi swastika, [that] arouses anger, alarm, or resentment in others on the basis of race, color, creed, religion, or gender." But Viktora appealed his conviction to a Minnesota district court, claiming that the law violated his right to free speech. The district court agreed with the appeal, formally called *R.A.V. v. City of St. Paul*, and overturned Viktora's conviction and struck down the law on two grounds. First, the court said that the St. Paul ordinance was too broad, since it could apply to any act that angered someone else. Second, it ruled that the First Amendment prevented St. Paul from banning cross burning as a form of expression. The court cited a 1989 U.S. Supreme Court decision, *Dallas, Texas v. Gregory Johnson*, which ruled that flag burning was protected by the First Amendment.

In that case, the Supreme Court had ruled that Dallas could not outlaw the burning of the American flag simply because it disliked the unpatriotic message implied by the act. Likewise, the district court ruled that St. Paul could not outlaw cross burning on the grounds that it opposed bigotry.

But the case did not end there. The city of St. Paul appealed to the Minnesota Supreme Court, which upheld the law by saying that cross burning was not a form of speech that deserved First Amendment protection. The Minnesota court ruled that the St. Paul law was not overly broad because it applied only to "fighting words," words which would provoke a reasonable person to violence. Fighting words were the subject of a 1942 U.S. Supreme Court decision, *Chaplinsky v. New Hampshire*, which stated that words "which by their very utterance inflict injury or tend to incite an immediate breach of the peace" are not protected by the First Amendment. In the Minnesota court's opinion, St. Paul could ban cross burning as a form of fighting words regardless of the message it expressed. The court argued that St. Paul had a "compelling interest in protecting the community against bias-motivated threats to public safety and order" which outweighed the First Amendment's protection of expressions of bias.

The U.S. Supreme Court next took up the case and on June 22, 1992, reversed the decision of the Minnesota court. The Supreme Court justices unanimously agreed that the St. Paul law was too broad, rejecting the argument that it would only be applied to fighting words. But they sharply disagreed on St. Paul's right to ban cross burning as an expression of racial bias. Justice Antonin Scalia, writing the Court's decision in the case, argued that the First Amendment precisely forbids discrimination by governments against certain viewpoints and so forbids St. Paul from outlawing expressions of racial hatred. He claimed that "the only interest distinctively served by [the St. Paul law] is that of displaying the City Council's special hostility towards the particular biases" against race, color, creed, religion, or gender; therefore, he concluded, the law violated the First Amendment. In an addendum disagreeing with Scalia's argument, Justice John Paul Stevens contended that because cross burning as an expression of racial hatred is particularly harmful it could be singled out for special penalties. "Conduct that creates special risks or causes special harms may be prohibited by special rules," he asserted. Stevens added that extending First Amendment protection to cross burning gives it more protection than some other forms of speech (such as commercial advertising) that are regulated yet still considered legitimate.

State of Wisconsin v. Todd Mitchell

The decision in the Minnesota case had an immediate impact on hate-crime cases in other states. On the day following the ruling, the Wisconsin Supreme Court cited Scalia's opinion as it struck down Wisconsin's hate-crime statute in the case formally known as *State of Wisconsin v. Todd Mitchell*. The case began in October 1989, when Todd Mitchell, a black nineteen-year-old, and a group of his friends were discussing *Mississippi Burning*, a controversial movie about Ku Klux Klan terrorism in the 1960s. Catching sight of a young white boy, Mitchell said to his friends, "You all want to fuck somebody up? There goes a white boy! Go get him!" Members of the group then attacked the white fourteen-year-old, beating him so severely that he was left in a coma for four days. Although he did not participate in the beating, Mitchell was tried and convicted of felony aggravated battery and received a sentence of two years. And because the court determined that his crime was motivated by hate, he received an additional two years under Wisconsin's Penalty Enhancement Statute. The statute, based on the ADL's model hate-crime law, provides increased penalties for a crime when the victim is intentionally selected because of "the race, religion, color, disability, sexual orientation, national origin or ancestry of that person."

Claiming that the extra punishment violated his right to free speech, Mitchell appealed the increased sentence. On June 23, 1992, the Wisconsin court overturned Mitchell's enhanced sentence (by this time he had already served the original two years) and nullified the penalty enhancement statute on the grounds that it violated First Amendment protection of speech. Using the decision in *R.A.V.* as a guide, the Wisconsin court ruled that the increased sentence punished Mitchell for his racial bias: The statute "violates the First Amendment directly by punishing what the [Wisconsin] legislature has deemed to be offensive thought." The court argued that Mitchell would not have received the additional sentence had he selected a black victim instead of a white one.

The state of Wisconsin appealed this decision to the U.S. Supreme Court, which on June 11, 1993, reversed the Wisconsin court's ruling. The justices of the Court unanimously agreed that the penalty enhancement approach did not violate the First Amendment. Chief Justice William Rehnquist, writing the opinion, argued that penalty enhancement punished conduct and not speech: Unlike the Minnesota law struck down in *R.A.V.*, the Wisconsin statute punished the act of choosing a victim based on race and not the racial bias itself. "Moreover, the Wisconsin statute singles out for enhancement bias inspired conduct because this conduct is thought to inflict greater individual and societal harm," Rehnquist maintained. Because of the greater harm involved, he argued, greater penalties could be applied.

The ADL applauded the Supreme Court ruling in *Wisconsin v. Mitchell* as an affirmation of its model hate-crime statute. "Hate crimes laws are necessary, because the failure to recognize and effectively address this type of crime can cause an isolated incident to fester and explode into widespread community tension," the ADL proclaimed. The nature of hate crimes makes them more harmful to society than ordinary crimes and so they warrant enhanced penalties, the organization argues. But civil libertarian Nat Hentoff disagrees with the Court's ruling, arguing that hate crimes are no more harmful than other violent crimes. "Wouldn't it have been just as outrageous if the assailants [in the Mitchell case] had beaten a fourteen-year-old black boy?" he asks. Enhanced penalties punish bigoted thoughts and therefore violate the First Amendment, Hentoff maintains.

By the end of 1994, according to the ADL, thirty-five states as well as the federal government had enacted hate-crime laws that follow the penalty-enhancement approach upheld by the Supreme Court in June 1993. The effectiveness and constitutionality of such laws are among the issues debated in *Hate Crimes: Current Controversies.*

Chapter 1

Are Hate Crimes a Serious Problem?

CURRENT CONTROVERSIES

Chapter Preface

A report presented in March 1995 by the Washington-based National Gay and Lesbian Task Force (NGLTF) indicates that hate crimes against gays and lesbians increased dramatically in the five-year period from 1989 to 1994. "The gay community is under siege in this country. We are fighting an epidemic of violence," claims NGLTF spokesman Robert Bray. He notes that, paradoxically, the rise in violence against gays has occurred at the same time that gays have gained greater prominence and acceptance in some parts of American society.

Matt Foreman of the New York City Gay and Lesbian Anti-Violence Project agrees, saying, "Whenever [the gay] community is given greater visibility in the media . . . violence goes up." In recent years, gays and lesbians have gained greater visibility in the media through their movement for civil rights protection and the campaign for AIDS awareness. But according to Foreman, when the media cover these issues they "'balance' their coverage by giving time to anti-gay fanatics." The views of such fanatics appeal to people's biases against the gay community, Foreman believes, taking away support for civil rights for gays and making it easier for some to target gays with violence.

According to columnist Thomas Sowell, however, it is the tactics and agenda of gay rights activists—an agenda he says is supported by the media—that increase opposition to civil rights protection for gays and lesbians. "Shrill demands and blatant disregard of other people's rights and feelings have become standard among [gay] activists," he asserts. Opposition to any aspect of the gay activists' agenda, Sowell contends, is quickly silenced with accusations of "homophobia." When legitimate opposition to the gay rights agenda is silenced in the media, Sowell believes, hostility toward gays and lesbians increases. "Those [in the media] who are trying to make homosexuals sacred cows are helping to make them targets" of violence, he concludes.

The causes of violence targeted at minority groups such as gays and lesbians, and whether such crimes are a serious problem, are among the issues debated in the following chapter.

Anti-Semitic Violence Is Increasing

by Craig Horowitz

About the author: *Craig Horowitz is a contributing editor of* New York *magazine.*

On a cool, sunny Saturday near the beginning of October 1992, twelve-year-old David was in synagogue studying, singing, and hanging out with his friends. At around 5:30, having spent the entire afternoon indoors, he desperately wanted to get some air. David grabbed his coat and two friends, and they took off into the streets of Riverdale [a neighborhood of New York City] to salvage the last piece of a perfect fall day. Just before six, his companions thought they should get back, but David hesitated. He wasn't quite ready. The early-evening air felt too good on his face, and the streets looked too inviting in the soft twilight. "Go on," he told them. "I'll meet you at the synagogue in ten or fifteen minutes."

Anti-Semitic Harassment Turns Violent

David had barely walked one block by himself when he approached the intersection of 236th Street and the Henry Hudson Parkway. It was quiet. Though it wasn't quite dark yet, David noticed that some streetlamps were just beginning to flicker purple. At the corner, a black Toyota Camry was parked by the curb, and five teenage boys were sitting inside—three whites, one Asian, and one black. When David reached the car, one of the whites got out. "Hey, Jew boy," he yelled. David kept walking. "Hey, don't ignore me, you dirty Jew." David walked a little faster and told the teenager who was following to leave him alone. David didn't panic—he had been taunted and even chased before. Quite a few times, in fact. Still, this was the first time he'd had to face it alone.

When he crossed the street, the teenager ran after him, grabbed him, and hurled him against the wall of an apartment building. "F——ing Jew," he screamed as he started punching. David began to fight back, and three more teenagers jumped out of the car. They dragged him into an alley between two buildings and beat

Excerpted from "The New Anti-Semitism" by Craig Horowitz, *New York*, January 11, 1993. Reprinted by permission.

18

him—punching and kicking him in the face, the stomach, and the ribs. "You're not so tough now, are you, Jew boy?" said the original attacker. When they'd had enough, they turned and walked away, leaving David in the alley, badly bruised but not seriously injured. The shirt and tie he had on for the Sabbath were soiled and torn, and his black suede yarmulke was on the ground next to him.

A Rash of Hate Crimes

On the morning of that same day—October 3—someone had burned Nazi symbols into a hallway carpet in a Roosevelt Island apartment building. On October 6, a man was leaving a Brooklyn synagogue with his wife and daughter when they were approached by two men. One of the assailants slapped the man's yarmulke off his head and yelled, "Gotcha." He "yoked" the man and cut him before running away down Avenue H when the man's wife shrieked. On October 10, at 5 P.M., a twenty-four-year-old woman was walking near the Henry Hudson Parkway with her seven-year-old brother, who was wearing a yarmulke, when a car with six men inside pulled up. The men screamed, "F——ing Jew!" and threw a lighted cigarette at the woman. Later that day, a Hasidic man was walking in the Westwood area of Staten Island when two men tried to drag him into the blue Jeep they were driving.

The next night, the attacks continued. A twenty-seven-year-old woman was stopped at a traffic light in Greenwich Village when four people in a BMW pulled alongside her, yelled anti-Semitic epithets, and threw a tire iron through her rear window. Two days later, a twenty-three-year-old Hasidic man was walking on Carroll Street in Brooklyn when someone asked him for a cigarette. When he said he didn't have one, the man knocked him to the ground and pummeled his face, calling him a "dirty Jew." Indeed, during a three-and-a-half-week period that began on September 27—the day that marked the start of the holiest days of the Jewish calendar—there were nineteen criminal acts of anti-Semitism recorded by the New York City Police Department's Bias Unit.

For many, the hatred reached its dénouement at the end of the month in State Supreme Court in Brooklyn. At 5:20 on October 29—following a delay of more than two hours so that several hundred police officers could be brought in—a jury of six blacks, four Hispanics, and two whites announced that they had found seventeen-year-old Lemrick Nelson Jr. not guilty of killing Australian Hasidic scholar Yankel Rosenbaum during the August 1991 rioting in Crown Heights (sparked when Gavin Cato, a black child, was accidentally struck and killed by a Hasidic driver). And in that singular moment, when the results produced by the criminal-justice system disappointed and devastated so many people, Jews in New York suddenly knew that what they had sensed for so long but rarely

> *"During a three-and-a-half-week period . . . there were nineteen criminal acts of anti-Semitism."*

talked about was true: Attitudes were changing, intolerance was on the rise, and they were becoming strangers in their own city.

The Lid Comes Off of Intolerance

As it turned out, however, the Nelson verdict was not the climax, only a beginning. The religious violence continued. At 9 P.M. on Saturday, December 12, 1992, sixty-two-year-old Rabbi Shaya Apter was attacked in front of the synagogue where he lives, on the lower East Side. A Romanian who escaped the Nazis, the rabbi was stabbed twice in the stomach by a lone Hispanic man. Several hours later, in Borough Park, a gang attacked three eighteen-year-old Jews in a parking lot, pulling one from his car and punching him in the eye. Earlier in the day, in one of the stranger episodes, a fourteen-year-old Staten Island girl had shouted anti-Semitic slurs at thirty-three-year-old Yechiel Leiter and then ordered her dog to attack him (the dog failed to respond). The girl struck again on Sunday, December 13, this time successfully, when she instructed her dog to maul a fifteen-year-old. The boy fell to the ground when the dog bit him, and the girl kicked him in the head. On December 14, Joseph Fredrich, a twenty-nine-year-old Hasidic man visiting from England, was robbed as he emerged from the subway at Kingston Avenue and Eastern Parkway at 11 P.M. Two blacks held a knife to his throat, yelled, "Kill the Jew!" and took his cash, his watch, and some Chanukah gifts he was carrying.

> *"Attitudes were changing, intolerance was on the rise, and [Jews] were becoming strangers in their own city."*

"Some of us at one point believed," says Abraham Foxman, the national director of the Anti-Defamation League (ADL), "that we were going to come up with the antidote, the panacea for anti-Semitism. Realistically, however, what we've learned is that the best we're going to be able to do is to keep a lid on the anger and the ugliness. But right now, for some reason, the sewer covers have come off."

That Jews should now feel threatened, unwelcome, even powerless, in what in terms of sheer numbers has always been the most Jewish of American cities—the most Jewish city in the world—is perhaps the best measure of just how deep the new anti-Semitism reaches.

The Nature of Anti-Semitic Attacks Has Changed

The bias attacks were occurring at such a quick clip that Mayor David Dinkins's office was having trouble keeping up. "This was more than just the usual holiday bump-up," says Herbert Block, the mayor's assistant for Jewish affairs. "There was one Sunday when we were trying to put out a statement on an incident that happened Saturday night, and literally, as the statement was being written, reports about two other incidents came in within half an hour of each other." But if the numbers are cause for concern, they tell at best only part of the story.

Tracking anti-Semitic attacks is one thing; examining their nature and character is something else entirely. Though any bias crime is obviously a hostile act, these most recent episodes were particularly vicious and personal. As long as anti-Semitism was reflected in crimes of property damage—swastika graffiti, knocking over gravestones, and the like—it was an issue but not necessarily a serious one. As often as not, these acts could easily be dismissed as the work of teenagers emboldened by alcohol. Suddenly, the problem was no longer that simple. "The quality of the attacks has clearly changed," says New York City Human Rights Commissioner Dennis deLeon. "In the past, there were more anti-Semitic incidents of property damage than any other kind. Now there seem to be more one-on-one personal assaults."

With the volume already turned up too high, activity during the second half of October 1992 pushed the decibel level even further. A poll released by the American Jewish Committee revealed that nearly half of all New Yorkers believe that Jews have too much power and influence in the life and politics of the city. Fully 66 percent of New York's Hispanics and 63 percent of blacks said they believed this to be true. Conducted over summer 1992 by the Roper Organization, the poll also revealed—perhaps not surprisingly, given the other results—that 37 percent of the Jews in New York believe that anti-Semitism is a major problem, and 58 percent said it has gotten worse during 1992.

This was no longer simply about the murder of a twenty-nine-year-old Hasidic Jew from Australia who was in the wrong place at the wrong time. Nor was it any longer about the seven women and five men on the jury who believed that nine cops from three different commands had somehow concocted their stories. And finally, it wasn't even about what Mayor Dinkins did or didn't say after the verdict, and what he did or didn't do during and after the riots. As painful as it was for his fellow Hasidim, and for Jews all over the city, to imagine Yankel Rosenbaum lying on the hood of a Lincoln Continental on a hot August night bleeding to death from a stab wound, the murder had become only one piece of a much larger picture. Crown Heights was now a symbol for Jews—as Yusuf Hawkins [whose August 1989 murder in the Bensonhurst neighborhood of New York City was incited by a crowd of whites] and Howard Beach [where in December 1986 a crowd of white teenagers attacked three blacks, resulting in the death of one] were for the black community—of alienation and anger that had been building for some time.

> *"That Jews should now feel threatened . . . [in New York City] is perhaps the best measure of just how deep the new anti-Semitism reaches."*

"Crown Heights prompted the Jewish community to put things together," says Dr. Diane Steinman of the American Jewish Committee. "It was a watershed event. . . . It's almost like we've reached the mountaintop and it's a blizzard up there, and we'd better find a way to get down, because it's dangerous."

Jews were now regularly giving voice to their disaffection and to their belief that the city didn't work for them anymore, just as blacks in Crown Heights claimed they weren't getting their fair share. . . .

A More Insidious Anti-Semitism

In the middle of November 1992, the Anti-Defamation League released a study of prejudice in America, yet the results were all but lost in the daily thicket of news related to Crown Heights. The first comprehensive, nationwide survey of its kind since 1981, it found that one in five American adults—nearly 40 million people—holds anti-Semitic beliefs. Numbers aside, the salient finding of the ADL study, like that of the Roper poll done in New York City, is that anti-Semitism has a new character and a new set of rules. In the past, American anti-Semitism was essentially a social disease, a prejudice that found its expression in predictable forms—not wanting to live next door to a Jew, work with a Jew, marry a Jew, and so on. But now, according to the studies,

> *"Though any bias crime is obviously a hostile act, these most recent episodes were particularly vicious and personal."*

the number of people with these feelings is negligible. Anti-Jewish attitudes have instead become more insidious, resembling the anti-Semitism that was prevalent in Europe in the first part of this century. The charges: Jews have too much power and are more loyal to Israel than to America.

Norman Podhoretz, the editor-in-chief of *Commentary* and a leading neoconservative intellectual, points out that these feelings have been "percolating in the culture" for more than twenty years. "The idea that Jews in America have too much power first arose in the late sixties. It was associated with the idea that justice is a proportional distribution of the goods of this world, in accordance with the size of the group an individual belongs to. Quotas is what it came down to. It was then that this notion arose that Jews, who were 2.5 or 3 percent of the population, were getting more than their fair share."

What the recent studies really don't explain—perhaps because there is no cogent explanation—is the enduring nature of anti-Semitism. How does one make sense of the fact, for example, that the ADL study finds that contact with Jews does not affect the anti-Semitic beliefs of respondents? In his recently published book *Antisemitism: The Longest Hatred*, historian Robert Wistrich writes, "Free-floating antisemitism, for which the actual presence of Jews is almost immaterial, thrives on archetypal fears, anxieties and reflexes that seem to defy any rational analysis."

The Politics of Intolerance

What also seems to defy rational analysis is the degree to which expressions of hate and intolerance have become acceptable. In Crown Heights, it took days before the murder of Yankel Rosenbaum was even *called* a crime of bias. In pop culture—rap music and heavy metal in particular—hostility toward Jews, blacks, gays, women, and virtually anyone who is not like "us" routinely goes unremarked upon. In the political season of 1992, appeals to the darker side of voters' primal instincts seemed almost as common as the basic stump speech.

What did Republican national chairman Rich Bond mean exactly when he said of the Democrats, "They are not America"? What was Democratic presidential candidate Jerry Brown thinking about when he stood outside the New York Stock Exchange in April 1992 and said in hauntingly familiar language—as reported in *The New Republic*—that he would "drive the moneylenders out of the temple"? Or former Secretary of State James Baker, who, when asked at a meeting of high-level administration officials about his hostility toward Israel, said, "F—— the Jews. They didn't vote for us anyway"?

Vice-President Dan Quayle made his contribution with his now-infamous frontal attack on the "cultural elite." Whatever one's view on the issue, the vice-president's tone as much as his phrasing made many people uncomfortable, clearly echoing the populist anti-Semitic rhetoric that began in the thirties and would for several decades wrap Hollywood, Jews, and Communism into a neat little anti-American package. Many people simply saw *cultural elite* as a euphemism for *Jewish elite*. Addressing a Clinton fund-raising dinner, in fact, director Mike Nichols opened by saying, "We can drop the Republican code for 'cultural elite.' Good evening, fellow Jews."

The Cultural War and Anti-Semitism

Then there's the vexing case of Pat Buchanan, onetime candidate for the Republican presidential nomination and full-time bellicose columnist and talking head. "Friends, this election is about much more than who gets what," he said when he addressed the Republican Convention in August 1992. "It is about who we are . . . what we stand for as Americans. There is a religious war going on in this country. It is a cultural war, as critical to the kind of nation we shall be as the Cold War itself, for this war is for the soul of America.". . .

Podhoretz thinks Buchanan's anti-Semitism—the kind cloaked in the comfortable rhetorical cloth of mainstream politics—has been seeping into the public debate for some time. "There was a growing acceptability within the culture of very virulent attacks on Israel that became difficult to distinguish from old-fashioned anti-Semitism.

"Anti-Jewish attitudes have . . . become more insidious."

You saw it first with Gore Vidal on the left and then with Pat Buchanan on the right. Why has this come to a boil now? My guess is that it's a matter of a gradual erosion of the restraints against this sort of open expression of hostility to Jews." This erosion has occurred, he says, as the Holocaust recedes. . . .

In the United States, there is a consensus that these are pessimistic, mean-spirited times marked all too often by the loss of civility and understanding.

Chapter 1

Where once Americans felt locked in what Dr. Martin Luther King called "a network of inescapable mutuality," today there is a danger of what Podhoretz calls the "balkanization of American culture"—the loss of a clear, collective sense of common cultural and social goals. Rather than an ecumenical spirit, there is only tribal hostility—something all too evident in Crown Heights. Even after federal and state authorities agreed to investigate the riots and the murder, even after admissions that the police made errors in judgment, and even after Mayor Dinkins's televised Thanksgiving 1992 plea for harmony, little has changed. People are still afraid, still angry, and still feel betrayed.

Gay-Bashing Is a Hate Crime

by George M. Anderson

About the author: *George M. Anderson is an associate editor of* America, *a weekly Catholic publication, and the former pastor of St. Aloysius Church in Washington, D.C.*

People who think "hate crime" is a nonstarter as a behavioral category—or who don't want "gay-bashing" included within it—should talk, as I did recently, with Lieutenant Bill Johnston of the Boston Police Department. Johnston heads the department's Community Disorders Unit, which investigates cases of bias crime; as such, he sometimes acts as a decoy in bars, both straight and gay, where attacks have been common. Interviewed by phone, he made clear why he thinks bias crime is crime with a difference, and why he includes gay-bashing within it.

Antigay Violence As Bias Crime

"When I was a decoy in a straight bar where robberies had been taking place," he said, "I was just robbed. When I was a decoy in a gay bar I was not simply robbed, I was also beaten." When back-up officers arrived to make arrests, he added, the men who beat him were surprised that their behavior was taken seriously. "They said, 'Oh, he's only a fag'—as if they had been engaged in no more than a weekend sport."

The more familiar bias crimes rise out of racial, ethnic, or religious prejudice: crossburnings by the Ku Klux Klan, swastikas painted on synagogue walls, name-calling, physical attacks on African-Americans, Jews, Asians. Though some argue that it is improper to classify and punish crimes according to motive, supporters of bias crime laws argue it is necessary to track the incidence of bias crimes, and to punish them with special severity, because they can intimidate an entire class of people, and because they often include the threat or reality of violence.

There are indications that hate crimes in general are on the rise in the United States. The Anti-Defamation League reported an 11 percent increase in anti-Semitic incidents between 1990 and 1992. Dr. Howard Ehrlich, research director of the National Institute against Prejudice and Violence, said in an interview in Baltimore, Maryland, that the rise in hate crimes began in the mid-1980s, and reflects an overall escalation of violence throughout American society. Whereas earlier most of the violence was directed against property, today, he said, we are seeing "cruder and more personal forms of attacks."

That appears to apply in particular to attacks on gays. The National Gay and Lesbian Task Force Policy Institute asserts that antigay harassment and violence in five major U.S. cities jumped by 131 percent from 1990 to 1991. An earlier (1987) report on bias crime prepared for the National Institute of Justice, a branch of the U.S. Department of Justice, concluded that homosexuals may well have become the most frequent victims of hate violence today. A single instance, among many that could be cited, took place in the Montrose section of Houston, Texas, on July 4, 1991. A twenty-seven-year-old man, Paul Broussard, was beaten and stabbed to death outside a gay bar by a group of ten young men armed with knives and nail-studded two-by-fours.

Increased Visibility and Increased Violence

Dr. Ehrlich attributes the rise to the increased visibility of gay men and lesbians. This follows a pattern: "When a traditionally subordinate group becomes more visible, levels of conflict increase." He cited the harassment and attacks suffered by some Arab-Americans when the 1991 Persian Gulf War brought their presence into public awareness. Holocaust memorial services on college campuses, he said, are sometimes linked with an increase in anti-Semitic incidents. In the case of homosexuals, he points to such factors as the election of openly gay public officials, the emergence of AIDS, and the growth of churches like the MCC [Metropolitan Community Churches, whose members are predominantly gay]. Others might add the increasingly assertive (and, to many, offensive) tactics adopted by homosexual groups like ACT-UP [AIDS Coalition to Unleash Power] in demonstrations aimed at individuals, groups, and institutions, including the Catholic church, and in campaigns to enact or preserve statutes outlawing discrimination against homosexuals in housing and employment, establishing inheritance and health insurance rights for gay partners, or granting recognition of "gay marriage."

> *"Antigay harassment and violence in five major U.S. cities jumped by 131 percent from 1990 to 1991."*

Barry Goodinson, executive director of Dignity/USA, a national organization of gay and lesbian Catholics, and a member of our small inner-city parish in Washington, D.C., spoke with me about the varied forms that "gay-baiting" and "gay-bashing" can take. Goodinson, thirty-two, is a graduate of Saint John's Seminary and College in Boston, Massachusetts, and of Georgetown University in Washington, D.C. Sometimes, he said, the attacks are verbal. "I was walking with a male friend near Dupont Circle, when a passerby yelled 'faggot' at us," he recalled. Such attacks, he said, have become more and more common—proof, for him, of "the current high level of homophobia." He would include as another form of gay-bashing the 1992 ballot initiatives in Oregon and Colorado aimed at banning civil rights protections forbidding discrimination on the basis of sexual orientation. Oregon's, which would have required schools to teach that homosexuality is "abnormal, wrong, unnatural, and perverse," failed, but Colorado's less extreme measure forbidding "protective status based on homosexual, lesbian, or bisexual orientation" passed.

> *"Another form of gay-bashing [is] the 1992 ballot initiatives in Oregon and Colorado aimed at banning civil rights protections [for gays]."*

Defenders of such initiatives say that laws to protect homosexuals aren't necessary because gays and lesbians are already covered by civil rights laws and don't need "special" protection. But, according to sources like Boston's Lieutenant Johnston, gays are the object of attacks precisely because of their sexual orientation—and police efforts to respond to the problem are hindered because victims are often reluctant to press charges or even to contact the police because they fear harassment at work, loss of jobs, or alienation from their families if they do testify in court on the nature of the incident. Johnston recalled a 1990 case of a man who had been severely beaten. "There's no doubt it was an antigay attack," he said. "It took place in the South End [neighborhood of Boston], where there's a large gay presence, and the perpetrator was using terms demeaning to homosexuals." The police were ready to classify the episode as a bias crime, but were stymied by the victim's reluctance to prosecute. "Only in the gay community do you find this kind of fear," he added. "I never see it in bias crimes involving blacks or Hispanics."

Who Does the Gay-Bashing and Why?

Who are the gay-bashers? Known perpetrators are predominantly males in their teens or early twenties, often from middle-class backgrounds. A segment of the CBS program *Street Stories* aired in 1992 was based on a police decoy operation begun in Houston after the murder of Paul Broussard. It included an interview with a nineteen-year-old man who regularly drove into the Montrose section of the city with a friend to prey on homosexuals. He compared beating them to smashing pumpkins on Halloween; they did not appear to him as real people. "It just seems like they're their own race," he said. "I don't really feel no remorse about anything I ever did to a gay person. . . . It's just the way I grew up."

Lieutenant Johnston believes antigay attacks are socially encouraged. He notes that "gays are the only group in the United States that it's okay to beat up." and points out that even when police make an arrest and a victim is willing to testify, prosecutors may balk at prosecuting vigorously; when they do, they are often thwarted by judges who give lenient sentences. The assumption seems to be that the perpetrators are basically good kids who should not be burdened with a criminal record.

The Catholic Stance on Gay-Bashing

Religion also plays a role, in Johnston's view. "People fall back on their religious beliefs to justify their hate," he says. Some preachers do condemn homosexuality and "gay lifestyles" in terms that, to homosexuals, appear to brand them as evil persons not worthy to live. While both Catholic and mainstream Protestant authorities have generally supported laws banning housing and job discrimination against gays, and the Catholic bishops of Oregon and Colorado opposed the anti-gay referenda voted on in November 1992, most of the same churches have refused to alter their basic ethical teachings on homosexuality. The Catholic stance, which opposes discrimination against gays, while characterizing homosexual acts as objectively sinful, was complicated by a statement distributed to U.S. Catholic bishops by the Congregation for the Doctrine of the Faith (CDF) in July 1992 entitled "Some Considerations Concerning the Catholic Response to Legislative Proposals on the Non-Discrimination of Homosexual Persons." The document asserts that it is not unjust discrimination to oppose legislation protective of gay rights in areas like teaching, athletic coaching, adoptive parenting, and military recruitment. The Oregon bishops said there was no conflict between their opposition to the referendum and the CDF statement.

Some incidents in Oregon tend to support Dr. Ehrlich's view that increased visibility brings increased hostility against marginalized groups. According to the *National Catholic Reporter,* the pastor of one Oregon parish received a telephoned warning against publicizing the bishops' statement opposing the referendum; when it was ignored, vandals set fire to an office in the rectory and painted such phrases as "Catholics love gays" and "Kill Catholics and gays" within the church. The spokesperson for a group organized to fight the referendum—a grandmother who heads the Ecumenical Ministries of Oregon—reported receiving telephone threats saying she should be killed for betraying Christianity.

> *"Gays are the only group in the United States that it's okay to beat up."*

Dr. Ehrlich's thesis is pushed a step further by Gary David Comstock in a 1991 book, *Violence Against Lesbians and Gay Men,* which contends that heightened violence against gays fosters still greater insistence by gays and lesbians on becoming active in their own cause. That insistence was evident in our own parish a few weeks before the November 1992 meeting of U.S. bishops in Washington, D.C., when Barry Goodinson invited worshipers to sign a petition being circulated nationwide by New Ways Ministry, an advocacy group for gay Catholics. The petition, directed to the hierarchy, took specific issue with the CDF's apparent fear that legislative protections for gay men and lesbians could threaten family life, and contended that there is no empirical evidence to support such fear. Among the 14,000 persons across the country who signed the New Ways petition were two who are themselves bishops, Walter F. Sullivan of Richmond, Virginia, and Thomas J. Gumbleton of Detroit, Michigan. Many parishioners at Saint Aloysius signed, and so did I.

Hate Crimes Against Whites Are a Serious Problem

by Resisting Defamation

About the author: *Resisting Defamation is a San Jose, California, organization that combats stereotypes of and slurs against European Americans through sensitivity education.*

Larry Brown was an engaging Irish American boy living with his mother, father, and sister on San Jose, California's East Side until May 4, 1990. He was an energetic and friendly student, and he had big plans and was successful at projects once he decided on them.

The Hate Crime Against Larry Brown

He and his family lived in the most ethnically diverse section of San Jose. Latinos, African Americans, Asian Americans, and European Americans live side-by-side, and attend school and church together. Larry's best friend was an African American with whom he shared athletic interests.

San Jose is the third largest city in California, and the eleventh largest in the United States. It is remarkably free from ethnic strife compared to Oakland, San Francisco, Sacramento, and Los Angeles. San Jose is the county seat of Santa Clara County, the fifth largest industrial county in the United States.

On a sunny morning during class break on May 4, 1990, four Vietnamese men came to the school yard.

They came with a loaded gun. One man drove the car with the loaded gun to the campus. A second man took the loaded gun and passed it to the hands of the killer. A third man illegally trespassed on the high school grounds to harangue the students sunning themselves during class break.

The killer, the fourth man, entered the campus, shouted "white devil" at the innocent Larry Brown, and a moment later shot him in the back of the head

"Why Isn't Larry Brown Finishing His Sophomore Year in College This Spring," a paper by Resisting Defamation, May 4, 1994. Reprinted with permission.

with one of four bullets. Two bullets struck no one, and the final bullet rico-cheted off the paved playground and struck a young woman student in the back of the head. She happened to be the African American sister of Larry Brown's best friend at school. She has recovered completely.

Larry Brown died of his gunshot wound later in the afternoon on May 4, 1990.

The Reaction to the Shooting

The Latino school principal moved quickly to bring in counselors for Latino students. Local agencies provided counseling to the Asian American and African American students. The European American student minority, who had just seen their co-ethnic shot to death, were given no counseling about this mur-der whatsoever.

The principal decided at once that the faculty and students had to "put this be-hind them" and continued a planned major *Cinco de Mayo* carnival on the cam-pus for the next two days. [Cinco de Mayo is a national holiday of Mexico that celebrates the May 5, 1862, defeat of invading French forces by a smaller Mex-ican army at Puebla, southeast of Mexico City.] He has since paid a heavy price in community relations for his insensitivity in having a party on the school grounds before Larry's blood had time to dry.

A rumor mill among some school district adults maliciously commenced a vi-cious story that Larry Brown had somehow called this murder onto himself through anti-social activities of a racist sort, but the court hearings set the record straight that he didn't have a mean instinct in his body.

The principal and his wife, who work for the same school district, have addi-tionally been discredited because they send their three children to *private* schools in San Jose. Just think: if Larry Brown had attended the school to which his own principal sent *his* children, Larry Brown would be fin-ishing his sophomore year in college this spring [May 1994]!

> **"The killer . . . shouted 'white devil' at the innocent Larry Brown, and a moment later shot him in the back of the head."**

None of the state and local offi-cials who would ordinarily be ex-pected to speak out against such a hate crime did so. None of the city or county politicians has, to this day, expressed dismay about this hate crime.

The district attorney, George Kennedy, has refused to press hate crime charges against the confessed first degree murderer.

Kennedy has also declined to press accessory charges against the other three men: the driver of the car with the loaded gun, the man who gave the gun to the killer, and the man who illegally trespassed on the campus to harangue the stu-dents just prior to the shooting.

The killer pled guilty to first degree murder, was sent to a youth camp, and rejoined us in San Jose in 1994. His accessories remain free, unaccused, and uncharged with any crime.

Had the ethnicities of killer and accessories and that of the victim been reversed, San Jose would still be humming with hypocritical murmurs of outrage and dismay at "white racism" run amuck. There would be candlelight parades every May 4, and there would be annual prayer meetings.

None of these expressions of outrage has surfaced in connection with the racially-motivated murder of Larry Brown. San Jose's dominant political and media culture attempted to paper over this murder by ignoring it.

It wasn't until May 1992 that the County Human Relations Commission had a "minute of silence" to show a minimum of respect toward the dead boy.

European Americans Become Concerned

Not all was lost, however, because a portion of the community woke up after this murder. European Americans in particular, and parent groups in general, have become much more aware of the failure of law enforcement to protect students.

European Americans investigated and found that there was *no voice from the European American community* to insist on adequate services for their children.

African Americans, Latinos, and Asian Americans are organized to guarantee that their children are not slighted in criminal, civil rights, tutoring, and college preparation issues. But there was not one person in San Jose in 1990 to speak out against similar slights against European American students.

Spokespersons have since emerged to brave the wrath of the dominant political and media culture of San Jose which dictates that European Americans are never victims of hate crimes and are, in fact, always the perpetrators.

A major scandal ensued in 1992 when it became clear that District Attorney George Kennedy, far from embarrassment over his failure to do his job, was actively preaching through his staff the hate doctrine that there is a "profile" of hate crime perpetrators, and that the "profile" is young European American men between nineteen and twenty-six.

> *"The district attorney . . . has refused to press hate crime charges against the confessed first degree murderer."*

Interested groups exposed his lie by using San Jose Police Department statistics for 1991 and 1992 which conclusively show that European Americans carry out fewer hate crimes than their population share.

European Americans are about 45 percent of the population in San Jose, but in 1991 performed only 29 percent of hate crimes in San Jose and in 1992 performed only 35 percent of hate crimes in San Jose. This is not the sign of an ethnicity that provides the "profile" of the hate criminal.

As we research other geographical areas, the standard finding remains consistent: *European Americans perform a share of hate crimes in any community or any region, however defined, that is substantially smaller than their population share.*

Other Forms of Bias and Stereotyping

Another example of anti–European American bias is more subtle. The daily newspaper promotes it from time to time, and that is the "hate crime analysis" story. Typically the story will provide examples of hate crimes, perhaps eight in number.

When this type of story is closely examined, it will be noted that seven of the eight examples feature European American assailants, thereby suggesting that most hate crimes are carried out by European Americans. This is a kind of hate speech encountered over and over in hate crime news stories.

Another way that European Americans are defamed is simpler. Newspapers just don't report on hate crimes by non–European Americans. In 1991, for example, 71 percent of 85 local hate crimes were perpetrated by non–European Americans who provide about 55 percent of the population. There was only one news story in the local paper about such a perpetrator.

> *"European Americans carry out fewer hate crimes than their population share."*

In 1992, 65 percent of the 57 local hate crimes were perpetrated by non–European Americans. There were no local news stories at all about such hate crimes.

Larry Brown's murder motivated us to look beyond the words of politicians and reporters, and forced us to acknowledge that we will have to organize, research, and speak out about failures of our society and government to respond to crimes against European Americans and to provide necessary services for the safety and health of young European Americans.

He's not a sophomore at college this spring, but we are determined not to forget Larry Brown.

Anti-Semitism Is Not Increasing

by J. J. Goldberg

About the author: *J. J. Goldberg is the New York–based correspondent for the Israeli newspaper* Jerusalem Report.

When representatives of the nation's major Jewish community relations groups gathered in New York in December 1992 to draft their yearly statement on anti-Semitism, the mood was quiet and businesslike. As they do each year, participants sorted through a depressing array of facts and figures illustrating Jewish vulnerability in America. The Anti-Defamation League (ADL) presented its new poll, showing that one in five Americans holds pronounced anti-Semitic views. Panelists took note of the continuing plague of bias crimes against Jews, from graffiti to murder. Staff experts dissected the constitutional challenges being mounted against "hate crimes laws" intended to stop such crimes.

Anti-Semitism Has Declined

Amid all the reports and statistics, however, one fact received only cursory attention: that while ever growing numbers of Jews believe anti-Semitism in America is rising to crisis proportions, by nearly every available measure it is actually on the decline. Discrimination in housing, jobs and schooling, once endemic, has all but disappeared. State-sponsored anti-Semitism, long a defining fact of European life, is virtually unknown here. Hostility toward Jews, measured in public opinion polls, has been declining steadily for two generations. Events that seemed sure to provoke broad anti-Semitism, from the 1973 Arab oil boycott to the arrests of Israeli spy Jonathan Pollard in 1985 and Wall Street cheat Ivan Boesky in 1986, came and went without a blip.

Only one common measure of anti-Semitism has gone up of late: "anti-Semitic incidents." This includes not only graffiti but increasingly arson and assault as well. (Even this indicator declined in 1992—for the first time in a decade—dipping 8 percent according to ADL figures.) Still, it's not a key test

J.J. Goldberg, "Scaring the Jews," *The New Republic*, May 17, 1993. Reprinted by permission of *The New Republic;* © 1993, The New Republic, Inc.

to most experts. The ADL's 1991 total of 1,879 incidents, the all-time high, amounted to just five a day—mostly epithets hurled and swastikas daubed—in a nation of 250 million people.

This is not to say that anti-Semitism has disappeared. [Former Ku Klux Klan leader and one-time presidential candidate] David Duke and [Nation of Islam leader] Louis Farrakhan have become household names. Anti-Semitic tracts such as *The Protocols of the Elders of Zion* are being peddled nationwide by neo-Nazis and black separatists. And the 1991 riot in Crown Heights [a neighborhood of New York City], which left one Jew murdered because of his religion, cast a chill over Jews nationwide. "Among those people who have bigoted attitudes, there's a greater tendency to act out," says Jerome Chanes of the National Jewish Community Relations Advisory Council, which convenes the interagency Jewish task force on anti-Semitism. "For whatever reason, the taboos are breaking down."

"Hostility toward Jews, measured in public opinion polls, has been declining steadily for two generations."

But whatever the facts, Jewish anxiety is rising off the meter. The percentage of Jews who tell pollsters that anti-Semitism is "a serious problem in America today" has skyrocketed, from 45 percent in 1983 to nearly 85 percent in 1990. "It seems Jewish anxiety is well ahead of what's really out there," says David Singer, research director of the American Jewish Committee (AJC).

What the Polls Showed

What explains this national anxiety? Some observers suggest a sort of post-Holocaust stress syndrome that makes the Nazi horror loom ever larger in memory as it fades into history. Some say the media are more sensitive to anti-Semitism when it arises. Jewish agencies may cooperate, consciously or not, in what amounts to hype.

The American Jewish Committee made the news in October 1992 when it released its Roper poll showing that 47 percent of New Yorkers—including 63 percent of black New Yorkers—believe Jews have "too much influence." The ADL received even broader coverage a month later with its national poll, which called 20 percent of Americans (and 37 percent of blacks) anti-Semitic.

But few readers saw the poll's full findings, which showed long-term declines in anti-Semitic views. The ADL's 20 percent figure, for example, actually represented a one-third drop from 1964, when 29 percent of those polled were counted as anti-Semitic. The drop was consistent for blacks and whites alike.

Twenty percent—50 million—still seems like a lot. Put into context, however, it seems like a lot less. One 1991 study of prejudice, conducted by the National Opinion Research Center at the University of Chicago, found that Jews rank somewhere in the middle of Americans' esteem, below Protestants,

Swedes and Japanese but well ahead of Mormons, blacks, Filipinos and Poles. Jews even fared better than Wisians, a fictional group that researchers tossed in to test free-floating orneriness. Wisians ranked near the bottom of the fifty-eight groups offered, between Koreans and Arabs.

What the Polls Didn't Show

What's more, someone who says Jews are "too powerful" is not necessarily anti-Semitic. American Jews *are* powerful. Over the last quarter-century, bodies such as the ADL and the two AJCs (Committee and Congress), together with the American Israel Public Affairs Committee, the pro-Israel lobby, have become a serious force in Washington. They push hard not just for aid to Israel but for a broad agenda ranging from abortion rights to church-state separation. Win or lose, their opponents often conclude they were "up against some powerful political forces," as George Bush once said.

But "too powerful"? That may be a judgment call. Jews make up 2.5 percent of the population and 10 percent of the Senate. Paradoxically, many Jews still think of themselves as members of a helpless out-group. As a result, honest disputes sound like assaults. And if calling a group of people "too powerful" is a statement of prejudice, then Jews are not free of prejudice, either. Take the AJC poll that showed that 63 percent of black New Yorkers think Jews have "too much influence." It also found

> *"Paradoxically, many Jews still think of themselves as members of a helpless out-group."*

that 23 percent of Jews—more than any other group—believe blacks have too much influence. That detail never made it into the papers.

For years, the organized Jewish community has taken the position that you can't be too vigilant. Expose anti-Semites and they will fade away; leave them be and they will fester in the dark. "If I'm going to err, it's going to be on the side of caution," says ADL's national director, Abraham Foxman. "This is not an exact science. I'm sorry if I have offended some in the black or white community by being too quick to yell. The last time Jews didn't, they paid a very heavy price."

Nowadays there's an opposite danger: that too much vigilance will lead to isolation. Before World War II, anti-Semitism was defined as wanting to harm Jews. In the post-war era, it was broadened to include prejudice that might lead one to wish Jews harm. More recently, it's come to mean any stereotype—or disagreement—with the Jewish community. The very term has become a weapon. Overused, it can breed the resentment it is meant to expose.

When Are Stereotypes Anti-Semitic?

The ADL's 1992 poll of anti-Semitic attitudes found for the first time that some respondents regarded the stereotypes being tested—especially the idea that Jews "stick together more than most Americans"—as *positive* traits. Blacks in particular told pollsters they admired Jews for helping their own.

The finding caused an uproar among the ADL staff and delayed the poll's release for months. Some staffers argued that the poll should have been reconfigured. Others insisted "anti-Semitism is anti-Semitism," regardless of intentions. In the end they compromised, raising the poll's threshold for "most anti-Semitic" to six "yes" answers from five, the cutoff in the 1964 and 1981 polls. Some unknown number of the "50 million anti-Semites" in the poll are just folks who hold no animus against Jews.

In private, some Jewish agency staffers insist the alarmist tone set by a few national Jewish agencies, mainly for fund-raising purposes, is a key cause of Jewish anxiety. Fingers point most often at the ADL and the Los Angeles–based Simon Wiesenthal Center, both of which specialize in mass mailings warning of impending doom and urging donations. "People don't give if you tell them everything's O.K.," says a cynical staffer at one of the smaller agencies. People give generously to the Wiesenthal Center and the ADL.

Of course, the tactics of a few bureaucrats in New York or Los Angeles hardly explain the nationwide fear gripping American Jews, many of whom are barely aware of the ADL's existence. More likely, the masses are driving the leadership. Maybe it's time for the leadership to start leading, and tell their public the truth.

The Hate-Crime Label Is Used to Suppress Politically Incorrect Opinions

by William Norman Grigg

About the author: *William Norman Grigg is a senior editor of the* New American, *published by the John Birch Society.*

On April 23, 1990, President Bush signed the Hate Crime Statistics Act, a measure instructing the Justice Department to compile statistics about crimes motivated by prejudice based upon race, ethnicity, religion, and sexual "orientation." The passage of the act consummated seven years of effort on the part of the homosexual lobby. By including "sexual orientation" as a protected category, the Hate Crime Act circumnavigates America's moral consensus. Furthermore, for statistical purposes verbal "assaults" upon homosexuals are assigned the same weight as violent assault.

Hate Crimes and "Political Correctness"

Since George Bush signed the Hate Crime Statistics Act in April 1990, the federal government, many state and municipal governments, and various non-governmental "watchdog" groups have been at war with "improper" attitudes and unsanctioned opinions. A declaration of war upon an abstraction—such as "racism," "sexism," or "hate"—is a rationale for a perpetual crusade and an enlargement of State power.

Under the U.S. Constitution, the police authority of the State is intended to serve strictly-defined, limited objectives: It is to protect law-abiding citizens from crimes committed against their rights, persons, or property. But in recent years there has been an inversion in the State's priorities, best captured in an observation made by Karl Hess in the September 1992 issue of *Liberty* magazine:

Excerpted from "Hate Crimes" by William Norman Grigg, *The New American*, November 16, 1992. Reprinted with permission.

The hallowed saying that "sticks and stones may break your bones but words can never hurt you" is obsolete. Now, when the sticks and stones break your bones, in a riot, for instance, it is either your fault directly, or society's, and the bone-breaking is forgiven in the major media. But utter a phrase that *disturbs* someone, and outrage flares against the words that are said to be unbearably hurtful.

The Hate Crime Act has given legal expression to the academic phenomenon of "political correctness." The State is devoting its police authority to the task of attitude control and correction. In his memoir *Against All Hope*, former Cuban political prisoner Armando Valladares informs us that in Fidel Castro's jails, common prisoners—thieves, murderers, and the like—were treated much better than those who were jailed for crimes against the State. Similar priorities are being manifest in America as the hate crimes concept takes hold. In violation of the constitutional principle of equal justice under the law, a victim hierarchy is being established: If present trends continue, criminal penalties may soon be assigned on the basis of the victim's race, gender, or sexual "orientation" rather than the severity of the crime. Additionally, the State is devising ways of quarantining "incorrect" attitudes and political opinions. Religious liberty and freedom of speech are imperiled by the emerging anti–hate crimes regime.

> *"The Hate Crime Act has given legal expression to the academic phenomenon of 'political correctness.'"*

Political Psychotherapy

Contemporary penology emphasizes "rehabilitation" rather than retribution or the attempt to obtain restitution from criminals. We are urged to regard criminals as "sick" individuals who can be "cured" rather than moral agents who should be punished in compliance with the requirements of justice. It should not surprise us that the same social elite that has thus perverted penology also regards "improper" politics to be a disease that must be cured. . . .

In 1955, social scientist Daniel Bell edited and published a collection of essays entitled *The New American Right*. Eight years later he came out with an expanded version of this collection entitled *The Radical Right*. . . .

Bell described Americans on the "radical right" as "pseudo-conservatives" and insisted, "They have little in common with the temperate and compromising spirit of true conservatism in the classical sense of the word. [T]heir political reactions express a rather profound if largely unconscious hatred of our society and its ways—a hatred which one would hesitate to impute to them if one did not have suggestive clinical evidence."

Bell free-associated right-wing "extremists" with the Ku Klux Klan and insisted that conservative politics was merely a manifestation of "status anxiety." The various tenets of conservative politics, according to Bell, were surrogates for racial hostilities. In his opinion, one graduated from anti-black prejudice or anti-Semitism into conservative politics "much in the same way as the average American, if he can manage it, will move on from a Ford to a Buick." Among these disguised prejudices Bell listed "the incredibly bitter feeling against the United Nations." Other contributors to his book expanded the inventory of political opinions that arose from "submerged prejudice." In this fashion members of the political elite narrowed the compass of acceptable political opinion.

The Politics of "Resentment"

Reviewing Bell's volume, anti-statist Murray Rothbard notes, "The soft Marxists and liberals of the 1950s and '60s engaged in Marxo-Freudian psychobabble to infer, in the name of psychological 'science,' that their opponents were, well, kind of *crazy*."

Rothbard observes that the Bell volume referred to genuine conservatism as "the politics of resentment": "Anger by the good guys, the accredited victim groups, is designated as 'rage'. . . on the other hand, anger by the designated *oppressor* groups is not called 'rage,' but 'resentment.'" "Resentful" people—that is, conservatives and others who resist "correct" politics—are perceived as "trying to undo the benevolent rule of wise elites concerned for the public good." It is useful to recall that following the 1992 Los Angeles riots the Establishment cognoscenti urged us to understand the "rage" of the rioters; by way of contrast those same deep thinkers dismiss opposition to homosexuality (for example) as "the politics of resentment."

> *"Dissenters from the Establishment line are execrated as 'hate-mongers' and excommunicated from civic society."*

The Establishment has an obvious interest in neutralizing opposition by dismissing it as prejudice or "hate-mongering." Unapproved opinions are said to carry "code words" that disguise prejudice; the next logical step is to criminalize or otherwise restrict "hate speech." "Therapeutic" programs are imposed upon communities in an effort to reeducate the public. Of course, dissenters from the Establishment line are execrated as "hate mongers" and excommunicated from civic society.

"Homophobia" As a Psychological Disorder

The invention of the term "homophobia" to invalidate opposition to homosexuality is a variant of the Bell approach. In 1967, New York psychotherapist George Weinberg devised the term "homophobia," which he defined as an "obsessive fear or hatred of homosexuals." At the time that Weinberg devised his neologism, homosexuality was still regarded by the psychiatric community as an affliction. This changed in 1973 when, after a lengthy campaign of intimidation by militant homosexual groups, the American Psychiatric Association (APA) removed homosexuality from its list of psychological disorders. Weinberg was eventually given an award by the APA for inventing the term "homophobia."

Weinberg's term reflects a political agenda, not a therapeutic conclusion. In his view, "The prevalent negative attitudes toward homosexuals still cause immense hatred, not just to gays but to those close to them and to all the righteous." According to Weinberg, those attitudes need not find overt expression in order to cause harm: "Apart from the evil done to homosexuals, many people who do not act overtly against them want to erase them from the mind, to annihilate them mentally." For Weinberg and those of his persuasion, such "mental annihilation" is as much a violent act as a physical assault. Accordingly, the effort to eradicate "homophobia" postulates a government responsibility to eliminate "violent" thoughts.

Weinberg maintains that those who do not "affirm" homosexuals in their chosen lifestyle are homophobic. One cannot condemn the sin and love the sinner, Weinberg maintains. Furthermore, one who sees no reason to protect homosexuals is diagnosed as "mildly homophobic." Those who cite historical facts and present realities in opposition to the homosexual "rights" agenda are referred to as "intensely homophobic."

Weinberg maintains that homophobia is, in part, an "irrational fear of contagion," meaning that those who oppose homosexuality are unreasonably afraid that the "lifestyle" can be transmitted by contact with homosexuals. (Since sexual molestation of children is regarded by many homosexuals as an initiation ritual, this fear is hardly irrational.) But Weinberg frequently refers to "virulent homophobia"—as if devotion to traditional morality were a contagious disease.

Treating "Homophobia"

Because homophobia is a sickness, it must be contained and eliminated. Weinberg informs those who "suffer" from "homophobia" that they must be cured: "To solve the problem of homophobia would in my opinion do much more than give homosexuals a fair chance. It would release the homophobe from the bonds of his own fear and in many cases his own obsessions." That "disease," Weinberg observes, is found primarily among orthodox Jews, fundamentalist Christians, and traditionalist Catholics. This assumption has migrated from the fringes into the mainstream. A 1989 taxpayer-funded study produced by the National Research Council concluded that the Judeo-Christian perspective on homosexuality is a "deeply rooted social pathology."

> *"[Traditional] attitudes have been redefined as 'prejudices' and verbal expression of 'prejudice' has been re-christened 'violence.'"*

A method has been found to enlist the government in the effort to "cure" traditional attitudes regarding homosexuality. Those attitudes have been redefined as "prejudices" and verbal expression of "prejudice" has been re-christened "violence." These definitions have been used in reports on "anti-gay violence" released by the National Gay and Lesbian Task Force (NGLTF) every year since 1984.

The NGLTF defines homophobia as "unfounded and long-standing notions that gay people are sick, sinful, or predatory" and maintains that such notions "have fostered hostility that leads to anti-gay violence." Except for a few documented examples of physical assault, the "violence" cited by the reports consists mostly of verbal abuse. The 1984 survey reported that 86 percent of all "anti-gay violence"

> *"Clearly the definition of an 'anti-gay' crime is designed to serve the political interests of the homosexual movement."*

consisted of "verbal insults." Of the 5,463 reported incidents accounted for in the 1987 NGLTF report, 85 percent were verbal harassment, threats, vandalism, or police "negligence." According to the NGLTF, the police are guilty of hate crimes when officers wear rubber gloves while dealing with homosexual protesters, or when they interfere with homosexual liaisons in public restrooms.

Clearly the definition of an "anti-gay" crime is designed to serve the political interests of the homosexual movement rather than the cause of equal justice. In 1990, the "bias crime unit" of the New York City Police Department recorded 71 "anti-gay crimes." During the same period the New York Anti-Violence Project, using much more emancipated definitions, claimed to have recorded 403 "anti-gay crimes."

Even as the homosexual lobby has grown in political influence, Weinberg's concepts have percolated up through the federal bureaucracy. In 1987, the National Institute of Justice—the research arm of the Justice Department—produced a survey that ratified the assumption that of all minority groups, homosexuals are the most frequent victims of "hate" violence. In the same year, the National Institutes of Mental Health held a research conference on anti-gay violence, and the House Judiciary Committee first considered a "hate crimes" act.

Homosexual Hate Groups

The tendentiousness of the "hate crimes" concept is illustrated in the fact that neither the media nor the government ever refers to outrages wrought by homosexuals as "hate crimes," nor are homosexual hate groups referred to as such. ACT-UP (the AIDS Coalition To Unleash Power) is a group that has invaded religious services, threatened the lives of public officials, and disrupted television news programs. In spite of the group's amply-documented penchant for violence and disruption, members of ACT-UP have served on an advisory panel to the National Institutes of Health.

Jefferey Pollard, a founding member of ACT-UP/DC in the nation's capital, has revealed that members of his group have appealed to Adolf Hitler's *Mein Kampf* for tactical advice. Pollard candidly refers to the group as "fascist." Nor is that characterization properly applied only to the Washington, DC, chapter. Larry Kramer, a playwright and a founder of ACT-UP, told *OutWeek* magazine that he wishes that angry homosexuals would create a terrorist organization. Kramer is not without influence. He was featured as a member of America's "cultural elite" in the October 5, 1992, issue of *Newsweek*.

In the November/December 1990 issue of *Mother Jones* magazine, ACT-UP member Michael Petaglis lamented the "missed opportunities" at the 1990 International AIDS Conference in San Francisco: "We should have shut down the subway and burned city hall. I think rioting is a valid tactic and should be tried." Nor would Petaglis contain his ambitions to property damage: "If someone took out [murdered] [North Carolina Senator] Jesse Helms or [Representative] William Dannemeyer of California, I would be the first to stand up and applaud."

When ACT-UP invaded St. Patrick's Cathedral in New York City in December 1989, desecrated the host, and assaulted worshipers with profane verbal abuse, the incident was not designated a hate crime. In 1992 the Vatican urged Catholics to uphold traditional church teachings about homosexuality. *The Nation* magazine condemned the Vatican's admonition as a hate crime and suggested that ACT-UP should prepare for another attack upon the Church. This attempt to incite anti-Catholic violence followed *The Nation*'s publication of an essay by Gore Vidal, in which he declared, "I now favor an all-out war on the monotheists" because of their opposition to homosexuality (and other depravities cherished by Vidal).

> *"Neither the media nor the government ever refers to outrages wrought by homosexuals as 'hate crimes.'"*

In the effort to destigmatize homosexuality, marginalized activist groups have worked in collusion with unaccountable bureaucracies to bring about radical changes in government policy. The passage of the Hate Crime Statistics Act has encouraged much more collusion of this sort, as activist organizations, encouraged by the government and tax-exempt foundations, assemble "educational" efforts and form "watch-dog" groups. . . .

Fighting "Bigotry"

The Northwest Coalition Against Malicious Harassment (NWCAMH) held a conference in Eugene, Oregon, on October 23–25, 1992. Entitled "To Find Common Ground," the event drew an estimated 1,000 people; religious leaders, educators, and law enforcement officials were heavily represented at the conference. Attendees enrolled in workshops that peddled the politically correct party line in the name of fighting "bigotry."

Several workshops free-associated the religious right with hate groups like the KKK and the Aryan Nations. Opposition to abortion was described in one program as a species of prejudice. Another class examined "language as a weapon of hate" and suggested strategies for "neutralizing racist, sexist and homophobic [verbal] attacks."

One lecturer purported to explain "the relationship between the white supremacist movement and the movement for traditional family values." (Little attention was paid to the fact that millions of black, Oriental, and Latino Americans are laboring to restore traditional family values.)

Another session was set aside for a discussion of the "contemporary Far Right from the John Birch Society to the American Front" (the latter being a neo-Nazi cabal in Oregon). An overview of "Hate Crimes and the Law" was provided by former Oregon Attorney General David Frohnmeyer—the brother of John Frohnmeyer, former chairman of the National Endowment

> *"Apparently a politically incorrect vote is also a hate crime."*

for the Arts. The lesser-known Frohnmeyer is presently the dean of the University of Oregon law school.

Not only were politically incorrect opinions described as variants of "bigotry" and unsanctioned speech as a "weapon," but according to the NWCAMH those on the "extreme right" have no right to political participation. One workshop offered an "examination of ballot box bigotry" and the "right wing assault upon democracy and community." Apparently a politically incorrect vote is also a hate crime.

The Hate Crime Statistics Act is just one element of a subsidized assault upon traditional values. To many observers, the Establishment appears to be indifferent to the collateral damage being done to freedom of speech and religious liberty. The truly informed will recognize that such freedoms are the primary targets of that assault.

Anti-Gay Violence Should Not Be Labeled Hate Crime

by Jonathan Rauch

About the author: *Jonathan Rauch is author of* Kindly Inquisitors: The New Attacks on Free Thought *and a writer for the* Economist *in London, England.*

At 10:30 on a weeknight in the spring of 1991, Glenn Cashmore was walking to his car on San Diego, California's University Avenue. He had just left the Soho coffee house in Hillcrest, a heavily gay neighborhood. He turned down Fourth Street and paused to look at the display in an optician's window. Someone shouted, "Hey, faggot!" He felt pain in his shoulder and turned in time to see a white Nissan speeding away. Someone had shot him, luckily only with a pellet gun. The pellet tore through the shirt and penetrated the skin. He went home and treated the wound with peroxide.

Life for Gay People

Later that year, on the night of December 13, a seventeen-year-old named John Wear and two other boys were headed to the Soho on University Avenue when a pair of young men set upon them, calling them "faggots." One boy escaped, another's face was gashed and Wear (who, his family said, was not gay) was stabbed. Cashmore went to the hospital to see him but, on arriving, was met with the news that Wear was dead.

This is life—not all of life, but an aspect of life—for gay people in today's America. Homosexuals are objects of scorn for teenagers and of sympathy or moral fear or hatred for adults. They grow up in confusion and bewilderment as children, then often pass into denial as young adults and sometimes remain frightened even into old age. They are persecuted by the military, are denied the sanctuary of publicly recognized marriage, occasionally are prosecuted outright for making love. If closeted, they live with fear of revelation; if open, they must

Jonathan Rauch, "Beyond Oppression," *The New Republic*, May 10, 1993. Reprinted by permission of *The New Republic*; © 1993 by The New Republic, Inc.

daily negotiate a hundred delicate tactical issues. (Should I bring it up? Tell my boss? My co-workers? Wear a wedding band? Display my lover's picture?)

There is also AIDS and the stigma attached to it, though AIDS is not uniquely a problem of gay people. And there is the violence. One of my high school friends—an honors student at Brophy Prep, a prestigious Catholic high school in Phoenix, Arizona—used to boast about his late-night exploits with a baseball bat at the "fag Denny's." I'm sure he was lying, but imagine the horror of being spoken to, and about, in that way.

If you ask gay people in America today whether homosexuals are oppressed, I think most would say yes. If you ask why, they would point to the sorts of facts that I just mentioned. The facts are not blinkable. Yet the oppression diagnosis is, for the most part, wrong.

Homosexuals Are Not "Oppressed"

Not wrong in the sense that life for American homosexuals is hunky-dory. It is not. But life is not terrible for most gay people, either, and it is becoming less terrible every year. The experience of gayness and the social status of homosexuals have changed rapidly in the last twenty years, largely owing to the courage of thousands who decided that they had had enough abuse and who demanded better. With change has come the time for a reassessment.

The standard political model sees homosexuals as an oppressed minority who must fight for their liberation through political action. But that model's usefulness is drawing to a close. It is ceasing to serve the interests of ordinary gay people, who ought to begin disengaging from it, even drop it. Otherwise, they will misread their position and lose their way, as too many minority groups have done already.

"Oppression" has become every minority's word for practically everything, a one-size-fits-all political designation used by anyone who feels unequal, aggrieved or even uncomfortable. I propose a start toward restoring meaning to the notion of oppression by insisting on *objective* evidence. A sense of grievance or discomfort, however real, is not enough.

By now, human beings know a thing or two about oppression. Though it may, indeed, take many forms and work in different ways, there are objective signs you can look for. My own list would emphasize five main items. First, direct legal or governmental discrimination. Second, denial of political franchise—specifically, denial of the right to vote, organize, speak or lobby. Third—and here we move beyond the strictly political—the systematic denial of education. Fourth, impoverishment relative to the non-oppressed population. And, fifth, a pattern of human rights violations, without recourse.

> *"'Oppression' has become every minority's word for practically everything."*

Objective Signs of Oppression and Gays

Any one or two of those five signposts may appear for reasons other than oppression. There are a lot of reasons why a people may be poor, for instance. But where you see a minority that is legally barred from businesses and neighborhoods and jobs, that cannot vote, that is poor and poorly educated and that lives in physical fear, you are looking at, for instance, the blacks of South Africa, or blacks of the American South until the 1960s; the Jews and homosexuals of Nazi Germany and Vichy France; the untouchable castes of India, the Kurds of Iraq, the women of Saudi Arabia, the women of America 100 years ago; for that matter, the entire population of the former Soviet Union and many Arab and African and Asian countries.

And gay people in America today? Criterion one—direct legal or governmental discrimination—is resoundingly met. Homosexual relations are illegal in twenty-three states, at least seven of which specifically single out acts between persons of the same sex. Gay marriage is not legally recognized anywhere. And the government hounds gay people from the military, not for what they do but for what they are.

Criterion two—denial of political franchise—is resoundingly not met. Not only do gay people vote, they are turning themselves into a constituency to be reckoned with and fought for. Otherwise, the Patrick Buchanans of the world would have sounded contemptuous of gay people at the 1992 Republican convention, rather than panicked by them. If gay votes didn't count, Bill Clinton would not have

> *"Not only do gay people vote, they are turning themselves into a constituency to be reckoned with."*

stuck his neck out on the military issue during the primary season (one of the bravest things any living politician has done).

Criterion three—denial of education—is also resoundingly not met. Overlooked Opinions, Inc., a Chicago market-research company, has built a diverse national base of 35,000 gay men and lesbians, two-thirds of whom are either not out of the closet or are only marginally out, and has then randomly sampled them in surveys. It found that homosexuals had an average of 15.7 years of education, as against 12.7 years for the population as a whole. Obviously, the findings may be skewed if college-educated gay people are likelier to take part in surveys (though Overlooked Opinions said that results didn't follow degree of closetedness). Still, any claim that gay people are denied education appears ludicrous.

Criterion four—relative impoverishment—is also not met. In Overlooked Opinions' sample, gay men had an average household income of $51,624 and lesbians $42,755, compared with the national average of $36,800. Again, yuppie homosexuals may be more likely to answer survey questions than blue-collar ones. But, again, to call homosexuals an impoverished class would be silly.

Criterion five—human rights violations without recourse—is also, in the end, not met, though here it's worth taking a moment to see why it is not. The number of gay-bashings has probably increased in recent years (though it's hard to know, what with reporting vagaries), and, of course, many gay-bashers either aren't caught or aren't jailed. What too many gay people forget, though, is that these are problems that homosexuals have in common with non-gay Americans. Though many gay-bashers go free, so do many murderers. In the District of Columbia last year, the police identified suspects in fewer than half of all murders, to say nothing of assault cases.

> *"If any problem unites gay people with non-gay people, it is crime."*

Gay-Bashing and Crime

And the fact is that anti-gay violence is just one part of a much broader pattern. Probably not coincidentally, the killing of John Wear happened in the context of a year, 1991, that broke San Diego's all-time homicide record (1992 was runner-up). Since 1965 the homicide rate in America has doubled, the violent crime arrest rate for juveniles has more than tripled; people now kill you to get your car, they kill you to get your shoes or your potato chips, they kill you because they can do it. A particularly ghastly fact is that homicide due to gunshot is now the second leading cause of death in high school–age kids, after car crashes. No surprise, then, that gay people are afraid. So is everyone else.

Chances are, indeed, that gay people's social class makes them safer, on average, than other urban minorities. Certainly their problem is small compared with what blacks face in inner-city Los Angeles or Chicago, where young black males are likelier to be killed than a U.S. soldier was in a tour of duty in Vietnam.

Gay-Bashing Is Not Oppression

If any problem unites gay people with non-gay people, it is crime. If any issue does not call for special-interest pleading, this is it. Minority advocates, including gay ones, have blundered insensitively by trying to carve out hate-crime statutes and other special-interest crime laws instead of focusing on tougher measures against violence of all kinds. In trying to sensitize people to crimes aimed specifically at minorities, they are inadvertently desensitizing them to the vastly greater threat of crime against everyone. They contribute to the routinization of murder, which has now reached the point where news of a black girl spray-painted white makes the front pages, but news of a black girl murdered runs in a round-up on page D-6 ("Oh, another killing"). Yes, gay-bashing is a problem. But, no, it isn't oppression. It is, rather, an obscenely ordinary feature of the American experience.

Of course, homosexuals face unhappiness, discrimination and hatred. But for everyone with a horror story to tell, there are others like an academic I know, a tenured professor who is married to his lover of fourteen years in every way but legally, who owns a split-level condo in Los Angeles, drives a Miata, enjoys prestige and success and love that would be the envy of millions of straight Americans. These things did not fall in his lap. He fought personal and professional battles, was passed over for jobs and left the closet when that was much riskier than it is today. Asked if he is oppressed, he says, "You're damn straight." But a mark of oppression is that most of its victims are not allowed to succeed; they are allowed only to fail. And this man is no mere token. He is one of a growing multitude of openly gay people who have overcome the past and, in doing so, changed the present.

Junk the Oppression Model

"I'm a gay person, so I don't live in a free country," one highly successful gay writer said recently, "and I don't think most straight people really sit down and realize that for gay people this is basically a totalitarian society in which we're barely tolerated." The reason straight people don't realize this is because it obviously isn't true. As more and more homosexuals come out of hiding, the reality of gay economic and political and educational achievement becomes more evident. And as that happens, gay people who insist they are oppressed will increasingly, and not always unfairly, come off as yuppie whiners, "victims" with $50,000 incomes and vacations in Europe. They may feel they are oppressed, but they will have a harder and harder time convincing the public.

They will distort their politics, too, twisting it into strained and impotent shapes. Scouring for oppressions with which to identify, activists are driven further and further afield. They grab fistfuls of random political demands and stuff them in their pockets. The original platform for the April 1993 March on Washington [for gay rights] called for, among other things, enforced bilingual education, "an end to genocide of all the indigenous peoples and their cultures," defense budget cuts, universal health care, a national needle exchange program, free substance-abuse treatment on demand, safe and

> *"Yes, gay-bashing is a problem. But, no, it isn't oppression."*

affordable abortion, more money for breast cancer "and other cancers particular to women," "unrestricted, safe and affordable alternative insemination," health care for the "differently-abled and physically challenged" and "an end to poverty." Here was the oppression-entitlement mentality gone haywire.

Worst of all, oppression politics distorts the face of gay America itself. It encourages people to forget that homosexuality isn't hell. As the AIDS crisis has so movingly shown, gay people have built the kind of community that evaporated for many non-gay Americans decades ago. You don't see straight volunteers queuing up to change cancer patients' bedpans and deliver their groceries. Gay people—and unmarried people generally—are at a disadvantage in the top echelons of corporate America, but, on the other hand, they have achieved dazzlingly in culture and business and much else. They lead lives of richness and competence and infinite variety, lives that are not miserable or squashed.

The insistence that gay people are oppressed is most damaging, in the end, because it implies that to be gay is to suffer. It affirms what so many straight people, even sympathetic ones, believe in their hearts: that homosexuals are pitiable. That alone is reason to junk the oppression model, preferably sooner instead of later.

"Get Used to It"

If the oppression model is failing, what is the right model? Not that of an oppressed people seeking redemption through political action; rather, that of an ostracized people seeking redemption through personal action. What do you do about misguided ostracism? The most important thing is what Glenn Cashmore did. After John Wear's murder, he came out of the closet. He wrote an article in the *Los Angeles Times* denouncing his

> *"The insistence that gay people are oppressed is most damaging . . . because it implies that to be gay is to suffer."*

own years of silence. He stepped into the circle of people who are what used to be called known homosexuals.

This makes a difference. The *New York Times* conducted a poll on homosexuals this year and found that people who had a gay family member or close friend "were much more tolerant and accepting." Whereas oppression politics fails because it denies reality, positive personal example works because it demonstrates reality. "We're here, we're queer, get used to it," Queer Nation's chant, is not only a brilliant slogan. It is a strategy. It is, in some ways, *the* strategy. To move away from oppression politics is not to sit quietly. It is often to hold hands in public or take a lover to the company Christmas party, sometimes to stage kiss-ins, always to be unashamed. It is to make of honesty a kind of activism.

Gay Americans should emulate Jewish Americans, who have it about right. Jews recognize that to many Americans we will always seem different (and we are, in some ways, different). We grow up being fed their "culture" in school, in daily life, even in the calendar. It never stops. For a full month of every year, every radio program and shop window reminds you that this is, culturally, a Christian nation (no, not Judeo-Christian). Jews could resent this, but most of us choose not to, because, by way of compensation, we think hard, we work hard, we are cohesive, we are interesting. We recognize that minorities will always face special burdens of adjustment, but we also understand that with those burdens come rewards of community and spirit and struggle. We recognize that there will always be a minority of Americans who hate us, but we also understand that, so long as we stay watchful, this hateful minority is more pathetic than threatening. We watch it; we fight it when it lashes out; but we do not organize our personal and political lives around it.

Gay people's main weapons are ones we already possess. In America, our main enemies are superstition and hate. Superstition is extinguished by public criticism and by the power of moral example. Political activists always underestimate the power of criticism and moral example to change people's minds, and they always overestimate the power of law and force. As for hate, the way to fight it is with love. And that we have in abundance.

Hate Is Not a Crime

by Tom Metzger

About the author: *Tom Metzger is the founder of White Aryan Resistance in Fallbrook, California, which publishes the* WAR *newspaper.*

It was Malcolm X who announced to the public that with John F. Kennedy's assassination in 1963, "the chickens have come home to roost."

The Government vs. White Men

For this bit of down-home observation, white liberals and conservatives were aghast and cried foul.

With decades of Iron Heel foreign bribery (aid) and meddling (invasions), the US was the subject of unending hatred.

At the same time, millions of non-white parasites have crossed our borders, bringing disease along with all their foreign squabbles.

Since the civil wrongs laws were forced down our throats, watchmen of the race have been nursing an increased hatred of our perverted institutions. By the '80s, many of us jumped the right-wing ship due to its complete lack of success and its incessant whining and groveling. By 1983 it became obvious that both the Constitution and the so-called Democratic process had become a cruel joke.

Soon a white revolutionary group named The Order broke out of the stranglehold of the right-wing and kicked ass—robbing banks and engaging in a host of other pro-Aryan activities.

April 19, 1995, brought white racist Richard Snell's murder at the hands of the Iron Heel [Snell received the death penalty in Arkansas for two murders] and was the anniversary of the Waco, Texas, Massacre. [On April 19, 1993, the Branch Davidian sect's compound in Waco burned, killing 72 people, during a Federal Bureau of Investigation/Bureau of Alcohol, Tobacco, and Firearms attempt to arrest sect members.] We will also never forget Samuel and Vicki Weaver. [The Weaver family members were killed in August 1992 during an attempt by U.S. marshals and FBI agents to arrest Randy Weaver.]

During 1994–95 an emergence of the right-wing militia phenomenon hap-

Tom Metzger, "Editorial," *WAR*, May 1995. Reprinted with permission.

pened. The militia, as a serious military threat to the Iron Heel, is next to nothing. However, it does tie down a lot of Iron Heel agents.

The impression I get is that the Oklahoma action [the bombing of the Murrah Federal Building in Oklahoma City on April 19, 1995] was more "payback" than an act of terrorism.

The mass media look like fools. Initial reports were that the Nation of Islam claimed responsibility. Next, Arabs were blamed, and pseudoterrorist "experts" were trotted out. Next, it was the nasty and evil white supremacist militia members who were believed guilty, so they trotted out Sleeze Dees [Morris Dees, founder of the Southern Poverty Law Center].

When I saw the drawing of John Doe #2 [an unidentified suspect in the Oklahoma bombing investigation] I immediately thought Mexican, and the last name of the army deserter arrested in California sounded very Mexican. In short, there was and continues to be so much misreporting

> *"Can you truthfully say there is no one that you extremely dislike?"*

and a total lack of objectivity on the part of the media that I doubt even the most complacent sheeple will look to the media in the future.

If I understood my terrorist reading, the whole purpose of terrorism is not to win by one act, but to divide people into groups and make the government overreact.

Clinton and the mass media have played into this scenario. Most of the weekend militia revolutionaries will be scared off since they want to be "popular." Those who were bothered by the Waco incident will note that the Clintons and the media were not concerned with the killing of children when it was state sponsored terrorism. Thus the whole initial purpose of terrorism, weeding out the weak and further dividing people into camps, has been accomplished. You can bet that legislation will be enacted which will be seen as additional "proof" of a coming police state.

Even with the wrong understanding and fuzzy logic on the race issue, militias will continue unknowingly to furnish spin-off "lone wolves" for a more serious and covert struggle.

In the meantime, dive to periscope depth; run silent and run deep. Iron Heel depth charges are already breaking through the waves. The weak will head for their holes. The phony leaders will conjure up another flim-flam story to cover up their cowardice; but in the end, *might will still be right*, as in all the ages past. Either rise to the threat or run. There is no other solution.

Discrimination Is Natural

Lets talk about hate crime. Since most people are hypocrites, they will swear up and down that they don't hate anyone. When you ask if they love, like trained seals they will clap and say, "Oh, yes, we love." The dictionary description of hate is simply extreme dislike. Now, can you truthfully say there is no one that you extremely dislike? If you extremely dislike someone or something, then you naturally discriminate against them. Discrimination is as old as man and animal.

A rabbit discriminates against a fox. The same is true when a white man observes Negroes, Latrinos and Asians overrunning his territory. If the white man is not flawed physically or mentally, he will know that more of them means less of us. At some point the increased numbers of them will mean the end of us, pure and simple. Neither you nor the rabbit needs a Harvard education to understand basic addition and subtraction.

The rabbit is programmed to run as long and as fast as it can. Many white people take this course of action, but eventually there is no place to run.

They are cornered like the rabbit and rightfully become a fine meal.

Fortunately, the white man has the ability to think on a higher level. Unfortunately, his mind over the years became dull and clouded by myths and stories which weakened his hate abilities. In most cases, from birth, we are told to suppress hatred and embrace tolerance. Tolerance toward an invader or enemy of course is suicide. An invader of the gene pool cannot be tolerated in any way. If the rabbit or the deer took a few seconds to ponder toleration, their species would have been extinct long ago. When the baboon sees a lion walking toward him there is not a split second to ponder if this is a loving lion or a hateful lion. Nothing personal. The lion wants to eat the baboon and the baboon chooses not to be eaten. This is how it should be with the white man. It's not personal; it is pure survival. If the protection of one's habitat and gene pool from alien races is hatred, then it is logical and should be accepted as such.

> *"White man, you have the greatest reason in history to kill."*

The social engineers and Jewish intellectuals are fools with all their drivel about rights, ethics and the sanctity of life; There is no such thing. It is false logic forced onto the public at large. These myths will never work for long, and Nature always makes payback a bitch.

Race Hatred Is Not the Worst Crime

As for so-called crimes, the logic is reversed. A person who has a strong reason such as race to kill for should be afforded much more latitude than one who commits a crime for no reason. Today many are killed without the slightest logic. A person submits, is robbed and then murdered for no direct reason. A person who commits a senseless crime then is afforded much more lenience than a person who can state in court a specific reason why he killed.

For example, in the Old West, when someone was caught for horse stealing, he was shot on the spot or hung. The reason was clear. Without a horse, you and your children could die of hunger because you lost your horse. Hate crime?

Of course not; just plain logic and reason.

An Eskimo's hunting ground is invaded and his dogs are stolen. Without them he will die. Logic: track the thief and execute him.

Today white men are in a box created by alien forces. Each day millions of white men who know the truth in their bones cower down in fear of so-called hate crime laws. Not one of us totally escapes this threat. Your country is invaded, your neighborhoods invaded, your women are carried off and you are told to be tolerant, turn the other cheek, learn to get along. In short to surrender.

When you obey millions of years of natural development and logic, you are called a hater and it is true. Don't deny it. Of course we hate, with a perfect hatred. The premise is correct, the logic is correct, and the answer is correct. White man, you have the greatest reason in history to kill. Is it a hate crime? It is surely hate, but a crime? I don't think so. You are being compressed every day into a tighter, heavier mass of hatred.

Sooner or later, no matter how dismal it may look, that nucleus will be split like an atom and the social explosion which will occur will be like nothing before seen. It will be the time of Ragnarok [the great battle between good and evil in Norse (Aryan) mythology]. At that time all the philosophers, media, priests, preachers and humanists will be blown away as chaff in the wind, by Nature's long-suffering battle ax.

THIS IS WAR!

Chapter 2

Should Racist Hate Speech Be Limited?

Hate Crime and Free Speech: An Overview

by Kenneth Jost

About the author: *Kenneth Jost is a staff writer for* CQ Researcher, *a weekly news and research report published by Congressional Quarterly, Inc.*

St. Paul, Minnesota, enacted a local hate crime ordinance in 1982. Instead of adopting the Anti-Defamation League's (ADL) penalty-enhancement model [which provided increased penalties for crimes in which the victim was selected because of race, religion, or sexual orientation], however, St. Paul decided to create a new offense: bias-motivated disorderly conduct. Under the ordinance, anyone who "places on public or private property a symbol, object, appellation, characterization or graffiti" that "arouses anger, alarm or resentment in others on the basis of race, color, creed or religion" was guilty of the misdemeanor offense of disorderly conduct. The city amended the law in 1989 to specifically include a burning cross or a Nazi swastika in the prohibitions and in 1990 to prohibit actions based on sexual prejudice.

Hate Crime or Free Speech

In the summer of 1990, prosecutors invoked the St. Paul ordinance for the first time. A group of teenagers was charged with placing a burning cross in the front yard of Russ and Laura Jones, who had recently become the first black family to move into a white working-class block in East St. Paul. Besides the St. Paul ordinance, the defendants were also charged with committing a racially motivated assault in violation of the state's hate crime law.

The defendants in the case included Robert A. Viktora, then seventeen, a high school dropout and a "skinhead"—a rapidly growing, youth-oriented group that preaches violence against blacks, Jews and gays. Viktora's court-appointed attorney, Edward J. Cleary, decided to challenge the St. Paul ordinance on constitutional grounds. Cleary did not contest the state charge against his client, but he said the local ordinance was overbroad because it directly punished "expressive" conduct. "In a country that values free speech, we should not have a law that says that expressing certain ideas, however offensive they may be, is in itself a crime," Cleary told one reporter.

The Ramsey County [Minnesota] juvenile court judge who heard Viktora's plea agreed and struck the law down. But in January 1991, the Minnesota Supreme Court revived the law. The court narrowly construed the law to apply only to what the U.S. Supreme Court had called in a 1942 case (*Chaplinsky v. New Hampshire*) "fighting words"—words that have "a direct tendency to cause acts of violence by the person to whom, individually, the remark is addressed." Under that construction, the state court concluded, the law was valid.

On June 10, 1991, the U.S. Supreme Court decided to review Viktora's case, which was formally called *R.A.V. v. St. Paul*, since juveniles are ordinarily not identified by name in juvenile court cases. The high court's action signaled a likely inclination to overturn the law. And even many supporters of the law conceded it had problems. The Anti-Defamation League filed a brief defending the law—as narrowed by the Minnesota court—even though officials acknowledged the ordinance went beyond the ADL's recommended statute.

> *"The justices voted unanimously to strike down the St. Paul ordinance, but they divided into two camps in explaining the decision."*

Ramsey County prosecutor Tom Foley, who was to argue the case before the Supreme Court, also acknowledged the law could not be applied literally. "If the cross had been burned down at the corner, at the middle of the day, at a protest, that's probably not something you could prosecute," Foley told a reporter on the eve of the arguments. "What if it's midnight, and right in front of the Joneses' house? That's closer to the line."

A Divided Court

The Supreme Court's decision on June 22, 1992, however, went further than the parties to the case or most observers had expected. The justices voted unanimously to strike down the St. Paul ordinance, but they divided into two camps in explaining the decision. A minority of four justices concluded that the law was overbroad because, even under the Minnesota court's ruling, it could be applied to protected forms of expression. On that basis, the four justices said, the law had to be struck down, but a narrower one might survive.

A five-justice majority, however, concluded that the ordinance was unconstitutional because it impermissibly singled out for prosecution specific types of expression—racial, religious or sexual insults—on the basis of their content. " The First Amendment does not permit St. Paul to impose special prohibitions on those speakers who express views on disfavored subjects," Justice Antonin Scalia wrote for the majority.

Scalia emphasized that the cross-burning could have been punished under several other laws—some of them carrying stiffer penalties than the St. Paul ordinance. But to pass constitutional muster, he said, any law limiting forms of expression had to be free of "content discrimination." A law targeting a particular kind of bigotry would not pass that test.

The four justices in the minority sharply challenged Scalia's reasoning and indirectly accused him of harboring a broader, unstated agenda. Justice Byron R. White said Scalia's rationale would prevent the use of civil rights laws in cases where racial epithets or sexual harassment created a "hostile work environment." Justice Harry A. Blackmun implied that Scalia's real goal was to nullify campus speech codes. "I fear that the Court has been distracted from its proper mission by the temptation to decide the issue over 'politically correct speech' and 'cultural diversity,' neither of which is presented here," Blackmun wrote.

Some observers outside the court also saw evidence of a conservative agenda in Scalia's opinion—and in the way the justices divided. Scalia led a predominantly conservative bloc that also included Chief Justice William H. Rehnquist and Justices Anthony M. Kennedy, David H. Souter and Clarence Thomas. There was a more liberal cast to the four-justice minority of White, Blackmun, John Paul Stevens and Sandra Day O'Connor.

Supporters of hate crime laws tried to counter a broad reading of the court's decision. ADL officials issued statements saying that hate crimes were still against the law and that their approach of increasing penalties for bias-motivated offenses would be upheld. But before the summer ended, state supreme courts in Wisconsin and Ohio had reached the opposite conclusion and decided to strike down hate crime laws directly modeled after the ADL proposal.

Hate Crimes Violate the Free Speech Rights of Victims

by Charles R. Lawrence III

About the author: *Charles R. Lawrence III is a professor of law at Stanford University in Palo Alto, California.*

In the early morning hours of June 21, 1990, long after they had put their five children to bed, Russ and Laura Jones were awakened by voices outside their house. Russ got up, went to his bedroom window and peered into the dark. "I saw a glow," he recalled. There, in the middle of his yard, was a burning cross. The Joneses are black. In the spring of 1990 they had moved into their four-bedroom, three-bathroom dream house on 290 Earl Street in St. Paul, Minnesota. They were the only black family on the block. Two weeks after they had settled into their predominantly white neighborhood, the tires on both their cars were slashed. A few weeks later, one of their cars' windows was shattered, and a group of teenagers had walked past their house and shouted "nigger" at their nine-year-old son. And now this burning cross. Russ Jones did not have to guess at the meaning of this symbol of racial hatred. There is not a black person in America who has not been taught the significance of this instrument of persecution and intimidation, who has not had emblazoned on his mind the image of black men's scorched bodies hanging from trees, and who does not know the story of Emmett Till. (Emmett Till, a fourteen-year-old boy from Chicago, was killed while visiting relatives in Mississippi in 1955. His alleged "wolf whistle" at a white woman provoked his murderer.) One can only imagine the terror which Russell Jones must have felt as he watched the flames and thought of the vulnerability of his family and of the hateful, cowardly viciousness of those who would attack him and those he loved under cover of darkness.

Excerpted from "Crossburning and the Sound of Silence: Antisubordination Theory and the First Amendment" by Charles R. Lawrence III, *Villanova Law Review*, vol. 37, no. 4 (1992), pp. 787ff. Reprinted with permission.

Free Speech vs. the Victims' Rights

This assault on Russ Jones and his family begins the story of *R.A.V. v. City of St. Paul*, the "hate speech" case decided in 1992 by the United States Supreme Court. The Joneses, however, are not the subject of the Court's opinion. The constitutional injury addressed in *R.A.V.* was not this black family's right to live where they pleased, or their right to associate with their neighbors. The Court was not concerned with how this attack might impede the exercise of the Joneses' constitutional right to be full and valued participants in the political community, for it did not view *R.A.V.* as a case about the Joneses' injury. Instead, the Court was concerned primarily with the alleged constitutional injury to those who assaulted the Joneses, that is, the First Amendment rights of the cross burners. [The majority opinion of the Court ruled that the St. Paul ordinance was unconstitutional because it targeted the viewpoints expressed by certain acts like cross burning while allowing other viewpoints to be expressed—ed.]

There is much that is deeply troubling about Justice Antonin Scalia's majority opinion in *R.A.V.* But it is the utter disregard for the silenced voice of the victims that is most frightening. Nowhere in the opinion is any mention made of the Jones family or of their constitutional rights. Nowhere are we told of the history of the Ku Klux Klan or of its use of the burning cross as a tool for the suppression of speech. Justice Scalia turns the First Amendment on its head, transforming an act intended to silence through terror and intimidation into an invitation to join a public discussion. In so doing, he clothes the cross burner's terroristic act in the legitimacy of protected political speech and invites him to burn again.

> *"Nowhere in the [R.A.V.] opinion is any mention made of the Jones family or of their constitutional rights."*

"Let there be no mistake about our belief that burning a cross in someone's front yard is reprehensible," writes Justice Scalia at the close of his opinion. I am skeptical about his concern for the victims. These words seem little more than an obligatory genuflection to decency. For even in this attempt to assure the reader of his good intentions, Justice Scalia's words betray his inability to see the Joneses or hear their voices. "Burning a cross in *someone's* front yard is *reprehensible*," he says. It is reprehensible but not injurious, or immoral, or violative of the Joneses' rights. For Justice Scalia, the identity of the "someone" is irrelevant. As is the fact that it is a *cross* that is burned.

When I first read Justice Scalia's opinion it felt as if another cross had just been set ablaze. This cross was burning on the pages of *United States Reports*. It was a cross like the cross that Justice Roger B. Taney had burned in 1857, [in the *Dred Scott v. Sanford* decision, which held that blacks were not U.S. citizens], and that which Justice Henry Billings Brown had burned in 1896 [in the *Plessy v. Ferguson* decision, which upheld segregation]. Its message: You have no rights which a white man is bound to respect (or protect). If you are injured by this assaultive act, the injury is a figment of your imagination that is not constitutionally cognizable.

Hate Speech Harms the Rights of Victims

For the past couple of years I have been struggling to find a way to talk to my friends in the civil liberties community about the injuries which are ignored in the *R.A.V.* case. I have tried to articulate the ways in which hate speech harms its victims and the ways in which it harms us all by undermining core values in our Constitution.

The first of these values is full and equal citizenship expressed in the Fourteenth Amendment's Equal Protection Clause. When hate speech is employed with the purpose and effect of maintaining established systems of caste and subordination, it violates that core value. Hate speech often prevents its victims from exercising legal rights guaranteed by the Constitution and civil rights statutes. The second constitutional value threatened by hate speech is the value of free expression itself. Hate speech frequently silences its victims, who, more often than not, are those who are already heard from least. An understanding of both of these injuries is aided by the methodologies of feminism and critical race theory that give special attention to the structures of subordination and the voices of the subordinated.

Free Speech vs. Discrimination on College Campuses

My own understanding of the need to inform the First Amendment discourse with the insights of an antisubordination theory began in the context of the debate over the regulation of hate speech on campus. As I lectured at universities throughout the United States, I learned of serious racist and anti-Semitic hate incidents. Students who had been victimized told me of swastikas appearing on Jewish holy days. Stories of cross burnings, racist slurs and vicious verbal assaults made me cringe even as I heard them secondhand. Universities, long the home of institutional and euphemistic racism, were witnessing the worst forms of gutter racism. In

> *"Hate speech harms its victims and . . . harms us all by undermining core values in our Constitution."*

1990, the *Chronicle of Higher Education* reported that approximately 250 colleges and universities had experienced serious racist incidents since 1986, and the National Institute Against Prejudice and Violence estimated that 25 percent of all minority students are victimized at least once during an academic year.

I urged my colleagues to hear these students' voices and argued that *Brown v. Board of Education of Topeka, Kansas* (1954) and its antidiscrimination principle identified an injury of constitutional dimension done to these students that must be recognized and remedied. We do not normally think of *Brown* as being a case about speech. Most narrowly read, it is a case about the rights of black children to equal educational opportunity. But *Brown* teaches us another very important lesson: that the harm of segregation is achieved by the meaning of the message it conveys. The Court's opinion in *Brown* stated that racial segregation is unconstitutional not because the physical separation of black and white children is bad or because resources were distributed unequally among black and white

> "**Brown** *held that segregated schools were unconstitutional primarily because of the message segregation conveys.*"

schools. *Brown* held that segregated schools were unconstitutional primarily because of the message segregation conveys—the message that black children are an untouchable caste, unfit to be educated with white children. Segregation stamps a badge of inferiority upon blacks. This badge communicates a message to others that signals their exclusion from the community of citizens.

Discrimination Conveys a Message

The "Whites Only" signs on the lunch counter, swimming pool and drinking fountain convey the same message. The antidiscrimination principle articulated in *Brown* presumptively entitles every individual to be treated by the organized society as a respected, responsible and participating member. This is the principle upon which all our civil rights laws rest. It is the guiding principle of the Equal Protection Clause's requirement of nondiscriminatory government action. In addition, it has been applied in regulating private discrimination.

The words "Women Need Not Apply" in a job announcement, the racially exclusionary clause in a restrictive covenant and the racial epithet scrawled on the locker of the new black employee at a previously all-white job site all convey a political message. But we treat these messages as "discriminatory practices" and outlaw them under federal and state civil rights legislation because they are more than speech. In the context of social inequality, these verbal and symbolic acts form integral links in historically ingrained systems of social discrimination. They work to keep traditionally victimized groups in socially isolated, stigmatized and disadvantaged positions through the promotion of fear, intolerance, degradation and violence. The Equal Protection Clause of the Fourteenth Amendment requires the disestablishment of these practices and systems. Likewise, the First Amendment does *not* prohibit our accomplishment of this compelling constitutional interest simply because those discriminatory practices are achieved through the use of words and symbols.

The primary intent of the cross burner in *R.A.V.* was not to enter into a dialogue with the Joneses, or even with the larger community. . . . His purpose was to intimidate—to cast fear in the hearts of his victims, to drive them out of the community, to enforce the practice of residential segregation, and to encourage others to join him in the enforcement of that practice. The discriminatory impact of this speech is of even more importance than the speaker's intent. In protecting victims of discrimination, it is the presence of this discriminatory impact, which is a compelling governmental interest unrelated to the suppression of the speaker's political message, that requires a balancing of interests rather than a presumption against constitutionality. This is especially true when the interests that compete with speech are also interests of constitutional dimension.

Verbal Assaults Are Discrimination

One such interest is in enforcing the antidiscrimination principle. Those opposed to the regulation of hate speech often view the interest involved as the maintenance of civility, the protection of sensibilities from offense, or the prohibition of group defamation. But this analysis misconstrues the nature of the injury. "Defamation—injury to group reputation—is not the same as discrimination—injury to group status and treatment." The former "is more ideational and less material" than the latter, "which recognizes the harm of second-class citizenship and inferior social standing with the attendant deprivation of access to resources, voice, and power," according to the National Black Women's Health Project.

The Title VII paradigm of "hostile environment" discrimination best describes the injury to which victims of racist, sexist and homophobic hate speech are subjected. When plaintiffs in employment discrimination suits have been subjected to racist or sexist verbal harassment in the workplace, courts have recognized that such assaultive speech denies the targeted individual equal access to employment. These verbal assaults most often occur in settings where the relatively recent and token integration of the workplace makes the victim particularly vulnerable and where the privately voiced message of denigration and exclusion echoes the whites-only and males-only practices that were all-too-recently official policy.

Robinson v. Jacksonville Shipyards, Inc. (1991), a Title VII case that appears to be headed for review in the Supreme Court, presents a clear example of the tension between the law's commitment to free speech and its commitment to equality. Lois Robinson, a welder, was one of a very small number of female skilled craftworkers employed by Jacksonville Shipyards. She brought suit under Title VII of the Civil Rights Act of 1964, alleging that her employer had created and encouraged a sexually hostile, intimidating work environment. A U.S. District Court ruled in her favor, finding that the presence in the workplace of pictures of women in various stages of undress and in sexually suggestive or submissive poses, as well as remarks made by male employees and supervisors which demeaned women, constituted a violation of Title VII "through the maintenance of a sexually hostile work environment." Much of District Court Judge Howell

> *" 'Hostile environment' discrimination best describes the injury to which victims of . . . hate speech are subjected."*

Melton's opinion is a recounting of the indignities that Ms. Robinson and five other women experienced almost daily while working with 850 men over the course of ten years. In addition to the omnipresent display of sexually explicit drawings, graffiti, calendars, centerfold-style pictures, magazines and cartoons, the trial record contains a number of incidents in which sexually suggestive pictures and comments were directed at Robinson. Male employees admitted that the shipyard was "a boys' club" and "more or less a man's world."

The local chapter of the American Civil Liberties Union (ACLU) appealed the District Court's decision, arguing that "even sexists have a right to free speech." However, anyone who has read the trial record cannot help but wonder about these civil libertarians' lack of concern for Lois Johnson's right to do her work without being subjected to assault.

The trial record makes clear that Lois Robinson's male colleagues had little concern for advancing the cause of erotic speech when they made her the target of pornographic comments and graffiti. They wanted to put the usurper of their previously all-male domain in her place, to remind her of her sexual vulnerability and to send her back home where she belonged. This speech, like the burning cross in *R.A.V.*, does more than communicate an idea. It interferes with the victim's right to work at a job where she is free from degradation because of her gender.

Hate Speech Limits Free Speech for Others

But it is not sufficient to describe the injury occasioned by hate speech only in terms of the countervailing value of equality. There is also an injury to the First Amendment. When Russ Jones looked out his window and saw that burning cross, he heard a message that said, "*Shut up, black man, or risk harm to you and your family.*" It may be that Russ Jones is especially brave, or especially foolhardy, and that he may speak even more loudly in the face of this threat. But it is more likely that he will be silenced, and that *we* will lose the benefit of his voice.

> "*When Russ Jones . . . saw that burning cross, he heard a message that said, 'Shut up, black man, or risk harm to you and your family.'*"

Professor Laurence H. Tribe has identified two values protected by the First Amendment. The first is the intrinsic value of speech, which is the value of individual self-expression. Speech is intrinsically valuable as a manifestation of our humanity and our individuality. The second is the instrumental value of speech. The First Amendment protects dissent to maximize public discourse, and to achieve the great flowering of debate and ideas that we need to make our democracy work. Both of these values are implicated in the silencing of Russ Jones by his nocturnal attacker.

For African-Americans, the intrinsic value of speech as self-expression and self-definition has been particularly important. The absence of a "black voice" was central to the ideology of European-American racism, an ideology that denied Africans their humanity and thereby justified their enslavement. African-American slaves were prevented from learning to read and write, and they were prohibited from engaging in forms of self-expression that might instill in them a sense of self-worth and pride. Their silence and submission was then interpreted as evidence of their subhuman status. The use of the burning cross as a method of disempowerment originates, in part, in the perpetrators' understanding of how, in the context of this ideology, their victims are rendered subhuman when they are silenced. When, in the face of threat and intimidation, the oppressors' victims are afraid to give full expression to their individuality, the oppressors achieve their purpose of denying the victims the liberty guaranteed to them by the Constitution.

> *"First Amendment law ignores the way in which . . . racism silences people of color."*

When the Joneses moved to Earl Street in St. Paul, they were expressing their individuality. When they chose their house and their neighbors, they were saying, "This is who we are. We are a proud black family and we want to live here." This self-expression and self-definition is the intrinsic value of speech. The instrumental value of speech is likewise threatened by this terrorist attack on the Joneses. Russ and Laura Jones also brought new voices to the political discourse in this St. Paul community. Ideally, they will vote and talk politics with their neighbors. They will bring new experiences and new perspectives to their neighborhood. A burning cross not only silences people like the Joneses, it impoverishes the democratic process and renders our collective conversation less informed.

Regulating Private Behavior to Guarantee Equality

First Amendment doctrine and theory have no words for the injuries of silence imposed by private actors. There is no language for the damage that is done to the First Amendment when the hateful speech of the cross burner or the sexual harasser silences its victims. In antidiscrimination law, we recognize the necessity of regulating private behavior that threatens the values of equal citizenship. Fair housing laws, public accommodations provisions and employment discrimination laws all regulate the behavior of private actors. We recognize that much of the discrimination in our society occurs without the active participation of the state. We know that we could not hope to realize the constitutional ideal of equal citizenship if we pretended that the government was the only discriminator.

But there is no recognition in First Amendment law of the systematic private suppression of speech. Courts and scholars have worried about the heckler's veto, and, where there is limited access to speech fora, we have given attention to questions of equal time and the right to reply. But for the most part, we act as if the government is the only regulator of speech, the only censor. We treat the marketplace of ideas as if all voices are equal, as if there are no silencing voices or voices that are silenced. In the discourse of the First Amendment, there is no way to talk about how those who are silenced are always less powerful than those who do the silencing. First Amendment law ignores the ways in which patriarchy silences women, and racism silences people of color. When a woman's husband threatens to beat her the next time she contradicts him, a First Amendment injury has occurred. "Gay-bashing" keeps gays and lesbians "in the closet." It silences them. They are denied the humanizing experience of self-expression. We *all* are denied the insight and beauty of their voices. . . .

In the rush to protect the "speech" of cross burners, would-be champions of the First Amendment must not forget the voices of their victims. If First Amendment doctrine and theory is to truly serve First Amendment ideals, it must recognize the injury done by the private suppression of speech; it must take into account the historical reality that some members of our community are less powerful than others and that those persons continue to be systematically silenced by those who are more powerful. If we are truly committed to free speech, First Amendment doctrine and theory must be guided by the principle of antisubordination. There can be no free speech where there are still masters and slaves.

Speech Codes Are Necessary to Fight Racism on Campuses

by William R. Cotter

About the author: *William R. Cotter is the president of Colby College in Waterville, Maine.*

In January 1993, as a group of black women gathered outside a high-rise dorm at the University of Pennsylvania joyfully—and noisily—marked the rounding of their sorority, hateful words—"nigger," "bitch," "fat ass"—pelted them from the rooms above. In another incident at Penn in 1993, black students allegedly seized almost every copy of the daily campus newspaper because they objected to the opinions of a columnist. Both events—and the university's response to them—put Penn and its president, Sheldon Hackney, at the center of an increasingly volatile conflict between free speech and racial harassment.

Free Speech vs. Racial Harassment

The university took no immediate action against the students involved in the newspaper incident, though when Hackney was nominated by President Clinton to head the National Endowment for the Humanities, a Penn spokesperson told the press that the students would be subject to disciplinary action. And they should be, because what they did was equivalent to tearing down a poster or heckling a speaker into silence. Their act constituted a clear violation of free speech.

In contrast, Penn moved swiftly against the one student who admitted taunting the sorority sisters, (although he personally said he simply called them "water buffalos") and the attention that case received raises troubling questions about the right—indeed, the obligation—of colleges and universities to protect all members of their communities from all forms of abuse while giving priority to our fundamental commitment to freedom of expression.

Right now, on editorial pages across the country, in Congress and in the broader arena of ideas, a battle is being fought that may redraw the boundaries of free speech. Some say speech of all kinds should be protected. Others, myself included, say private colleges not only have the legal *right* to enforce speech codes that prohibit verbal harassment, they have a *responsibility* to do so.

Balancing Free Speech and Civility

At first blush it may seem incongruous for a college president to advocate any restriction on speech. Colleges and universities were designed as havens for the free and open exchange of ideas. One of the oldest traditions we have—the tenure system—was instituted partly to allow academics to pursue their ideas without fear of losing their salaries along with a king's favor or a university president's approval. I am dedicated completely to the preservation of tenure and of colleges as sanctuaries of unfettered thought.

> *"Colleges not only have the legal* **right** *to enforce speech codes that prohibit verbal harassment, they have a* **responsibility** *to do so."*

But as the president of a private college, I have a unique trust. Unlike state universities, which are bound by constitutional interpretations that increasingly restrict their ability to act against verbal harassment, private colleges (except in California) are free to enact speech codes. So my peer presidents and I are presented with a challenge: to balance the need for free speech with the need to provide a civil atmosphere for all of our students. Indeed, the easy way out would be to refuse to institute sanctions against any kind of speech. But that would be irresponsible, and college presidents should not walk away from this challenge. After all, we do not preside over institutions that are the equivalents of Hyde Park Speakers' Corner [in London], where hate speech can be spewed and passersby have the option to stop and listen or to keep going, secure in the knowledge that they probably will never see the speaker again. Colleges, especially small colleges like Colby College, in Waterville, Maine, are more like families; members of these communities cannot avoid each other for long, and they certainly cannot—and should not have to—avoid common walkways for fear of being harassed verbally.

Increased Racism on College Campuses

The Penn case is only the most recent in a string of incidents in which students were subjected to such abuse. In 1991, a student was expelled from Brown University for yelling anti-Semitic, anti-homosexual and racist epithets from his room into a common courtyard. At Colby, we have disciplined both black and white students for racial taunts. The Universities of Michigan and Massachusetts—and many others—have grappled with hate graffiti. Officials in the University of California system warn of a "backlash" against Asian-American students. Occidental College, also in California, recently became enmeshed in conflicting state and federal lawsuits after they announced that they planned to hold disciplinary hearings under their sexual harassment policy against a group of fraternity men who ran to a sorority singing about mutilating women's genitalia with a chain saw. In each case, the colleges and universities involved have tried to reconcile their commitment to free speech with their desire to guard against verbal harassment—especially of minority students and women.

Words wound. The old rhyme that ends "but names will never hurt me" wasn't true for the women at Penn. I suspect it isn't true for any of us. Hurtful words can resonate in our lives more deeply than superficial physical injuries—a fact recognized recently by U.S. Roman Catholic bishops, who noted that "violence in any form—physical, sexual, psychological or verbal [emphasis mine]—is sinful." People who use words as weapons against others should find no shelter at our colleges and universities. This can occasionally involve written words, such as racist, misogynist, or anti-Semitic notes affixed to the door of a dormitory room or on the customary classroom seat of an intended victim. However, most written speech, in college newspapers for example, advocating even outrageous views must normally be unfettered unless it descends to libel or constitutes such a vicious, personal attack on an individual or a small group that it would be the equivalent of proscribed verbal harassment.

> *"Hurtful words can resonate in our lives more deeply than superficial physical injuries."*

College administrators have striven for many years to build diverse communities on their campuses, communities that reflect the makeup of the nation as a whole—and we've done so with support from the U.S. Supreme Court and others outside higher education. But it is not enough to *admit* a diverse student body. We have an obligation to protect those who are vulnerable to physical and verbal harassment. By definition, educational institutions must provide an atmosphere in which learning can take place. Order is required for meaningful discussion, and support for those who may feel vulnerable is necessary if they are to participate in the educational process. Speech that injures or silences people limits participation and impedes education.

Calls for Abolishing Speech Codes

Nevertheless, many in the media, in Congress and even in the American Civil Liberties Union (ACLU) seem insensitive to the obligation of a college to create a civil atmosphere.

In 1992, a *Wall Street Journal* editorial condemned Colby, along with Penn, Stanford University, the University of Minnesota, the University of Florida and Brown University, for trying to curb verbal harassment. The editorial misquoted and distorted Colby's policies and subsequently failed to print a clarifying letter from me. In June 1993, the *Journal* took pride in the turmoil they helped cause at Penn and called for the abolition of all speech codes, even the most carefully crafted and sparingly used. "We were happy to have played some part in bringing . . . the case at Penn to wider public attention," the editors wrote.

> But it is important to understand how unexceptional that case was. That this awful intimidation and self-censorship flourishes elsewhere is caused by the fact that so many schools are led by what are simply weak men. . . . [W]hat we learned at Penn and elsewhere is that it is time for the speech codes to go. Abolish them. They are a blot on the idea of a university.

No. Carefully drawn speech codes are an essential part of the university's obligation to preserve an environment where free speech can flourish. Would the *Journal*—or any newspaper—permit its employees to hurl racial, sexist or anti-Semitic epithets at each other in the newsroom on the grounds that free speech must be protected? Of course not. Nor should colleges allow such behavior.

The *Journal* also criticized 200 members of Harvard's class of 1993 for turning their backs on General Colin Powell as he delivered his commencement address, even though the *Journal* usually champions such examples of free expression. In this case I agree with the *Journal*. Some of us "weak men" (and women) in higher education work hard to guarantee the right of controversial speakers to be heard on our campuses and implore our students and faculty to listen to opposing views. When rumors reached me that some faculty members and students were considering a boycott of Colby's 1993 commencement because Bob Dole was to address the ceremony, I objected in a public forum. I told the assembled senior class and the faculty that such an action would not only be impolite, since Senator Dole was a guest of the college, but would violate the most basic understanding of the obligation to listen—particularly in an academic community whose purpose is the pursuit of knowledge.

> **"Speech that injures or silences people limits participation and impedes education."**

We are obliged to make special efforts to seek out contrary opinions and to encourage others to do so, and boycotting speakers—before we have even given them a chance to be heard—seems to me almost as offensive as interfering with free speech itself. Of *course* I recognize the importance of free speech, but I draw the line when speech is used not to communicate ideas but simply to injure others.

Congressional Action to Abolish Speech Codes

Not only do newspapers such as the *Journal* rail against policies designed to promote verbal civility on campus, so do many conservatives in Congress—with, oddly enough, the blessings of the ACLU.

In 1991, Congressman Henry Hyde introduced HR 1380 to amend Title VI of the Civil Rights Act of 1964 "to protect the free speech rights of college students." His bill would have applied First Amendment prohibitions that now affect only state institutions (including public universities) to private colleges. Lower federal courts have struck down verbal harassment codes enacted at state universities in Michigan and Wisconsin, although the U.S. Supreme Court has not yet passed on their constitutionality. But the Court's 1992 decision in *R.A.V. v. City of St. Paul, Minnesota,* may have elimi-

nated even the "fighting words" exception to the First Amendment established a half century ago, so hate speech codes at state universities may be unconstitutional even when they try to restrain "fighting words." How-

> *"I draw the line when speech is used not to communicate ideas but simply to injure others."*

ever, the Supreme Court has yet to rule directly on this issue, and I hope that some state university administrators will stand by needed codes and appeal any adverse lower court decisions until there is a definitive Supreme Court ruling.

In earlier cases, the Supreme Court has specifically encouraged colleges to recruit a diverse student body and has held, in the public school context, that administrators of public institutions have broad powers to guarantee an orderly and civil atmosphere. It is possible, therefore, that the Court might uphold a carefully tailored state university speech code.

Colleges Must Combat Bigoted Speech

When he introduced his bill, Hyde said, "I do not condone bigoted speech, but driving such sentiments underground through academic sanctions does not eliminate bigotry. It just makes it fester. Instead, we should unleash the most effective weapon of the democratic society—more speech."

More *bigoted* speech? More epithets thrown from one side to the other and back? More drunken shouting from windows? Does that increase understanding? Does that help individuals explore unpopular opinions? Is there a difference between speech and harassing epithets? If so, how can a line be drawn and what should colleges do?

The ACLU endorsed the Hyde bill, and its president, Nadine Strossen, appeared with Hyde when he introduced it. Yet the ACLU tells us in other policy papers that "colleges and universities have an affirmative obligation to combat racism, sexism, homophobia, and other forms of bias." They advise a college to "utilize every opportunity to communicate through its administrators, faculty and students its commitment to the elimination of all forms of bigotry on campus." But if colleges cannot respond meaningfully to bigoted speech or hate graffiti aimed at students, how can we fulfill that commitment? Would simple condemnation of uncivil speech restore the feeling of belonging and security to which all students are entitled? I doubt it.

I, along with officials from other colleges, met with Mr. Hyde to explain the difficulty we face in trying to ensure both free speech and freedom from verbal assault. I told him about a white Colby student who had jeered the opposing team at a hotly contested basketball game with racial taunts. Colby security officers warned the student, then removed him from the gym, and he subsequently was denied his sport's captaincy. Mr. Hyde agreed that the college should have taken action in that case. But Hyde's proposed legislation and the *Journal*'s advice would prevent private colleges from taking such steps if they wished to continue receiving federal money.

Michael Grieves, the executive director of the conservative, Washington-based Center for Individual Rights, says his organization would not have defended the expelled Brown University student. (Center lawyers successfully defended Professor Michael Levin of City College of New York, who was under investigation for saying that blacks are intellectually inferior to whites, as well as a George Mason University fraternity that held an "Ugly Woman" contest in which a young man appeared in blackface.) "There is a real distinction," says Grieves, "between genuine speech and being a lout and having nothing to say at all." I agree, and this crucial distinction is exactly what the colleges must try to define.

> *"If colleges cannot respond meaningfully to bigoted speech, . . . how can we fulfill that commitment [to eliminate bigotry]?"*

A Fairer System for Handling Complaints Is Needed

So, am I saying that I believe students who cross the line between free speech and verbal abuse ought to be expelled immediately? Absolutely not. No one learns anything that way. But how can we protect, even *invite* unpopular speech and controversial opinions—including those that touch on matters of race, religion or gender—while censuring verbal harassment? By creating a system for airing complaints that everyone can trust to be genuinely fair.

Both the University of Pennsylvania student who admitted shouting at the black sorority sisters and the women themselves say the case was handled badly. Five months after the complaint was lodged—after a storm of publicity—the women dropped the charges, saying that not only had they been harassed, they had been "further victimized by the media and, thereafter, by the judicial process and agents of the university."

Over the years, Penn has developed an intricate system for reviewing campus disciplinary matters—but that intricacy lends itself to the kind of unwanted publicity and outside interference Penn suffered in 1993. It was a very public airing of Penn's dirty laundry, and in the end, nobody benefited much—and the causes of racial harmony and free speech were both damaged.

On most of our campuses these incidents are handled through the student judicial process—and that almost always results in a loss of confidence by everyone, "winners" and "losers" alike, in the fairness of the institution. Student/faculty judicial boards simply aren't equipped to handle such tricky matters.

I think we should develop quick, effective systems for clearing the air after an incident of verbal harassment by getting the parties together to talk. If that fails and some sort of mediation is required, there should be a private, impartial, non-judicial hearing.

In these emotionally charged cases, colleges and universities should be able to call on arbitrators. Each party in the dispute could choose one person from a list of lawyers, civil rights leaders, journalists, counselors, clergy and others willing to serve and those two could select the third. The panel would then make its findings promptly, using procedures it—and not the college—determined.

> *"We should develop quick, effective systems for clearing the air after an incident of verbal harassment."*

Taking a case to a panel, not to a courtroom, might encourage more talk on campus about the twin values of free speech and freedom from harassment. At the very least, that procedure would not fan the distrust that typically accompanies these incidents. And maybe those who have suffered abuse, such as the Penn sorority sisters, could actually end up feeling whole and cherished and respected by their colleges instead of torn and bloodied by the process.

Political Correctness Does Not Censor Free Speech

by Linda S. Greene

About the author: *Linda S. Greene is a professor of law at the University of Wisconsin.*

When men open doors for women, they often say with a smile, "I know this is not politically correct but. . . ." The request by groups that the literary canon be expanded to include the works of people of color and women has been denominated an example of political correctness. Efforts to diversify faculty also meet the political correctness charge, and concerns about pornography, hate speech, and sexual harassment are tarred by the same politically correct brush. The now broad usage of the phrase makes succinct characterization problematic, but in general the most serious charge of political correctness is an accusation that one espouses a cramped, narrow orthodoxy, or worse, censorship of free expression. At the extremes, critics of "political correctness" include charges of authoritarianism.

Hate Speech Leads to Violence

Our discourse on hate speech has been fundamentally altered by the charge of political correctness; it has changed the discussion from one that focuses on purveyors of hate to one that focuses on objectors to hate. In this context, the charge of political correctness is a clever rhetorical phrase that has turned a debate about racism and its lingering manifestation into a debate about censorship.

During the 1960s civil rights movement, we observed film footage that graphically portrayed the violence associated with racist epithets. This footage helped us to understand the relationship between hate speech and the question of equality both emotionally and intellectually. We were officially embarrassed and ashamed of these frank demonstrations of hate. And we seemed to understand that words as well as actions played a key role in a régime of separation and subordination. We also knew that certain words were audible reminders of an ideology of racial supremacy and inferiority, and that such language signaled a rejection of the ideal of equality we hoped to belatedly embrace.

For a moment it seemed that we were clear about racist hate speech. We concluded that it was the expression of the ideology of racial inferiority which had been central to our constitutional and popular culture. Pursuant to new civil rights statutes, our judges ruled that racially hostile environments violated the law. Official rules as well as customs eradicated the use of racial epithets from public life and required the punishment of public figures if they repeated their private verbal indiscretions. There was no public argument, on any ground, that racist speech was harmless or useful. Or perhaps there was no one willing to make that case.

The New Public Argument

Now, however, we do have a public argument about the permissibility of racist speech. The pre-1965 public argument was that racist speech conveyed truthful and appropriate messages about the worth of those maligned. The old public argument was fairly similar to the private argument. But the new public argument eschews the endorsement of specific language and the endorsement of racial inequality. The new public argument is that any curtailment or punishment of racist speech not only would violate First Amendment principles but also would have a chilling effect on freedom of expression.

The new public argument is much more attractive than the old ones. In the first place, the new argument appropriates a major premise difficult to refute—that liberty and freedom of speech are fundamental. In addition, the new public argument avoids the messy and embarrassing discussion of the particular words that users of racist speech hurl to remind certain people that they are not equal and that they are still at risk. The new public argument is also attractive to a wider range of people, some of whom are prominent and above reproach, intellectually and professionally, and provides the proponents of racist ideology some new and respectful bedfellows. The public argument does everything a good public argument should do—it provides a lofty and unassailable rationale for behavior that one could not directly defend. Moreover, these arguments may be asserted without discussing the particular behavior at all. And the new public argument "spins" the arguments against racist speech into arguments against liberty, choice, and freedom.

> *"The most serious charge of political correctness is an accusation that one espouses . . . censorship of free expression."*

It is tempting to focus solely on the charge of censorship and ignore the role the charge plays in obscuring the full dimensions of the problem of racial harassment. The charge is an attractive one because we instinctively associate free speech with our important notions of freedom. But the effectiveness of political correctness charges depends on the degree to which censorship accusers can maintain this discussion at a high level of abstraction because it avoids any affiliation with those who actually engage in racial harassment.

In addition, those who focus on censorship also fail to identify or specifically discuss the words or ideas contained in the speech they aim to protect. How different the reaction to discussions of hate speech might be if the opponents of speech regulation framed their arguments in affirmative terms that embrace both the language and the acts empowered by these abstract arguments. It is the use of abstractions and the maintenance of a high level of generality in the discussion of freedom and liberty that give the censorship charge its force.

> *"The new public argument 'spins' the arguments against racist speech into arguments against liberty, choice, and freedom."*

The core question, then, is whether we should be satisfied with a formal equality that in substance continues a pattern of the subordination of groups, despite their recent access to employment, housing, and education.

Arguments framed in terms of political correctness become arguments against public responsibility for the transformation of institutions and the end of institutional racism. In fact, they are implicit arguments that individuals may determine institutional policy by deciding whether to harass and how viciously. They are also implicit arguments that harassed individuals must bear the costs of resistance to their enjoyment of full citizenship and self-fulfillment. The arguments against institutional environmental measures are arguments for a privatization of responsibility for equality and abdication of institutional responsibility for substantive institutional transformation. The foes of political correctness want to privatize the question of the liberty of individuals to speak freely. Historical victims of racism bear the costs of this privatization policy.

Deliberately, this essay avoids a legal focus. The harms caused by the antipolitical correctness movement transcend legal issues. The movement creates doubt about the legitimacy of policy that addresses language and environmental concerns and applies an anticonstitutional tar to those who propose to address questions of harmful language and expressive conduct. The movement creates a political and cultural climate tolerant of hate and hostile to the enjoyment of equal participation in society by previously excluded groups.

Free Speech Absolutism

In addition to these problems caused by the antipolitical correctness movement, the movement also rests its case on broadly conceived free speech principles that, while important, do not support the grand claim that all speech suppression is unconstitutional. A cursory review of free speech doctrines past and present reveals that free speech absolutism has never been the law of the land. We permit the regulation of speech in the context of intellectual property; we sanction for plagiarism; and we permit damages for libel and defamation.

Our constitutional law permits the suppression and punishment of obscenity and the regulation of advertising (for example, we permit the punishment of misleading or false statements in a prospectus offering to sell securities). Until recently, we assumed that the prohibition of sexual and racial harassment in our schools was yet another example of a circumstance in which a strong societal interest justified some limitation on speech. How ironic that we miss the outcry against the above-noted examples of speech suppression but hear a loud chorus where the speech implicates the very selfhood and dignity of individuals.

To be fair, there are important First Amendment concerns at stake when the government suppresses any speech, including hate speech. Over the last twenty-five years, the Supreme Court has incrementally and substantially embraced the general notion that government acts unconstitutionally when it suppresses speech on the basis of the subject matter or viewpoint expressed. These decisions are grounded on the Court's conclusion that important values underlie the First Amendment—the autonomy of individuals and their freedom of conscience, the search for truth, the importance of public debate on political issues—and that these values may be compromised by governmental suppression of speech. These are sound values, but they are not necessarily compromised by the suppression of racial hate speech.

> *"The objectives that underlay some efforts to suppress speech . . . may be so important . . . as to justify some narrowly drawn protective measure."*

In the case of hate speech—the use of epithets and similar words with which the speaker intends to cause emotional harm and grievous insult—an analysis may not simply yield the same value compromising result. For example, questions of autonomy, conscience, and free will have implications for the person addressed as well as the speaker, and we cannot dismiss the autonomy and conscience-formation concerns of the hearer of derogatory words that are chosen to destroy confidence and effectiveness. In addition, the general importance of facilitating the search for truth in a free marketplace of ideas both assumes that racial hate is just another idea rather than an original and enduring flaw in our historical experience and also assumes that the epithets contribute to that search.

And, the importance of open debate on political issues is uncontested, but when the specifics of the viewpoint implicated in epithets is excavated, we may conclude that we have closed debate on the issues of equal rights, or that there are many other arenas for the continuation of the debate. We also can conclude that epithets which disturb the peace by provoking violent response compromise the hearer's ability to participate in that debate by destroying confidence and interfering with the ability of others to regard the individual and her group as equal participants in that debate. Finally, the objectives that underlay some efforts to suppress speech—nondiscrimination in the workplace, in the acquisition and retention of housing, or in the pursuit of an education—may be so important to the hearer's ability to participate vigorously in the polity as to justify some narrowly drawn protective measure.

RAV v. St. Paul

These general observations aside, the most recent Supreme Court decision on hate speech, the cross-burning case of *RAV v. City of St. Paul, Minnesota,* does not foreclose policies that curtail hate speech. Some confusion is expected and normal because all members of the Court found unconstitutional a statute that punished a Klan-type cross burning on the property of a black family. The result justifies legitimate concern about the future constitutionality of any code or law that punishes hate speech, but a closer examination of the various rationales shows that the Court has not foreclosed all racial and hate speech suppression.

The five-justice majority opinion in *RAV*, written by Justice Antonin Scalia, said that racist hate speech—in this case personalized cross burning—could not be singled out for suppression while the government permitted other kinds of invective that might provoke violence. In the words of the opinion, "the First Amendment imposes . . . a 'content discrimination' limitation upon the State's prohibition of proscribable speech." According to the Court, the problem with the ordinance was that it applied only to fighting words on the basis of race, color, creed, or religion and that this limitation embodied both content discrimination and viewpoint discrimination.

> *"In certain circumstances all members of the Court would sanction suppression of racial hate speech."*

However, the majority decision did suggest that the state might criminalize threats of violence as long as it did not select the threat of violence to be criminalized on the basis of the content of the speech used. The majority decision also suggested that the state might criminalize, regulate, or punish a type of conduct—such as sex discrimination—and prohibit sexually derogatory words to make the prohibition against sex discrimination effective.

The remaining four Justices agreed that the ordinance was unconstitutional but on different grounds. Justice Byron R. White (with Harry A. Blackmun, Sandra Day O'Connor, and John Paul Stevens) wrote both to express disagreement with the majority rationale and to suggest another theory upon which the statute was unconstitutional. Justice White's opinion concluded that the statute was unconstitutional because it punished both protected speech (that which simply hurt feeling and did not provoke violence) and "fighting words," a category of unprotected speech. Thus, these Justices suggested that a law or code that focused on fighting words which provoked violence would be constitutional.

And though Justice Stevens agreed with Justice White that the ordinance was unconstitutionally overbroad, he wrote separately to emphasize his view that the "scope of protection provided expressive activity depends in part upon its content and character as well as on the context of the regulated speech. The distinctive character of a university environment or a secondary school environment influences our First Amendment analysis." A close reading of these opinions reveals that there may be ample room for debate about the constitutionality of hate speech codes and laws, and the *RAV* case did not categorically foreclose them. Rather, the case suggests that in certain circumstances all members of the Court would sanction suppression of racial hate speech.

In any event, while constitutional law determines the range of legal options, the social and political climate determines whether government will fully exercise its options. In a curious way, the foes of political correctness have made it "politically incorrect" to contemplate or advocate speech suppression under any circumstance. They have certainly achieved their censorship aims by raising the stakes of opposition to racial harassment.

The discourse of political correctness thinly veils an underlying and persistent unease about fundamental questions of social transformation in institutions and in society at large. In this regard, its effect is similar to that of "reverse discrimination" and "innocence" language in contexts of remedies for discrimination. Both charges—reverse discrimination and "political correctness"—divert attention from fundamental questions about the content of equality for historically excluded groups to questions of privilege for historically included groups. The charges create new "victims" who assert rights violations rather than stake claims of historical privilege. These sound-bite discursive strategies provide effective ideological cover to proponents of a limited version of equality that tolerates token entry but still requires submission to subordinating practices.

The charge of political correctness is an intriguing social phenomenon that has provided much fun at great cost. The charge has diverted our attention from the second-generation problem of equality—the terms of inclusion in previously segregated institutions. The role of harassment and intimidation in the maintenance of subordination is both historical and enduring. While foes of political correctness charge the imposition of orthodoxy, their efforts support the survival of an orthodoxy far more troubling—that racial harassment is both ordinary and privileged. There is much room for debate over the appropriateness of particular measures. But the argument that restraint of racial harassment is impermissible is the equivalent of the untenable proposition that individuals must accept rights—housing, education, employment—under subordinating conditions. The charge that measures to provide more than token equality impose political correctness obscures the equality dimension of racial hate speech. The censorship charge cloaks permissiveness on racism in a lovely philosophical garment. The time has come to strip it away and look directly at the ugliness it conceals and protects.

Hate Speech on Radio Is a Problem

by Kenneth S. Stern

About the author: *Kenneth S. Stern is a program specialist on anti-Semitism at the American Jewish Committee in New York City.*

Day and night, across the country, hosts and callers express opinions on every topic imaginable. Some, heard by millions, are entertaining and thought-provoking. Others are bigoted and hurtful. Some hosts will bait people to draw out hate. Others will give air time to neo-Nazis and Ku Klux Klansmen. Listen to talk radio long enough and you, too, will be a target, no matter what your heritage, religion, race, sex, or sexual orientation.

Bigotry on the Radio

"Is it possible," a caller asks on WABC in New York, "that the lower intelligence of blacks, as documented by William Shockley, is responsible for the complete lack of morality in the blacks, especially toward children?"

"The Jew-Commies only parade around with this [president of Poland, Lech] Walesa to trick the western banks into giving them money," a spokesman for an extremist organization claims in a call to WTEL in Philadelphia, "and then they will transfer these funds to Israel or to New York."

"It's normal practice," a caller on WWDB in Philadelphia explains, "for Italian people to squeeze every cent they can out of you. Underhanded dealing seems to be very prevalent among Italians."

Should bigoted opinions be allowed on radio? How should talk-show hosts handle ignorance and hatred? What should stations do when hateful opinions are championed by hosts? How much government regulation is there—or should there be—of the industry? What can individuals and community groups do? How important is radio, anyway? If you think there are easy answers to these questions, you are mistaken. It is not simply a matter of a choice among, or drawing a better line between, the ideals of free speech and of respect for others. Radio is a

Excerpted from Kenneth S. Stern, "Hate on Talk Radio," *USA Today* magazine, July 1992; © 1992 by the Society for the Advancement of Education. Reprinted with permission.

profit-oriented industry. Controversy sells—and bigotry is controversial.

Talk radio was born in 1921 when six New England governors followed Massachusetts' Speaker of the House to WBZ-AM's (Springfield, Massachusetts) microphone. The first talk-radio subject?—farming.

Today, there are hundreds of talk stations in markets of every size around the country. There are twice as many stations that bill themselves as "talk" than there were in the mid-1980s, and "10 years from now," predicts Michael Harrison, publisher of the trade journal *Talkers*, "talk will be the dominant form of radio. As a matter of fact, I see it as being one of the only forms of radio." If he is right—and recent trends such as the expansion of talk onto FM and cable TV suggest he might be—will bigotry become an even more welcome guest on our airwaves?

> *"Controversy sells—and bigotry is controversial."*

The Beginning of Hate Radio

That radio and bigotry is a dangerous mix is not a matter of opinion, but fact. Hitler and Stalin used radio, and an American, Father Charles E. Coughlin, known for his vicious anti-Semitism, was one of the most powerful radio personalities ever. Imagine listening to the radio in 1938 and hearing an eloquent, vibrant personality explaining why the Nazis had "levied a fine of approximately $400,000,000 against the 600,000 German Jews resident in Germany. In all countries Jews are in the minority," he indicated. "They have no nation of their own. [They are] a closely woven minority in their racial tendencies; a powerful minority in their influence; a minority endowed with an aggressiveness. . . . It is the belief of the present German government [that Jews] were responsible for the economic and social ills suffered by the Fatherland."

So why should Jews be fined? Millions of radio listeners heard Coughlin state:

> Nazism was conceived as a political defense mechanism against communism. [N]ot $400,000,000, but $40,000,000,000 . . . of Christian property was appropriated by [the Bolsheviks who were put in power by] the Jewish Bankers. [Why] was there . . . silence on the radio and in the press? Ask the gentlemen who control the three radio chains. Ask those who dominate the destinies of the financially inspired press. Surely these Jewish gentlemen must have been ignorant of the facts . . . that Nazism is only a defense mechanism against communism.

The reaction against Coughlin was swift. The *Detroit Times* reported that more than 100 telephone calls and 25 telegrams and letters were received by one station alone protesting the program. Rather than curtail his venom, Coughlin built ratings on the criticism. He painted himself the victim of unfair attacks by an evil conspiracy designed to deprive Americans of truth—*his* truth. Coughlin was a major force on radio until his opinions became no longer just anti-Semitic but treasonous. With the American entrance into World War II against the Nazis, he lost his audience.

There is no Father Coughlin terrorizing people over the airwaves today, but there could be. The dynamics are the same. The draw of radio is not fairness or a better-thought-out opinion. People listen to be entertained. Father Coughlin, despite his evil message, was riveting. Those few who took to the airwaves to decry him were not.

Outright vs. Subtle Bigotry

Talk radio is, above all else, cheap programming. All that is needed is a host, an engineer, a producer, and a telephone. The beauty of radio—and its danger—is that it is instantaneous. Call-in shows are live. Anything can be said. The host can reply with almost anything in return. Some say bigoted things, play on the caller's bigotry, or let callers make hateful assertions, without comment in return.

Clear-cut cases of bigotry will get hosts into trouble. On January 18, 1988, Frank Turck of WBEC-FM, Pittsfield, Massachusetts, began his program by saying, "It's Martin Luther King Day. Let's break out the watermelon and fried chicken." That was the "last straw," said the station's program director. Turck had been warned before about racist comments. In 1987, Steven White of WKRI-AM, Providence, Rhode Island, was fired for calling drug dealers "niggers" and "spics." In 1990, Tim Lennox of WERC-AM, Birmingham, Alabama, was suspended indefinitely. He had been upset that a colleague's car had been vandalized, allegedly by a black male. In response, he banned black callers from his show. Those are the "easy" cases for station management. The airing of bigotry usually is more complicated.

One morning, on WABC in New York City, a caller to the Dave Dawson and Roger Skibiness program identified himself as "Lenny from Bay Ridge," which he labeled "Giuliani country." The city was in the midst of a racially charged mayoral campaign, and Rudolph Giuliani was the white Republican candidate. As Skibiness and Dawson sat silently, Lenny went into a lengthy diatribe about Jews and blacks, how the Jews were backing the black Democratic candidate, David Dinkins. If Dinkins won, he warned, the city would be swamped with "black welfare parasites." When Lenny finished his attack, without interruption, the hosts simply went on to the next call.

> *"Some [radio hosts] say bigoted things, ... or let callers make hateful assertions, without comment in return."*

Soon "Laura from Brooklyn" was on the air. She said she was Italian, not black or Jewish, and was upset at the hosts for letting Lenny spew his bigotry unchallenged. Skibiness, in a mocking tone, yelled, "Shut up, you bigot!," then went to the next caller. Dawson and Skibiness apparently thought their method of ignoring, and then validating, Lenny's bigotry would be more entertaining than confronting it. That vignette is a microcosm of the problem of bigotry on the air.

What the Government Does

The Federal Communications Commission (FCC), based in Washington, D.C., licenses and regulates broadcast media. In the early days, broadcasters tended to fear the FCC. "I remember when I was a new broadcaster in the 60s," recalls Michael Harrison, "I thought if you said one word on the air, a squad car would pull up with the FCC police, and they'd throw you in jail." Broadcasters now know that almost anything is fair game.

In 1987, the FCC adopted rules against broadcasting of any "material that depicts or describes, in terms patently offensive as measured by contemporary community standards for the broadcast medium, sexual or excretory activities or organs." In other words, stations could be chastised for broadcasts that "did not necessarily use the seven 'dirty words,'" according to the FCC. "Indecent" material, as the FCC calls it, is prohibited from the air during hours that children might be listening. "Obscene" material always is prohibited.

The FCC's rules against obscenity and its concern for the overexposure of violence to children on television are different from its approach to bigotry on the air, which is "Hands off." Asked about bigotry on talk radio, the FCC supplies Mass Media Bureau Publication 8310-37, "Call-in or 'Open Mike' Programs," and Mass Media Bureau Publication 8310-75, "The FCC and Freedom of Speech." The salient point of these leaflets is: "The Commission is barred by law from trying to prevent the broadcast of any point of view."

Some critics of talk radio complain that, if the FCC is going to interfere with the freedom of broadcasters to air indecent, obscene, or violent material, why should it not also regulate the airing of bigotry? Certainly, more people have been harmed by intergroup hatred than by obscene language. The answers, beyond the legal proscription of the First Amendment against interference with expression, are compelling.

First, how would one define expressions that are to be deemed illegal? Nazi beliefs? Sexist views? Lenny of Bay Ridge's dislike of blacks? As tough as it is to define obscenity, it is all the more difficult to define views that are so extreme and hurtful as to warrant suppression.

Second, even if the government could articulate some standard, would we really want it intruding on what could be heard on the airwaves? There is, after all, a dial, and people can turn off what they find offensive. Intrusion into and regulation of opinion also will chill individuals from uttering what they believe. Talk radio, for all its problems, is honest; callers say what they think. The shadow of "Big Brother" would harm our freedoms much more than the ramblings of a thousand bigots.

Also, simply because government may not be able to pass a law to cure a societal problem does not mean that the situation cannot be addressed otherwise.

Too often, regulation is seen as the only option for achieving societal change. Bigotry *can* be discouraged on radio. The industry, the community, and the audience can have an impact.

That's Entertainment

Anyone who expects that talk-radio hosts, like journalists, will regulate their opinions in the quest for fairness, balance, and objectivity doesn't understand the medium. Talk radio is not journalism. It has no pretense of being fair. Talk is, first and last, entertainment, opinionated and subjective.

The key to being a good talk-show host is to have a personality that comes through like a laser and a point of view. Howard Stern, the "king of shock," draws an audience because people expect him to be outrageous. They want to see what limit of impropriety or bad taste he will challenge next. Rush Limbaugh, who champions extreme conservatism, has created a loyal following who can count on a strong, if, on occasion, excessively stated, point of view. Both, regardless of their message, are skillful entertainers.

Most talk-radio personalities today are male, conservative, and white. There are differences of opinion as to why that is so. Some, such as Harrison of *Talkers*, think the conservative bent is "a reflection of the fact that the nation has developed a relatively conservative political philosophy," although he thinks "there will be liberals as well as conservatives again" on talk radio.

Bill McMahon, a consultant for talk-radio stations around the country, agrees that the conditions exist for a better balance in the future. Interviewed in *Talkers*, he said, "One of the things that bothers me the most is when I talk to a program director, and I say to them, okay, what are you looking for, and the first thing they define is whether they want a liberal or a conservative. . . . I mean if we're talking politics to the people we hire, it just, all of a sudden, takes over the radio station." A good talk-show host, he claims, is a "great observer of life" and a great entertainer.

These characteristics, rather than political line, help define the success of the New York–based, but nationally heard, Rush Limbaugh—today's number one talk-show host. Limbaugh—who takes on "Feminazis, Environmental Wackos, Humaniacs, and the Art and Croissant Crowd"—is, first and foremost, an entertainer, who attacks "with half my brain tied behind my back to make it fair."

> *"Bigotry **can** be discouraged on radio."*

Some see him as pandering to bigotry. One host stated: "There are people who exploit bigotry. Sometimes I tune into Rush Limbaugh, and I just can't believe what he's doing." Harrison, on the other hand, regards him as a talent without any malice. "I think that Rush Limbaugh is a very complex entity who, on short notice, given a shallow listening, you could get the impression [that he dabbles in bigotry]. Rush Limbaugh is, if anything, a tongue-in-cheek satirist of those things. I believe he's a true artist, although there is the danger that someone might misunderstand him."

Regardless of whether Limbaugh is perceived correctly or incorrectly, he defines what makes a talk-show host a success. He has all the characteristics that make a great radio entertainer. If radio station executives around the country try to imitate his popularity by hiring hosts who copy Limbaugh's politics, their efforts will fail. Limbaugh is successful because he has great entertainment attributes.

> *"Talk [radio] is, first and last, entertainment, opinionated and subjective."*

Political Potential

Talk-show hosts have organized successful and nearly successful campaigns to block Congressional pay raises, repeal mandatory seatbelt laws, oppose tax increases, and stop the imposition of tolls on roads.

What radio personalities say about political issues can have a tremendous impact. However, there is another, perhaps greater, danger that comes not from the *ad hoc*, promotion-generating campaigns, but from those with a larger design for talk radio. The Liberty Lobby now has a foothold in talk radio and is poised to expand its influence.

The Liberty Lobby is a right-wing, anti-Semitic organization founded by Willis Carto. It publishes the newspaper *Spotlight* (with a circulation of about 100,000) and has, as offshoots, the Populist Party (former Ku Klux Klan leader David Duke was its 1988 presidential candidate) and the Institute for Historical Review, a producer of journals, videos, tapes, pamphlets, and diatribes denying the existence of the Holocaust.

The Liberty Lobby, which promotes talk shows of its own, also has purchased the Sun Radio Network, affiliated with nearly 200 AM and FM stations around the country. On many Sun-affiliated stations, or directly from a satellite, listeners can hear "Radio Free America" and "Editor's Roundtable." The first, a call-in show that airs five nights a week, promotes guests such as "controversial engineer Fred Leuchter of Massachusetts." According to the Liberty Lobby, "Leuchter is being attacked by Zionist groups who resent his engineering report on the alleged gas chambers at Auschwitz. Essentially, Leuchter investigated and found the allegation that millions of people were gassed to be physically impossible." The "Editor's Roundtable," hosted by *Spotlight* editor Vince Ryan, is a discussion program, regularly reflecting the conspiratorial, anti-Semitic philosophy of the Liberty Lobby.

Fighting Bigotry on the Air

As potentially useful a tool as talk radio is for hateful political philosophies, it is equally capable as a tool to foster better intergroup relationships. Again, the key to using the medium is not the dictation of doctrinaire belief, but the exploitation of its entertainment value.

There are hosts who take bigotry head-on, rather than run from it or exploit it. Part of a successful approach is a matter of professionalism and skill; another is a commitment against bigotry, regardless of political philosophy; and a third is personality. Hosts have to be themselves and do what's comfortable for them in confronting bigotry.

There are some easy things to do, as a general rule. "If someone calls up and says something that's a slur," says host Arnie Arneson (of WNHV-AM, White River Junction, Vermont), "I stop them. That's the first thing I do, and I remind them that I have a problem with their perception."

"If it's overt and clear," explains host Jim Althoff (of KING-AM, Seattle, Washington), "I stop things right there. If it's something like, 'Well, those people, you know how those people are,' I'll call them on it. I say, 'Well, what do you mean, those people?'"

Mike Castello, Daynet's program director, sees the handling of bigotry as a matter of professionalism. "You're in control; you make the stupidity of their opinion manifest. You make them look like the biggest fool. Say, for example, someone says something hateful against blacks. 'Come on, now,' you say, 'let me hear some more. Was this taught to you in your *home*? Was this taught to you in *school*?' asked with an incredulous voice. The idea is to make them embarrassed to go on."

Barry Farber of Daynet smiles at the thought of handling bigotry. "You can hear it coming, it's the cold 'I.' It's the 'I used to like Israel, but . . . .' You can hear the anger. You can hear it in their voice. I hold my temper. I say, 'Anyone intelligent enough to dial seven digits on a telephone certainly knows,' and in a calm voice I tell him the facts. That Israel is surrounded . . . keep my temper and respond with tact. 'I don't blame you,' I say, 'You

> *"The [right-wing, anti-Semitic] Liberty Lobby now has a foothold in talk radio and is poised to expand its influence."*

have learned from a heavily financed propaganda machine, which works to convince you. . . .'"

Each of these approaches differs in accordance with the personality of the hosts, but all are effective. None is an attempt to win an argument. Each is designed to hold, entertain, and educate an audience.

A usual complaint about talk-show hosts is that they let bigots go on unanswered. None of these hosts does that. Like a Rush Limbaugh, they are in control. Yet each, in his or her own way, stops the bigotry, and uses it to teach tolerance, rather than exploit it for ratings.

The fact that each will not let bigots air their views unchallenged in and of itself keeps the bigots from calling. "Shows get a reputation after a while," says Jim

Althoff. "Someone will think, 'Well, geez, so and so will not let me get on with this, so why bother.'"

Arnie Arneson agrees. "I think that's really what show hosts can do. They can either accommodate that type of bigotry, or they can set the stage where that's not acceptable behavior. My listeners understand, I won't tolerate it.". . .

Halting Hate

Owners of stations should take seriously their responsibility to serve the public interest. They should seek out and promote talk-radio talents who use their entertainment skills to improve human relations.

Hosts should not see themselves as the possessors of all knowledge. If the show's format allows for guests, high-quality people should be available to plug in by phone. Owners should consider hiring hosts who have attached themselves to a network of experts, including journalists and lawyers.

Stations should screen calls.

Hosts should study their craft and see the effective handling of bigotry as a matter of professionalism.

Professional associations, such as NARTSH [National Academy of Radio Talk Show Hosts], should offer seminars and workshops that provide hosts with information, ideas, and skills needed to handle bigotry and bigoted propaganda as opportunities for positive, entertaining, and educational programming.

Professional associations should work with community groups and universities to study how bigotry is handled in the talk medium.

Hosts and stations that handle bigotry well should be recognized by the community through awards and other public acknowledgements.

Community groups should monitor local stations, either in coalition with others or in cooperation with universities.

Stations should be challenged and approached when bigotry is not handled well on the air. Affected groups should not go to the station alone—they should come with as broad a coalition as possible. In extreme cases, if moral incantations fail, actions designed to impress that pandering to bigotry will harm the station's revenue should be considered.

Community groups should write letters to the station, documenting what it is doing well, and what it is doing poorly regarding bigotry. Copies of the letters should be sent to the FCC.

Community groups should hold forums to discuss bigotry in the talk media. Talk-show hosts, program directors, station owners, and managers should be invited to participate. A dialogue between industry and community should be created.

Community organizations should become resources for the talk industry, providing quality information and guests.

Individuals should write to stations, both to commend and complain. They should call in when they hear bigotry and help confront it.

Individuals should alert community groups about hate on talk radio.

Racist Speech Should Be Protected by the Constitution

by David Cole

About the author: *David Cole is a professor of law at Georgetown University in Washington, D.C.*

Since 1989, the Supreme Court has been asked to decide whether the state may regulate three types of controversial symbolic speech: flagburning, nude dancing, and crossburning. An innocent observer reviewing the Court's answers might well conclude that the Court is more concerned with protecting flags and moral sensibilities than racial minorities. After all, four Justices felt that the sanctity of the flag justified criminalizing its desecration and five Justices upheld a requirement that dancers wear pasties and G-strings to protect public morality, while all nine Justices agreed in 1992 that a prohibition of crossburning and other racist speech was unconstitutional.

Can Government Regulate Harmful Speech?

But the full picture is more complicated. Each case sparked sharp disagreements among the Justices, none more so than *R.A.V. v. City of St. Paul, Minnesota*, which reviewed the indictment of a white juvenile for burning a cross on a black family's lawn. The *R.A.V.* decision was unanimous only as to its bottom line, and only because the statute was so poorly drafted that every Justice could find some constitutional fault with it. On the core question raised by the case—the legitimacy of regulating racist expression—the consensus fractured into four divided opinions.

All three cases ask what might appear to be an easy question under the First Amendment: may government prohibit expression because it concludes that the message communicated is harmful or offensive? Justice William J. Brennan's decision for the majority in *Texas v. Gregory Johnson*, the flagburning case,

David Cole, "Neutral Standards and Racist Speech," *Reconstruction*, vol. 2, no. 1, 1992. Reprinted with permission.

characterized the answer to that question as the First Amendment's foundation: "If there is a bedrock principle underlying the First Amendment, it is that the government may not prohibit the expression of an idea simply because society finds the idea itself offensive or disagreeable." Yet the only Justice who voted consistently in all three cases was Justice Sandra Day O'Connor, and she ignored the principle by approving prohibitions on all three forms of expression. It appears that Justice Brennan's "if" was warranted; the First Amendment's "bedrock principle" is not as settled as his metaphor optimistically implied.

Freedom of Speech vs. Equality

Probably the most profound challenge in recent years to this would-be foundation of free speech jurisprudence comes from those who seek to regulate racist speech and pornography as civil rights violations. An increasing number of progressive scholars have begun to ask why speech may be regulated, for example, to protect against intangible harms to reputation, but not to remedy the injuries that racial epithets inflict. Similarly, they ask why it should be permissible to regulate obscenity in the interest of maintaining vague moral standards of the community,

> *"The Justices' disagreement about formal First Amendment doctrine is as much about . . . equality as it is about speech."*

but impermissible to regulate pornography in the interest of protecting women from sexual violence and discrimination. At bottom, these scholars charge that traditional First Amendment doctrine fails to take seriously the claim that racist speech and pornography silence and subordinate racial minorities and women, thereby doing harm to both speech and equal protection values.

Nor has the debate remained merely academic. A cadre of engaged scholars has begun to address these issues concretely through the law. On campuses across the country, law professors and students have drafted regulations of racially or sexually harassing speech and lobbied for their adoption. Professor Catharine MacKinnon, the principal theorist behind the regulation of pornography as a women's rights issue, has worked with several city councils, women's rights litigators in Canada, and the United States Congress to translate her theory into practice. (MacKinnon also submitted an amicus brief in *R.A.V.* in support of the St. Paul ordinance, on behalf of the National Black Women's Health Project.)

There is little doubt that the Supreme Court's *R.A.V.* decision was in part a response to these efforts, even though the ordinance at issue addressed neither racist speech on campus nor pornography. Justice Harry A. Blackmun put it most bluntly, stating: "I fear that the Court has been distracted from its proper mission by the temptation to decide the issue over 'politically correct speech' and 'cultural diversity,' neither of which is presented here today."

All of the Justices in *R.A.V.* addressed the issue primarily in terms of speech rather than equality, and some might suggest that this preoccupation with free speech explains the Court's unanimous result. But four Justices—Byron R. White, John Paul Stevens, Blackmun, and O'Connor—concluded that some regulation of racist speech is permissible, so the analysis is not so simple. A close reading demonstrates that the Justices' disagreement about formal First Amendment doctrine is as much about the unspoken issue of equality as it is about speech.

"Fighting Words" and Other Unprotected Speech

The doctrinal issue posed concerned the Court's "categorical" approach to the First Amendment. In reviewing regulation of expression, the Court has developed a general rule that government may not proscribe speech on the basis of its content, and a series of "categorical" exceptions to this rule, themselves defined by the content of speech. Certain categories of speech—such as obscenity, libel, speech posing a clear and present danger of illegal action, and fighting words—are said to be "unprotected" by the First Amendment and therefore subject to regulation. Thus, for example, while the state may not prohibit speech because its content is politically objectionable or sexually explicit, it may prohibit speech on the basis of its obscene content.

In *R.A.V.*, however, the implicit contradiction between the content-neutrality rule and its categorical exceptions came to a head. In an attempt to save the St. Paul ordinance from a First Amendment challenge, the Minnesota Supreme Court had narrowly interpreted the ordinance to apply only to the unprotected category of "fighting words." "Fighting words" are those individually targeted insults "likely to cause an average addressee to fight." This category is so narrow as to be in truth almost academic—so narrow that the Court has not upheld a single conviction for fighting words since the category was created in 1942.

> *"Government may proscribe fighting words generally, but cannot single out specific [racist] fighting words."*

The St. Paul ordinance was even narrower; it did not proscribe all fighting words, but only those which were likely to provoke retaliation "on the basis of race, color, creed, religion, or gender." It was this further selectivity, however, which created the constitutional issue: if the state may prohibit all fighting words because they are unprotected, may it prohibit a subset of fighting words that poses a particularly serious social problem?

St. Paul argued, and three Justices agreed in a concurrence by Justice White, that because fighting words are unprotected, government may proscribe any subset of them—including racist fighting words—without worrying about the First Amendment. But writing for a majority of five, Justice Antonin Scalia rejected this "greater includes the lesser" reasoning. He pointed out that simply because the state may penalize libel, an unprotected category of expression, does not mean that it may penalize only that subset of libel which is critical of the government. Just so, he held for the majority, government may proscribe fighting words generally, but cannot single out specific fighting words on the basis of their racist content.

As a First Amendment matter, Justice Scalia appears to have the better argument. When the Court says a category of expression is "unprotected," it does not mean that the expression is open to any and all regulation, but only that regulation along a particular content-based line is permissible. The state may penalize obscenity, libel, fighting words, and subversive speech, so long as it uses the specific content demarcations the Court has

> *"Bias crime laws, like laws against discriminatory housing or employment practices, do not violate the First Amendment."*

approved for each category. But once the state chooses to penalize a subset of one of those categories, it alters the content line and raises new First Amendment questions. Scalia's decision therefore reaffirmed the importance of close judicial scrutiny whenever the state seeks to regulate speech on the basis of a content line not previously approved as a category of "unprotected" speech.

Defining the Difference Between Speech and Action

The full implications of *R.A.V.* for regulations of racially motivated conduct are less than clear. One day after the decision was issued, the Wisconsin Supreme Court relied on it to invalidate a law that enhanced penalties for criminal conduct motivated by racial animus. But such bias crime provisions should be permissible under Justice Scalia's reasoning, which draws a sharp distinction between regulations of conduct directed at communicative content and all other attempts to penalize conduct. Where the government's interest in prohibiting conduct turns on the conduct's message, as in flagburning statutes, the law is treated as a regulation of speech. But where the government regulates conduct for an important non-communicative reason, such as a ban on all public burnings, flagburnings and crossburnings can be banned without infringing the First Amendment.

The state's interest in redressing the discriminatory impact of a bias-motivated physical assault does not stem from the assault's communicative character, but from the fact that the victim was singled out for assault because of his or her race. It is not so much what the act communicates, but what it does, that gives rise to the increased penalty. Bias crime laws, like laws against discriminatory housing or employment practices, do not violate the First Amendment because the regulatory interest is directed at the act of discrimination, not the expression of a discriminatory thought.

R.A.V.'s rationale raises more serious questions, however, regarding sexual and racial harassment. In dicta [opinions], Justice Scalia approved hostile work environment claims under Title VII of the Civil Rights Act of 1964, which are predicated on racist or sexist speech in the workplace. But here his reasoning is questionable. He maintained that when government prohibits conduct generally without reference to its communicative element (such as employment discrimination), it may incidentally restrict pure speech (racial and sexual harassment) that falls within the general prohibition.

This formulation, however, begs the critical question of when pure speech may be regulated as conduct. Surely the First Amendment places some limit on the type of speech that may be penalized as racial or sexual harassment. Yet Justice Scalia's analysis offers no guidance in divining that limitation. While it makes sense to direct First Amendment scrutiny to regulations of conduct directed at communicative content, it does not follow that where a regulation is not so directed the government may include any speech it desires within the prohibition.

Community Standards and Free Speech for Minorities

The core of the *R.A.V.* decision, however, is clear: singling out racist speech is unconstitutional because it fails the test of content neutrality. Such regulation is designed to protect particular groups by excising certain disapproved messages or forms of expression from the social vocabulary. By contrast, the established categories of unprotected expression maintain a formal neutrality among the citizenry: fighting words are defined by the harm they cause to the "average addressee," obscenity is defined by reference to general community standards, and libel is defined by injury to reputation. Unlike the harms of racist speech, everyone can presumably suffer the harms inflicted by these categories of expression.

But if racial and gender divisions shape our society, how do we even begin to define the standpoint of "the average addressee" or "the community"? In a divided society, the delineation of any such "neutral" standards is likely to be deeply contested, so that allowing the state to regulate speech along even formally neutral lines may permit the dominant majority to suppress the speech of the subordinate minority. Defining formal neutrality is likely to be deeply problematic in a pervasively unequal community.

Even when racial differences are not involved, neutral content lines can be elusive. In the 1991 nude dancing case [*Michael Barnes v. Glen Theatre*], for example, Justice Scalia concluded that a requirement that nude dancers wear pasties and G-strings was content-neutral because it was designed to further public "morality" rather than to suppress expression. He did not see any need to specify whose morality was being furthered, even though it was clearly not the morality of those who enjoy nude dancing. He did not account for how the absence of pasties and G-strings undermines public morality *except* by virtue of what it expresses. Nor did he explain, one year

> *"If racial and gender divisions shape our society, how do we even begin to define the standpoint of . . . 'the community'?"*

later in *R.A.V.*, why suppressing expression to further some citizens' views of public morality is more neutral than doing so to further equality.

Many of the Court's current categories of unprotected expression similarly reflect a failure to adhere consistently to content neutrality. Obscenity law, for example, fails the neutrality test by privileging the representation of "ordinary" sexual desires over those the majority deems "prurient" or morally depraved. And the fighting words doctrine favors the violent responses of listeners over the provocative messages of speakers.

Content Neutrality in an Unequal Society

All of this suggests that the content neutrality mandated by the First Amendment may be illusory. Indeed, Justice Scalia's strict insistence on content neutrality might be compared to his commitment to formal equality in equal protection jurisprudence. Both principles make sense in an ideal world, but suffer greatly in translation to the real world. On equal protection issues, Scalia's formalism leads him to treat affirmative action with as much suspicion as discrimination against African-Americans, making efforts to

> *"Justice White found that singling out racist fighting words was justified 'in light of our nation's long and painful experience with discrimination.'"*

redress racism through racially conscious means extremely difficult. Just so, his commitment to neutrality in speech regulation frustrates legislative attempts to respond to racial inequality by regulating speech.

The Justices who would have approved of a more carefully drafted prohibition of racist fighting words did so precisely because of the reality of racial inequality. Justice Stevens explained that "one need look no further than the recent social unrest in the nation's cities to see that race-based threats may cause more harm to society and to individuals than other threats." And Justice White found that singling out racist fighting words was justified "in light of our nation's long and painful experience with discrimination."

Is the First Amendment's content-neutrality principle morally and intellectually bankrupt in a world divided by social inequality? If neutrality is only an illusion, how can it override the concrete goal of equality? Professor Stanley Fish of Duke University has argued that there is no principled reason in the abstract to protect speech, and that therefore our tolerance of any particular speech must be determined by contingent, political arguments about whether that speech furthers or hinders social goals. In this view, suppression of racist speech is justified simply because such expression undermines our collective project of racial equality.

Others, such as Professor Charles R. Lawrence III of Stanford University, concede that there are First Amendment values to be weighed in the balance, but maintain that those values cannot be considered in the abstract, "by presupposing a world characterized by equal opportunity and the absence of societally created and culturally ingrained racism." Lawrence argues that in the real world of racial subordination, the First Amendment's "marketplace of ideas" will be purified by eliminating at least the most virulent forms of racist speech, which serve only to reinforce prejudice and to devalue and silence black participation.

Who Is a Minority?

The neutrality principle may begin to make more sense, however, once we remember what is often left out of the calculations of those who would prohibit racist speech. The victims of racist speech are not the only disadvantaged and silenced minority in the equation. Proponents of racist speech—Ku Klux Klan members, Nazis, and the like—are also a minority, and a particularly unpopular one at that. Tolerating racist speech may well have the effect of excluding members of racial minorities from full participation in the public debate. But suppressing racist speech even more certainly has the effect of excluding a minority from the debate—those who espouse racial hatred. What justifies suppressing the speech of one minority in order to protect another?

Of course, put this way, there is no room to be neutral: one of these two minority groups will suffer whatever the government does. At one level, the choice seems clear. One group seeks goals consistent with constitutional values and the other doesn't. Racists advocate an ideology of intolerance, disrespect, and subordination; regulators of racist speech pursue inclusion, mutual respect, and equality. But focusing on means instead of ends, it appears that racists have tempted their critics to stoop to their tactics. Those who would prohibit racist speech propose a strategy of intolerance and discriminatory silencing of certain (racist) messages. Racists, meanwhile, ask (no doubt cynically) that their ideas be equally respected and tolerated rather than suppressed. The content-neutrality principle demands that we not sacrifice means to ends,

> *"What justifies suppressing the speech of one minority in order to protect another?"*

but that demand seems especially harsh in this case, where the burden rests on only some within our community.

While the weight of that burden should not be underestimated, the regulative response is a mistake. In the end, the strongest argument for content neutrality may be a pragmatic judgment about the role of free speech in political struggle. The world would be a better place without racist speech. But it will not be a better place if we get there by using the fact that the majority now disapproves of racist speech to suppress that speech by force of law.

A Strict Adherence to Free Speech Is Best

If the history of political struggles over speech teaches us anything it is that the majority will most often seek to regulate the speech of the politically powerless. In fact, in a democratic society the only speech government is likely to succeed in regulating will be that of the politically marginalized. If an idea is sufficiently popular, a representative government will lack the political where-withal to suppress it, irrespective of the First Amendment. But if an idea is unpopular, the only thing that may protect it from the majority is a strong constitutional norm of content neutrality.

In the arena of speech, then, a strict adherence to content neutrality may be justified, not because the playing field is level, as Justice Scalia assumes, but precisely because it is not. Speech is a powerful tool for change for those dissatisfied with their position in society. It will remain that way only if, with vigor, we presumptively forbid the majority from suppressing speech of which it disapproves. The principle of content neutrality keeps open the possibility for political change.

It may well be that as long as society remains unequal, content neutrality will be an illusion. Others might call it an unrealized ideal. It certainly does not guarantee that disfavored expression will always be protected, as the nude dancing case demonstrates. But whether content neutrality is an illusion or an ideal, it is all that stands between the dissenter and the majority. And as long as society remains unequal, disadvantaged minorities will find themselves far more often in dissent. At this moment in history, the majority appears to agree that racist speech is repugnant, injurious, and deserving of suppression. But to empower the majority to regulate the speech of dissenters when the majority's values happen to be aligned with our own is a terrible mistake. This once, we would do better to side with Justice Scalia.

Restricting Speech Does Not Fight Racism on Campuses

by Jennifer Kelley

About the author: *Jennifer Kelley is on the staff of* Peace & Democracy, *the quarterly publication of the Campaign for Peace and Democracy.*

Over the last few years, the issue of restricting offensive speech has mushroomed into a ferocious and long-winded debate that has taken on a variety of forms and names—from "political correctness" to "fighting words" to "hate speech." On one side of the debate are those who favor limited or extensive restrictions on speech; on the other, those who believe the First Amendment guaranteeing the right to freedom of expression should be protected without qualification.

Racism Is Increasing on College Campuses

Issues of biased expression and speech restrictions on college and university campuses have been at the forefront of this debate. Although there is a growing reluctance to prolong what many view as a superficial and stalemated discussion of bias at the university, I would argue that the issue of free speech must continue to receive attention in the campus setting. The issue provides the opportunity to examine the appropriateness and effectiveness of efforts to curb intolerance and hatred through speech codes. With racism, sexism, sexual harassment, and homophobia on the rise on American college campuses, the academic community must continue to seek effective means of dealing with these and other forms of prejudice.

It is important to note that bias-related incidents on campuses have *increased* since the implementation of speech and civility codes, raising questions about the effectiveness of such codes. Universities, therefore, need to focus not on the wording of speech codes, the kinds of speech and conduct they target, or their enforcement, but rather on the validity of the principles behind the codes. This basic investigation of the philosophical justification for speech and civility

Jennifer Kelley, "Free Speech/Hate Speech: A Student's View," *Peace & Democracy News*, Winter 1992–93. Reprinted by permission.

codes is too often forgotten in the frantic effort to revise and perfect the wording of campus speech codes.

The fact of the matter is that controlling speech does not work; nor will it ever be an effective weapon against hatred and prejudice. It is ridiculous to suggest that anti-Semitism or homophobia, for instance, are simply forms of speech. Yet that is the implicit mentality behind policies that seek to eradicate prejudice by targeting individual acts of expression. Hatred is not simply a matter of semantics. It is a matter of ignorance and of violent, intolerant attitudes and practices.

We are presently facing a pivotal moment in the debate over free speech on campus. On June 22, 1992, the Supreme Court held a St. Paul, Minnesota, ordinance used to prosecute a teenager for burning a cross on the lawn of a black family to be an unconstitutional restriction of the right to free expression. At the same time, the Court's ruling left open the possibility that some restrictions on expression are valid. On campuses, the ruling has already inspired renewed efforts to reword campus speech codes to make them less vulnerable to constitutional challenges.

> *"Controlling speech does not work; nor will it ever be an effective weapon against hatred and prejudice."*

It is my belief that, rather than leading us to revive old strategies, the St. Paul decision should push us in a different direction—toward the far more difficult task of understanding the origins of hate and prejudice, and exploring more effective alternatives to speech and conduct restrictions. From my involvement with issues of free speech on campus, I have come to realize that speech codes are not only ineffective, but that they actually undermine progress toward greater tolerance. I have seen nothing as effective in the fight against hatred on campus as free, open, unrestricted expression and discussion of the issues—the kind of discussion speech codes seek to suppress. In the attempt to overcome narrow and hateful attitudes, and to develop tolerance for diversity, it is essential that differences among people are openly discussed and understood. Because ignorance helps to feed intolerance, protecting ignorance through censorship serves only to feed intolerance. Speech codes tend to create an atmosphere in which many issues are considered taboo and off-limits because of the sensitivity that surrounds them.

A Free Exchange of Ideas Is Needed

The most productive and worthwhile (if sometimes tense) discussions I have observed in the classroom have been those in which sensitive issues relating to social attitudes were directly confronted. Through these discussions, students revealed and challenged each other's assumptions. Many of my classmates and I left these conversations with a greater appreciation and acceptance of fellow-students' differences in race, religion, gender, or sexual orientation. Considering the value of the experiences, it would be unthinkable to consider restricting this free interchange of feelings and ideas.

While free expression is not a panacea that will eradicate prejudice and hatred, it can help to dispel ignorance. In addition to inculcating a tolerance of diversity, free expression tends to encourage personal empowerment, another important weapon in the fight against bias. Unfortunately, one cannot always count on being able to convince others that their intolerance is misguided. Those who are sometimes the objects of prejudice, however, become better equipped by open debate to combat the feelings of intimidation, oppression, and victimization that hateful words and acts engender. "Protecting" people from intolerant views through speech restrictions can do them a disservice by preventing them from confronting these views.

I have seen people strengthened by the experience of unrestricted expression at events like the annual Take Back the Night march for rape victims sponsored by students at Barnard College and Columbia University, and the huge yearly Gay Pride march on Fifth Avenue in New York City.

At the Take Back the Night event, women as well as men are able to find an alternative to fear, oppression, and hate through the sharing of experiences and feelings of solidarity and support. At the 1992 Gay Pride march, there were a number of protesters holding signs with messages objecting to homosexual lifestyles. The marchers did not call for restricting the expression of these biased views. Instead, as they passed the protesters, they confidently chanted "Shame, shame, shame." Witnessing and participating in such events make one highly conscious of the empowering nature of expression.

Free expression on campus (and in the rest of society) offers hope for changing intolerant attitudes, and provides an important means for overcoming the paralyzing sense of victimization these attitudes can create. Institutions of higher learning are theoretically supposed to provide an open and unrestricted marketplace of ideas. What is the purpose, then, of spending endless hours reading and discussing the forms in Plato's *Republic*, but ignoring his conception of the innate, caste-like differences between people, or understanding Augustine's faith, but denying his references to homosexuality and his view of women, or contemplating Richard Wagner's influence on twentieth-century music, but not his anti-Semitism and his influence on the National Socialist movement in Germany, and so on, just because these topics are deemed by some to be too touchy, too

> *"Free expression tends to encourage personal empowerment, another important weapon in the fight against bias."*

sensitive, too potentially offensive? What is to be gained from completely sterile studies that avoid controversy at all costs? The answer is nothing; furthermore, there is a lot to be lost. We must not sacrifice the integrity and value of institutions of higher education to hasty and ineffective efforts to discourage prejudice. It is therefore crucial that we stop the dangerous and counterproductive attacks on free speech, and refocus our efforts on developing real solutions to the problems of hatred and intolerance.

Conservative Values on Radio Are Wrongly Labeled Hate Speech

by Rush Limbaugh

About the author: *Rush Limbaugh is the host of a nationally syndicated talk radio and television show and the author of* The Way Things Ought to Be *and* See, I Told You So.

There are times in one's life that despite all the blood, toil, tears, and sweat expended in the pursuit of excellence, one really should lean back, light up a good cigar, take a sip of an adult beverage, and just savor the moment. My friends, this is one of those times.

Target Numero Uno

Thirty years after the inauguration of Lyndon Johnson's Great Society; twenty-five years after Woodstock; two decades after Richard Nixon's resignation; and two years after Democrats secured control of the White House and both chambers of Congress [in 1992], modern liberalism—exhausted and confused—is on the run. Three decades after Ronald Reagan's brilliant enunciation of conservative ideals at the end of the 1964 campaign, he told me, "Now that I've retired from active politics, I don't mind that you've become the number-one voice for conservatism in our country." And liberal fear is palpable.

Thus came the sizzling summer 1994 onslaught against me. "He's a showman, a showoff, and a jerk," wrote one pundit. "Chief propagandist for the revolution," said another. "A self-serving, hate-mongering liar," railed one writer. "A tool-shed-sized hate monger," said another. "Rush Limbaugh's ideology makes him a political dinosaur, which puts him on the endangered species list," wrote one critic. "Judge for yourself about that slabhead, Rush Limbaugh," said another.

The assault came from every corner of liberalism—from the White House and the *Washington Post*, from the *New York Times* and the *New Yorke*r, from the *Na-*

tion and the *New Republic,* from *Time* magazine and the *Los Angeles Times*, from C-Span and CNN, from *U.S. News & World Report* and *USA Today*, and from National Public Radio, the National Organization for Women, and the National Education Association (I'm leaving many out, but you get the picture). In the month that followed President Clinton's June 1994 attack on

> *"Liberals fear me because I threaten their control of the debate."*

me, I was mentioned in 1,450 stories, including the *South China Morning Post* and *Agence France Presse*, as tracked by a media database service.

Liberals have, in fact, elevated me to the role of leading political figure. Target Numero Uno. It is a role I have never sought. My goal has always been to host the most-listened-to radio and television shows in history and, in turn, charge confiscatory advertising rates. But as it happens, not only am I a performer, I am also effectively communicating a body of beliefs that strikes terror into the heart of even the most well-entrenched liberals, shaking them to their core.

The interesting question is, Why? Why do liberals fear me? I am not a distinguished member of Congress. I am not running for President. I do not control billions of dollars in taxpayer money. I can enact no policy, law, or regulation to affect a single American citizen's behavior. So why the high level of liberal emotion? This would seem to me to be a legitimate area of inquiry to be pursued by members of the mainstream media—but their own animus has prevented them from solid analysis of this phenomenon. Yet again, I must do their job for them.

Controlling the Debate

First, liberals fear me because I threaten their control of the debate. These are the facts: Twenty million people a week listen to my radio program on 659 stations nationwide, on short wave and Armed Forces Radio worldwide, while several million more watch my television show on 250 stations nationally. I am on the air seventeen-and-a-half hours a week. Add to that six million copies sold of my two books, *The Way Things Ought To Be* and *See, I Told You So*, and 475,000 monthly subscribers to *The Limbaugh Letter* after just two years in business.

What I do in this rather large *oeuvre* (a little literary lingo, there) is hard for pundits to peg. Media sages have not to this point been confronted with a conservative who is both commentator and entertainer. A conservative who traffics in satire, of all things—mostly liberal turf until now. A conservative who dares poke fun at liberal sacred cows, and who does so with relish, optimism, and good cheer. A conservative whose expression of core beliefs is unabashed, unapologetic, unembarrassed—and who has the best bumper music on the air.

How do I attract so many people? First, I approach my audience with enormous respect. I am absolutely convinced that the country contains vast numbers of intelligent, engaged citizens who are hungry for information and inspiration. These are people who play by the rules, who are working hard to raise their families, to strengthen their communities, to do the right thing—and to enthusiastically enjoy life in the process. They are proud to be counted among those who believe in God, American ideals, morality, individual excellence, and personal responsibility.

These are the people who are constantly told: "You are the problem. You aren't compassionate enough, you don't pay enough taxes, your selfishness and greed (which is how the desire to look after one's own family and improve one's lot in life is always defined) are destroying the country." These are the people whose most heartfelt convictions have been dismissed, scorned, and made fun of by the mainstream media. I do not make fun of them. I confirm their instincts, with evidence taken directly from pages of the daily papers and from television news programs. I explain what is actually in legislation. I quote what our esteemed members of Congress and the mainstream media actually say. I detail and analyze news stories (many of which don't get national play except on my programs) that demonstrate the absurdity of liberal policies.

"I *Am* Equal Time"

I have not attracted and kept my audience by being a blowhard, a racist, a sexist, a hatemonger. Those who make such charges insult the intelligence of the American people. If I were truly what my critics claim, I would have long ago, deservedly, gone into oblivion. The fact is, my audience knows I constantly champion rugged individualism. One of the most oft-heard phrases on my shows is this: "I want a great America made up of great individuals, an America where everyone is unshackled to be the best he can be." This is the philosophy that sends liberals into fits—because they know a country made made of strong, self-reliant individuals does not need them at all.

My tools are not "right-wing demagoguery," as is so often charged. My tools are evidence, data, and statistics. Economic analysis. Cultural criticism. Political comment. I demonstrate. I illustrate. I provide my audience with information that

> *"I have not attracted and kept my audience by being a blowhard, a racist, a sexist, a hatemonger."*

the mainstream media refuses to disseminate. And I do so in an entertaining, enjoyable way. That is why I always say my views and commentary don't need to be balanced by equal time. I *am* equal time. And the free market has proved my contention.

Despite claims from my detractors that my audience is comprised of mind-numbed robots, waiting for me to give them some sort of marching orders, the fact is that I am merely enunciating opinions and analysis that support what they already know. Thousands of listeners have told me, on the air, in faxes, letters, and by computer e-mail, that *I* agree with *them*. Finally, they say, somebody in the media is saying out loud what they have believed all along.

This hard evidence that huge numbers of ordinary Americans have privately rejected the tenets of liberalism is a genuine threat to the decades-long liberal dominance of American institutions. Conservatives—who have been shut out of the debate in the arena of ideas for a generation—are finally understanding the stunning truth that they are not alone. The marginalization of conservative ideas, a successful liberal tactic for thirty years, is over. Most Americans are, in fact, conservative. They may not always vote that way, but they live their lives that way. This fact has been successfully hidden from the population. Until now.

Beyond mere jealousy that their territory has been horned-in on, the political and cultural significance of this phenomenon has finally begun to dawn on liberals. One of the first signs of panic occurred back in the Outlook section of the *Washington Post* in February 1994. In "Day of the Dittohead," David Remnick opined: "Nearly all the hype about Limbaugh winds up on the entertainment pages. And yet there is very little in the press to suggest that he is, above all, a sophisticated propagandist, an avatar of the politics of meanness and envy. Limbaugh's influence is hard to gauge," Remnick continued. "But attention must be paid. . . . The left-wing media and the 'arts and croissants crowd,' as Limbaugh puts it, ignore him at their peril.". . .

> *"I represent middle America's growing rejection of the elites."*

Rejecting the Media Elites

The second reason liberals fear me is that I represent middle America's growing rejection of the elites. Americans are increasingly convinced they have been deceived by the so-called "professionals" and "experts"—particularly, but not exclusively, in the media. Seeing themselves as sacrosanct, the self-important media elite have adopted a religious zeal toward their business—which they actually consider a "mission." I pointed this out in my first book, but the situation has gotten both worse and more transparent. The *Washington Post's* advertising campaign for new subscribers states bluntly, "If you don't get it, you don't get it." Fortunately, most Americans don't get it. Meanwhile, the *New York Times Magazine* promotes itself as "What Sunday Was Created For," which might amuse the Creator, whom, I suspect, had something very different in mind when He did the creating. But that's just it. What you have here is the arrogance of power. And that is why so many people are looking elsewhere, and increasingly to me.

Of course, it is not just the media elites that Americans are rejecting. It is the medical elites, the sociology elites, the education elites, the legal elites, the science elites—the list goes on and on—and the ideas this bunch promotes through the media. Americans have been told our health care lags behind the rest of the industrialized world; it doesn't. They were told drugs are safe; they aren't. They were told free sex is liberating; it isn't. They were told massive welfare spending would help people get back on their feet; it hasn't. They were told that without government intervention on behalf of environmentalist wackos, the world would come to an end; it won't. They were told that religious people are dangerous to the country; they aren't.

An assistant managing editor for one regional newspaper actually wrote, "I despise the Rush Limbaugh show," throwing the pretense of journalistic objectivity to the winds. Most aren't so explicit, but their work reeks with animosity for my audience and me. . . .

Faith in Government

Third, liberals fear me because I'm validating the thoughts of the silent majority. Liberals seek to lull Americans to sleep with promises that government will take care of everything, if they will just fork over their money. I, on the other hand, challenge people to wake up. Millions already seriously question the wisdom of handing $1.5 trillion a year to the federal government when the post office cannot even deliver the mail on time—and actually throws away what it is too lazy to deliver. I provide the hard information, statistics, and specific details from the record to confirm many Americans' suspicions about government "efficiency." That is the sort of thing that infuriates liberals, who are wed to the idea that government is good, and the bigger the better.

New York Times columnist Anthony Lewis, in a revealing July 1994 article entitled "Where Power Lies," argued that "power does not reside only in the White House or government anymore." His worst nightmare, apparently. Instead, "those who seek to destroy faith in the American political system have considerable power now, power demanding attention." Lewis breathlessly explained that "Rush Limbaugh's game" is "to throw dirt on government and anyone who believes that society needs government. In his hateful talk about President and Mrs. Clinton and others in office, he is really trying to destroy public faith in our institutions."

The charge is preposterous. He admits he never listens to my program—"a pleasure I deny myself," as he puts it. As anyone in my audience will tell you, I defend the institutions and traditions which have made America great. But perhaps Mr. Lewis should go back and re-read some of his old columns for a clue about why

> *"I defend the institutions and traditions which have made America great."*

Americans are so upset with government today. In 1992 he wrote: "Hyperbole is to be expected of politicians. But deliberate lies? I think that kind of politics has brought this country close to disbelief in its political system." He was referring, unconvincingly, to George Bush—but a reader can be forgiven if our current president springs to mind. And that is just it. Official deception and dissembling are responsible for Americans' growing anger and frustration with government. I simply shine the light of truth on it. . . .

"I Am Not Running for Political Office"

Fourth and finally, liberals fear me because I am not running for political office, and thus I am invulnerable to the political attacks of liberals. "Demagogues . . . fizzle out because people weary of the act or because the political equation changes or because they face a real political challenge," insisted the *Nation*'s Alexander Cockburn in a July 1994 *Los Angeles Times* column. "There's almost no one out there fighting the political battles with Limbaugh in language ordinary people can understand and enjoy." The same month, leftist columnist Lars-Erik Nelson lamented in the *Washington Post*, 'There is no leftist equivalent to Rush Limbaugh."

Liberals treat me as if I were the Republican presidential candidate. But I have no interest in running for office. Why should I? I am setting the agenda right where I am—with something very simple: The truth. Liberals, who for so long have dominated the nation's institutions and who have tried so hard to dominate the nation's political agenda, flounder helplessly as a result. They understand how to fight a political challenge—war rooms, bus tours, direct mail, editorials, protests. They do not know how to fight a cultural challenge—the explosion of talk radio—except to try to regulate it out of existence (as in their attempts to revive the Fairness Doctrine, dubbed the "Hush Rush Bill" by the *Wall Street Journal*).

> *"I am setting the agenda right where I am—with something very simple: The truth."*

What is actually happening now is a threat to liberal control of America's institutions. And this phenomenon is not a political one. The American people are discovering once again what the Founders always intended—that the country's future is in their hands. It depends on parents raising their children; it depends on teachers pushing these children to excellence; it depends on grandparents teaching these children the traditional lessons of morality and virtue; it depends on pastors, priests, and rabbis pointing these children to the God who loves them.

The Most Dangerous Man in America

That is not to say politics or the presidency is not important; it is. Washington takes too much of our money and our liberties and reinforces the dangerous myth that government can provide security and happiness and success. Yes, Americans need to send men and women of character to Washington and state capitals. But politics is not everything.

That is my message, and that is why I am dangerous. Neither the 1994 nor 1996 election results will serve as the sole indicators of the impact of my programs, because the battle is not simply for political control; it is for re-establishing control of America's institutions. And because I am affecting the debate on how that can be achieved, liberals are apoplectic.

Many times I get calls on my show from people who rail against one liberal outrage or another and complain that the country is going down the tubes. That was certainly the reaction as liberals fired their salvos at me and my audience. But actually, the liberal extremists may well be on their last legs. Their power source, the Democratic Party and its leadership, is woefully out of touch. They simply cannot extricate themselves from bondage; their power base is a constituency of victimhood. The shrill tone and apocalyptic hyperbole that characterize liberal attacks on me are instructive, speaking volumes about their fear of becoming irrelevant.

Historians will remember 1994 as a watershed year in American politics. It was the year that modern liberalism, the ideology dominating nearly every important cultural and political institution in the country, tipped its hand, revealing its deep insecurity. The summer of 1994 will be remembered as the season that liberals, acutely aware of the seismic rumbles just below the surface of American politics and society, unleashed their fury against a man who is neither a politician nor a candidate for political office. It was the summer all hell broke loose against the "most dangerous man in America."

Liberals are terrified of me. As well they should be.

Chapter 3

Should Special Penalties Apply to Hate Crimes?

CURRENT CONTROVERSIES

Enhanced Penalties for Hate Crimes: An Overview

by Brent F. Stinski

About the author: *Brent F. Stinski is a journalist in Chicago, Illinois.*

When Robert Viktora and his friends took a couple of broken chair legs, crudely fashioned them into the form of a cross, then set it ablaze on the front lawn of an African-American family in St. Paul, Minnesota, they touched off a debate that remains clouded with uncertainty.

Cross Burning and Free Speech

Can the law regulate hate?

After that predawn attack in June of 1990 on the home of Russ and Laura Jones, Viktora was charged with violating a hate law that was newly written by the city of St. Paul. He claimed the ordinance denied him the right to free speech.

The U.S. Supreme Court agreed with Viktora in *R.A.V. v. City of St. Paul, Minnesota* (1992).

Reading from the Court's opinion offers little guidance. Despite the unanimous vote, the justices differed sharply in rationale, some taking a hands-off stance with near-libertarian overtones, others arguing that while the ordinance was sloppily written, its anti-hate intent merited consideration.

The opinion remains loaded with consequences for some forty-six states with hate legislation.

The majority opinion, written by Justice Antonin Scalia and joined by Justices William H. Rehnquist, Anthony M. Kennedy, David H. Souter, and Clarence Thomas, found the St. Paul ordinance to discriminate on the basis of conduct, in Scalia's words, a "presumptively invalid" regulation.

Although he conceded that the speech prohibited by *R.A.V.* fell in the unprotected category of fighting words—"conduct which itself inflicts injury or tends to incite immediate violence"—Scalia asserted that as far as government is concerned, fighting words are fighting words; St. Paul could not regulate those

Brent F. Stinski, "Can Hate Be Controlled? A Clouded Issue," *Human Rights*, Spring 1993; © 1993 by the American Bar Association. Reprinted by permission.

only demeaning "race, color, creed, religion or gender" and ignore others against traits which have also historically drawn bias-motivated affronts, such as sexual preference or union membership.

Differing Approaches to Free Speech

But the ordinance discriminated against "viewpoint" as well, Scalia wrote, arguing that while disallowing fighting words against certain minority groups, the same ordinance permits fighting words calling for tolerance of those groups. Thus abortion-rights protesters could not hurl anti-Catholic insults at a rally, but others could fling back abuses about "anti-Catholic bigots" at will.

In effect, wrote Scalia, "selectivity of this sort creates the possibility that the city is seeking to handicap the expression of particular ideas."

Justices Byron R. White, Harry A. Blackmun, John Paul Stevens, and Sandra Day O'Connor concurred, though at the same time appearing to search for constitutional shelter for other kinds of hate laws. The St. Paul law trespassed on constitutionally protected expression when it outlawed an expression which "arouses hate or resentment in others on the basis of race, color, creed" or other trait, they argued.

White faulted Scalia's content-neutral approach for slighting "long-established" First Amendment doctrine and recommended a categorical approach, in which certain forms of expression such as fighting words or pornography merit little if any constitutional protection.

Hence if the entire category fails to deserve protection, concluded White, particularly harmful regions can legally merit harsher punishment.

Stevens joined White's concurrence only in part, finding the content-neutral approach "just too simple" and the categorical approach to "sacrifice subtlety for clarity" by ignoring the innumerable settings in which hate words spring forth. Stevens perceived a hierarchy of regulation for expression: Political speech is allowed the most freedom, obscenity and fighting words the least.

> *"The rift from* **R.A.V. [v. City of St. Paul]** *reflects an historic tension between two justifications for free speech."*

Scalia's argument that fighting words cannot be regulated by content, Stevens concluded, perversely sets them equal to political speech.

The rift from *R.A.V.* reflects an historic tension between two justifications for free speech, say legal scholars. The "instrumental approach," described by constitutional scholar Ronald Dworkin in the June 11, 1992, edition of the *New York Review of Books*, follows the logic of White's dissent by justifying free speech for its productive ends—an informed electorate and accountable government.

Another approach reflected in Scalia's opinion supports free speech for its own sake. "Government insults its citizens . . . when it decrees that they cannot be trusted to hear opinions that might persuade them to dangerous or offensive convictions," wrote Dworkin.

Chapter 3

Free Speech vs. Hate-Crime Laws

Less than twenty-four hours after the *R.A.V.* decision came down, one state supreme court became the first of many to add new notes to that history.

Voting 5–2 [in the case *State of Wisconsin v. Todd Mitchell*], Wisconsin's Supreme Court cast down its "enhancement law," a hate statute similar to those in many states that boosted the offenses in which the victim was "intentionally selected" on the basis of "race, color, religion, disability, sexual orientation, national origin or ancestry."

A trial court used the law to lengthen the penalties of one of several African-American men who, after discussing a scene from *Mississippi Burning*, allegedly attacked a fourteen-year-old male walking nearby.

In ruling the law unconstitutional, the state supreme court cited in part the day-old *R.A.V.* precedent and argued the necessity to use speech to prove the intentional selection "threatens to chill free speech" and steps into the realm of "subjective mental thought." [The U.S. Supreme Court reversed the Wisconsin court's decision in June 1993, upholding the enhancement law.]

Two months later [in the case of *State (of Ohio) v. David Wyant*] Ohio nixed a 1987 law similar to that of Wisconsin, and though it credited the law's intentions, decided that the "thought crime" law could not constitutionally punish conduct based on the mental processes that motivate behavior.

In the same week as the Ohio decision, the Supreme Court of Oregon voted 7–0 to validate one of its enhancement laws, in part because speech serves as evidence in other instances— the words "I am going to kill you," for example, in an attempted murder case.

> *"There is a distinction between making speech the crime itself, or an element of the crime, and using speech to prove the crime."*

The court also argued that the law punishes committing certain acts and does not necessarily rely on speech. One could infer bias if every Saturday night a defendant traveled to Latino neighborhoods and assaulted a passerby who appeared to be Hispanic.

Wrote the Oregon court: "There is a distinction between making speech the crime itself, or an element of the crime, and using speech to prove the crime."

Yet the Oregon opinion still stokes questions. Much of it addressed a segment stipulating that two or more offenders must act in unison, and it noted that the downcast Wisconsin law contained no such clause. Enhancement critics say Oregon had reservations that would have kept it from hate laws dealing with sole offenders; enhancement proponents toss aside the comments, citing the unanimous approval and arguing that for all constitutional purposes, Oregon's laws mirrored those of other states.

Enhancement laws roused still more controversy when in New Jersey one superior court judge ruled an enhancement law suitable; another judge ruled it unconstitutional.

The Importance of Hate-Crime Laws

Supporters argue enhancement laws exist outside of the realm of free speech, and predict that unless the Supreme Court considers the enhancement issue, well-written laws in thirty-one states will be brushed aside by the momentum of *R.A.V.*

"The Supreme Court was very careful to say, 'We're not deciding this, we're not deciding that,'" said Simon Karas, of the Ohio Attorney General's Office, about the initial Court decision. "This Ohio case is not *R.A.V.*"

Instead of focusing on the speech issues of *R.A.V.*, enhancement laws penalize actions—in effect working like antidiscrimination laws which prohibit hiring or firing on the basis of race, sex, or another minority characteristic, says Anti-Defamation League lawyer Michael Sandberg.

> *"The need for enhancement statutes is clear and paramount, argue supporters."*

"Do those laws mean you are no longer able to believe what you want about Jews or African-Americans or gays? No," Sandberg says. "You can go on the radio and make your remarks if you want. But when you act upon that bias, then you can be in violation."

The need for enhancement statutes is clear and paramount, argue supporters. Gay bashing not only harms the victim, but it instills fear in the entire gay and lesbian community.

Supporters also contend that victims suffer more intensely when targeted for crime because of membership in a group. According to findings by the National Institute Against Prejudice and Violence, victims of ethnic violence suffer 21 percent more trauma symptoms than other victims of similar crimes.

Hate laws are important, says Southern Poverty Law Center lawyer Richard Cohen, because they work much like civil rights legislation did in the 1960s, by sending "an unmistakable statement to the public" that bias-motivated crimes are not tolerated.

Bob Purvis of the National Institute Against Prejudice and Violence, which has opposed campus hate speech codes but stood behind enhancement laws, speculated Justice Scalia wrote *R.A.V.* with broad justification in order to set a Trojan Horse should enhancement statutes come before the Court.

"He may not have the majority [now]," said Purvis. "The weight of analysis shifts when you're dealing with a physical attack instead of burning a cross."

Using Speech to Determine Motive

Though most acknowledge the different nature of hate-motivated crimes, opponents say the premises of current enhancement laws stand on loose constitutional ground.

"It's very difficult to prove what the aggravating factor is," said Robert M. O'Neil, a University of Virginia law professor. "There's no way to prove the essential element of such a case without taking speech into account."

Using speech to determine motive in the courtroom goes against the flow of analysis in *R.A.V.* and threatens to drastically chill speech by inspiring extensive searches into what the offender has written or said for evidence to prove motive at the moment of the offense.

Ohio public defender Susan Gellman, who in a widely recognized article in the *U.C.L.A. Law Review* criticized enhancement laws a year before *R.A.V.*, finds that laws which punish actions "based on" a perceived minority status fail to address the several motives of an offender.

> *"Opponents say the premises of current enhancement laws stand on loose constitutional ground."*

For example, she said, a defendant accused of holding up a Jewish man on Yom Kippur may have known nothing at the time of the crime of the holiday or the man's religion. The same defendant might have known the day and faith, but have acted more out of a desire for money than hatred for the Jewish community. In both cases the defendant could be guilty under several statutes, she believes.

"One problem is they're using the motive as a surrogate for effect," she says. "You can have the motive with no effect or you could have the reverse."

Gellman recommends creating a law which would specifically upgrade "offenses where the defendant acted with specific intent to create terror within a definable community or with specific intent to create a threat of further crime within a definable community."

Diane Zimmerman, a New York University professor of law and chair of the American Bar Association Individual Rights and Responsibilities Section's First Amendment Rights Committee, said enhancement statutes fail muster in that they select some biases as worse than others. She criticized state statutes like Oregon's—prohibiting crime based on the perception of the victim's "race, color, religion, national origin or sexual orientation"—which do not account for other "minority" attributes such as gender or age.

"I understand that when skinheads attack Jews, African-Americans, or Vietnamese, it has resonance in a long history," she says, "but so does it when people are picked out for other reasons. . . . If the penalties already follow, it just isn't clear why we need this."

Distinctions between biases carry, she adds, "a strong affinity to the kind of stuff that the Supreme Court said no to in the *R.A.V.* case."

Will Hate Crimes Increase?

Hate laws and codes in some form are direly needed, law enforcement officials, several legislators, and minority organizations maintain. "No matter what the ruling that we ultimately get from the Supreme Court," points out Michael Sandberg of the Anti-Defamation League, "hate crimes are still going to happen."

If long-term trends continue, they could happen with an even higher frequency. Though not enough time has elapsed to record any possible increases in hate crimes since *R.A.V.*, the Anti-Defamation League has tracked steady rises in hate-motivated anti-Semitic incidents since 1988, documenting a record high 1,879 in 1991.

Similarly, the National Gay and Lesbian Task Force and the Klanwatch Project of the Southern Poverty Law Center respectively find long-term growth in the numbers of gay bashing incidents and white supremacy groups.

"Any minority group you talk to would tell you they're experiencing an increase," said Patti Abbott, a spokeswoman for the Minneapolis-based Gay and Lesbian Community and Action Counsel. She said the recent L.A. riots and recession-ridden times—historically notorious for fostering hate offenses—have created a climate where "you don't have to put a hood on your head to want to lash out at minorities."

Special Penalties Should Apply to Hate Crimes

by Nadine Strossen

About the author: *Nadine Strossen is president of the American Civil Liberties Union.*

To further our constitutional values of equality, the government may impose harsher punishments upon crimes whose victims are selected on the basis of racial and other invidious discrimination.

Discriminatory Crimes

Opponents of laws authorizing such enhanced penalties have misleadingly claimed that they create "hate-speech crimes," and therefore violate the First Amendment. But these laws target acts that are more accurately described as "discriminatory crimes," and thus may be punished consistent with the First Amendment, so long as the laws are narrowly drawn and carefully applied.

If Wisconsin's discriminatory crime statute—which was upheld by the Supreme Court in the [*State of Wisconsin v. Todd Mitchell*] case—punished discriminatory ideas or expressions, the American Civil Liberties Union (ACLU) would oppose that statute. The ACLU has consistently opposed all laws that punish "hate speech" and successfully challenged the University of Wisconsin's hate-speech code on First Amendment grounds. However, Wisconsin did not punish Todd Mitchell for his discriminatory beliefs but for acting on those beliefs by participating in a vicious, near-fatal racist attack on a fourteen-year-old boy.

This fundamental distinction between protected thought and punishable conduct is central to both free speech jurisprudence and anti-discrimination laws. For example, landlords may believe in racial segregation, but they may not act on this belief by refusing to rent to prospective tenants of a certain race.

Anti-discrimination laws long have prohibited discriminatory acts that would not otherwise be illegal—for example, refusing to hire someone—because of society's consensus that such discriminatory acts cause special harms, not only to the imme-

Nadine Strossen, "Yes: Discriminatory Crimes," *ABA Journal*, May 1993; © 1993 by the American Bar Association. Reprinted by permission of the *ABA Journal*.

diate victim but also to the racial or other societal group to which the victim belongs, and to our heterogeneous society more generally. Why, then, shouldn't the law treat discriminatory criminal acts more severely than other criminal acts?

Promoting Equality Values

Unlike those who urge that all discriminatory crime laws are unconstitutional, the ACLU's position is that, if narrowly drafted and carefully enforced, such laws can avoid First Amendment pitfalls while promoting constitutionally protected equality values. Thus, the ACLU maintains that a defendant's words are only relevant if the government carries the heavy burden of proving beyond a reasonable doubt that they are directly related to the underlying crime and probative of his discriminatory intent.

Without this tight nexus, the defendant's thoughts, associations and expressions remain constitutionally protected and inadmissible. Accordingly, the ACLU has opposed certain discriminatory crime laws in some contexts. It has opposed Florida's law providing for an enhanced penalty if the crime "evidences prejudice," because this law on its face punishes a defendant's abstract thought without demanding a clear, specific connection between the prejudiced thought and a particular crime.

> *"Why . . . shouldn't the law treat discriminatory criminal acts more severely than other criminal acts?"*

In the *Mitchell* case, there was a sufficiently direct nexus between Mitchell's racially inciting statements and the brutal attacks they provoked to treat the statements as probative of his discriminatory intent. Addressing a group of other black men, Mitchell said, "Do you all feel hyped up to move on some white people?" When the victim approached a short time later, Mitchell said to the group, "You all want to f--- somebody up? There goes a white boy; go get him." He then indicated that the group should surround the victim. Immediately thereafter, group members ran toward the boy, surrounded him, and repeatedly kicked and punched him into unconsciousness.

Expression may constitute circumstantial evidence of discriminatory intent under discriminatory crime laws, as it does under other anti-discrimination laws. But the First Amendment does not bar the use of words to prove criminal intent or other elements of a crime. An accused kidnapper cannot raise a First Amendment objection to the introduction of a ransom note into evidence. Nor can a defendant who has made repeated, harassing telephone calls claim immunity from prosecution because his instruments of harassment were words.

The First Amendment protects the right to be a racist, to join racist organizations, to express racist beliefs—but not the right to engage in racist attacks. This critical distinction may be difficult to draw in particular situations. But to pretend it doesn't exist disserves constitutional values of both free speech and equality.

Penalty-Enhancement Laws Are Needed to Fight Hate Crime

by Steven M. Freeman

About the author: *Steven M. Freeman is director of legal affairs for the Anti-Defamation League.*

There is a profound irony to the current national preoccupation with hate crimes. The irony is that hate crimes are nothing new. They have exploded as a phenomenon on the public consciousness only recently, but in fact, crimes motivated by bigotry have plagued this nation since its earliest days. Racial assaults, cemetery desecrations, gay-bashings, and countless other forms of bias-motivated criminal conduct are a sad but very real part of American history—and unfortunately, they are still happening today.

The Anti-Defamation League's Fight Against Hate Crimes

Eight decades ago, when the Anti-Defamation League (ADL or League) was founded (in 1913), a particularly brutal, anti-Semitic crime—the lynching of a Jew named Leo Frank in Atlanta, Georgia—provided dramatic evidence of the need to combat criminal conduct motivated by bigotry.

As an agency dedicated to exposing and counteracting not only anti-Semitism, but all forms of prejudice, ADL takes considerable pride in the pioneering role we have played in calling attention to hate crimes. Our proactive efforts, including the model legislation we first drafted in 1981, stemmed from the conviction that the criminal justice system was not handling hate crimes adequately. Anti-Semitic crimes, our particular concern, were on the rise, and the traditional responsive components—media exposure, education, and more effective law enforcement—were not proving sufficient. Something new was needed.

The reason for our concern about hate crimes is readily apparent. Such crimes have a special emotional and physical impact that extends beyond the original

Steven M. Freeman, "Hate Crime Laws: Punishment Which Fits the Crime," *Annual Survey of American Law*, no. 4 (1992/93), pp. 581–85 (sans footnotes). Reprinted by permission of the *Annual Survey of American Law*, New York University School of Law.

victim. They intimidate others in the victim's community, causing them to feel isolated, vulnerable, and unprotected by the law. By making members of a specific group fearful, angry and suspicious, these crimes polarize cities and damage the very fabric of our society.

Failure to recognize and effectively address this type of crime can cause an isolated incident to fester and to explode into widespread community tension, perhaps leading to an escalating cycle of reprisals. This is especially true if the targeted group perceives that law enforcement officials are not taking their concerns seriously. As anyone who lived through the violence in Crown Heights, Brooklyn, in the summer of 1991 could testify, the harm caused by bias crimes cannot be measured solely in terms of property damage assessments or physical injuries. [In August 1991, a weekend of rioting erupted after a black child was killed by a car driven by a Jewish man.]

The Penalty-Enhancement Model

So, in 1981, ADL went to the drawing board and came up with a model statute. The ADL legislation was drafted to cover not just anti-Semitic crimes, but all hate crimes, and it was intended to complement other ADL counteraction measures—including the aforementioned media exposure, education, and more effective law enforcement.

In crafting its model statute, ADL drew inspiration from laws already on the books in Arizona, New York, and Oregon. The League adopted an approach which is centered around a "penalty-enhancement" scheme. Expressions of hate protected by the First Amendment's free speech clause are not criminalized. However, when bigotry prompts an individual to engage in criminal activity, a prosecutor can seek a stiffer sentence. The obvious intent of such legislation is not only to impose serious punishment on the perpetrators of hate crimes, but also to deter such crimes by making it clear that they will be considered particularly serious crimes and will be dealt with accordingly.

In promoting model legislation, ADL was cognizant of, and sensitive to, the First Amendment concerns which have been subsequently raised in a series of constitutional challenges, including the landmark Supreme Court case, *State of Wisconsin v. Todd Mitchell* (1993), [in which the court upheld a Wisconsin penalty-enhancement law], discussed below. The League is a staunch believer in the importance of the First Amendment's free speech clause, and takes seriously the adage

> *"[Hate] crimes have a special emotional and physical impact that extends beyond the original victim."*

that the best answer to bad speech is not censorship, but more speech. However, we remain convinced that hate crimes and hate speech are qualitatively different.

Certainly hate-motivated *violent* crimes are incompatible with the fundamental values which underlie the First Amendment. The "marketplace of ideas" cannot function effectively when a bigot crosses the line from speech to conduct. As the Northern and Southern California chapters of the American Civil Liberties Union said in an *amicus* brief they filed jointly with ADL in 1993, "violence and threats of violence undermine the search for truth by distorting the 'marketplace of ideas.' Violence substitutes coercion for persuasion, force for discussion and debate."

In that same *amicus* brief the authors observed that "violence also undermines the important First Amendment value of individual self-fulfillment and personal autonomy. At bottom, the right of free expression depends upon respect [for] the autonomy and integrity of others."

Hate-Crime Laws and Free Speech

Those who have challenged the penalty-enhancement approach on First Amendment grounds have frequently raised concerns about its potential "chilling effect" on speech. However, most hate crime statutes, including the ADL model, use the language "by reason of" or "because of"—making it clear that the connection between the perpetrator's selection of a particular victim and that victim's race, religion, ethnicity, or sexual orientation must be conclusively established. Moreover, the defendant receives the full protection of all the relevant rules of evidence, including an appropriate weighing of the prejudicial and probative value of

> *"Expressions of hate protected by the First Amendment's free speech clause are not criminalized."*

prior expressions of bigotry. A difference in race or other status between perpetrator and victim can never be sufficient proof, in and of itself, that a hate crime took place.

State legislatures and courts across the country have been persuaded that ADL's approach is constructive, and more than half of the states have enacted laws based on, or similar to, the ADL model. As of this writing, a federal hate crime bill [sponsored by Representative Charles Schumer] similar to the ADL model has been proposed in the United States Congress.

In June 1993, speaking in a clear and unambiguous voice, the United States Supreme Court validated the constitutionality of the penalty-enhancement concept. The Court's unanimous decision, in *Mitchell*, represents an important milestone in the struggle against criminal conduct motivated by bigotry.

In *Mitchell*, the Court specifically upheld a Wisconsin law based on the ADL model statute. The Wisconsin law enhances a defendant's penalty when the prosecution is able to prove that the defendant selected his or her victim because of race, religion, color, disability, sexual orientation, national origin or ancestry. The *Mitchell* case itself involved an attack on a white teenager by a young African-American.

In an emphatic and sweeping opinion written on behalf of all nine Justices, Chief Justice William H. Rehnquist noted that courts routinely look at a defendant's motive in the course of determining a sentence. He compared the Wisconsin statute to federal and state anti-discrimination laws which have previously been held constitutional, and drew a clear distinction between it and the St. Paul, Minnesota, ordinance which the Court found unconstitutional in a crossburning case in 1992 [*R.A.V. v. City of St. Paul*].

> *"Speaking in a clear and unambiguous voice, the . . . Supreme Court validated the constitutionality of the penalty-enhancement concept."*

Responding to the major argument advanced by opponents of the Wisconsin law, the Chief Justice firmly rejected any notion that the law punished the defendant's thoughts rather than his conduct. In his words:

> [T]he Wisconsin statute singles out for enhancement bias-inspired conduct because this conduct is thought to inflict greater individual and societal harm. For example, according to the State and its *amici*, bias-motivated crimes are more likely to provoke retaliatory crimes, inflict distinct emotional harms on their victims, and incite community unrest. . . . The State's desire to redress these perceived harms provides an adequate explanation for its penalty-enhancement provisions over and above mere disagreement with offenders' beliefs or biases.

The Chief Justice's reference to the state's *amici* was fitting given the outpouring of *amicus* support for Wisconsin's law. Among those who filed briefs, in addition to ADL, were the United States Justice Department; the Attorneys General of all forty-nine other states; thirty-five members of Congress; the cities of Atlanta, Baltimore, Boston, Chicago, Cleveland, Los Angeles, New York, Philadelphia, and San Francisco; the American Civil Liberties Union; the National Association for the Advancement of Colored People Legal Defense Fund; and a wide array of other civil rights groups representing many different minority communities. ADL's *amicus* brief on Wisconsin's behalf was joined by fifteen other law enforcement and civil rights organizations, including the International Association of Chiefs of Police, the National Gay and Lesbian Task Force, People for the American Way, and the Southern Poverty Law Center.

The Need for Hate-Crime Laws

The outcome in *Mitchell* was not a surprise. In fact, it was presaged by Justice John Paul Stevens, who had previously pointed out in *R.A.V.* that

> [c]onduct that creates special risks or causes special harms may by prohibited by special rules. . . . Threatening someone because of her race or religious beliefs may cause particularly severe trauma or touch off a riot, and . . . such threats may be punished more severely than threats against someone based on, say, his support of a particular athletic team. There are legitimate, reasonable, and neutral justifications for such special rules.

Not only is the penalty-enhancement approach sound, in our best judgment it works. Certainly, anyone who has ever spoken to the victim of a hate crime understands that crossburning is different from ordinary trespass; that a swastika daubing is different from ordinary vandalism; and that a gay-bashing or racial assault is different from an ordinary mugging. For victims of such incidents, penalty enhancement is a punishment which fits the crime.

> *"For victims of [hate crimes], penalty enhancement is a punishment which fits the crime."*

As to the effectiveness of hate crime laws as a deterrent, from an empirical standpoint the jury is still out. Of course, now that the Supreme Court has spoken, there is reason to be optimistic that additional states will enact such laws and that law enforcement officers and prosecutors will be more vigorous in implementing them. With increased awareness and enforcement, would-be perpetrators are more likely to get the message, and think twice the next time their bigotry tempts them to commit a bias-motivated crime.

Penalty Enhancement Does Not Punish Free Speech or Thoughts

by *Harvard Law Review*

About the author: *The* Harvard Law Review *is published eight times a year by the Harvard Law Review Association, Cambridge, Massachusetts.*

In recent years, violence, threats, and vandalism committed because of the race, religion, sexual orientation, or other such characteristic of the victim have increased at an alarming rate. Such incidents, commonly referred to as "hate crimes," inflict not only physical harm, but also unique psychic damage on their victims. Moreover, because a hate crime is directed not only at the individual victim, but also at the group to which the victim belongs, such violence tends to "escalate from individual conflicts to mass disturbances," according to the Oregon Court of Appeals, by exacerbating racial divisions among observers who sympathize with either the victims or the attackers. State and federal legislatures have taken various measures to combat this growing problem. In particular, many states have adopted "penalty-enhancement" statutes that increase penalties for certain crimes when committed because of the victim's race, religion, or national origin.

The Legality of Hate-Crime Laws

Recent legal developments, however, have cast doubt on the constitutionality of these penalty-enhancement statutes. In the summer of 1992, the supreme courts of Ohio and Wisconsin each found its state's penalty-enhancement statute to violate the First Amendment. In overturning the statutes, both courts cited *R.A.V. v. City of St. Paul, Minnesota*, in which the United States Supreme Court struck down on First Amendment grounds an ordinance banning the display of any symbol that "arouses anger, alarm or resentment in others on the basis of race, color, creed, religion or gender." The Supreme Court, however, in

Excerpted from "Hate Is Not Speech: A Constitutional Defense of Penalty Enhancement for Hate Crimes" by the *Harvard Law Review*, vol. 106 (April 1993); © 1993 by the Harvard Law Review Association. Reprinted with permission.

June 1993 reversed the decision in the Wisconsin case [*State of Wisconsin v. Todd Mitchell*]. . . .

Most penalty-enhancement statutes prescribe heightened penalties when certain crimes, independently punishable under other penal code sections, are committed because of the victim's race, color, religion, ethnicity, or other such characteristic. Penalties may be enhanced either by reclassifying the underlying offense as a more serious crime or by finding the defendant guilty of an additional offense of "intimidation" or "harassment." This popular penalty-enhancement approach [pioneered by the Anti-Defamation League (ADL)] lies at the center of the current controversy over the legality of hate-crime statutes. In Oregon, the state supreme court in 1992 upheld a penalty-enhancement statute against freedom of expression challenges brought under the state and federal constitutions. In Ohio and Wisconsin, however, such statutes were overturned by similar challenges. In other states, lower courts have produced conflicting holdings on this issue.

> *"Recent legal developments, however, have cast doubt on the constitutionality of these penalty-enhancement statutes."*

Arguments Against Penalty-Enhancement Statutes

The Ohio court in *State v. Wyant* and the Wisconsin court in *State v. Mitchell* each relied on arguments from a [1991 *UCLA Law Review*] article by Professor Susan Gellman, who served as lead defense counsel in the *Wyant* case. In her article, Gellman first claims that penalty-enhancement statutes violate the First Amendment for evidentiary reasons. Although the statutes do not prohibit speech as such, they do rely on speech as evidence of illicit motive; this evidentiary use of speech, Gellman argues, creates an unacceptable chilling effect. Under such statutes, not only would the defendant's words be directly related to the predicate offense, but "all of his or her remarks upon earlier occasions, any books ever read, speakers ever listened to, or associations ever held could be introduced as evidence that he or she held racist views and was acting upon them at the time of the offense," according to Gellman. This possibility, Gellman argues, will lead to "habitual self-censorship of expression" of racist ideas.

Gellman's second and more complicated argument posits that, by punishing bigoted motive, hate-crime statutes unconstitutionally infringe freedom of thought. Because penalty-enhancement statutes increase penalties for offenses independently punishable under different penal code sections, "the enhanced penalty must be for something more than the elements that constitute the predicate offense." The "something more" is the fact that the defendant acted "by reason of" or "because of" the victim's race, color, religion, or national origin. This element, according to the *Wyant* and *Mitchell* courts and Gellman, constitutes "no additional act or conduct beyond what is required to obtain a conviction under the predicate statutes. Thus the enhanced penalty results solely from the actor's reason for acting, or his motive."

Gellman maintains that although an underlying "predicate" offense such as an assault is punishable, the actor's motive for committing the offense is "pure thought and opinion" and, as such, is protected by the First Amendment. "[T]he state's power to punish the [predicate] action," she observes, does not "remove the constitutional barrier to punishing the thoughts." Because, in her view, penalty-enhancement statutes effectively punish thought, she concludes that such statutes are unconstitutional.

Response to the First Amendment Critiques

Before addressing each of the preceding arguments, it is important first to distinguish penalty-enhancement statutes from "hate-speech" statutes. In *R.A.V. v. City of St. Paul*, the Supreme Court struck down a speech ordinance which applied specifically to "symbol[s], object[s], appellation[s]," and the like. By contrast with hate-speech laws, penalty-enhancement statutes do not outlaw any types of "expression" recognized by the First Amendment.

Speech that conveys the idea of racial superiority, heinous though it may be, is protected under the First Amendment. Thus, the Supreme Court held in *R.A.V.* that speech falling within the category of "fighting words," although it may generally be regulated, is nonetheless a type of speech. Thus any government regulation of such speech must remain content-neutral. As the Court has repeatedly noted, however, the First Amendment does not give absolute protection to every act that has any communicative content. For example, every crime committed "expresses" the perpetrator's antisocial thoughts and ideas, but the First Amendment clearly does not shield such acts of "expression." To award a crime the status of protected speech would lead to horrific results: rape would be protected as an expression of the idea of misogyny, and assassination would be protected as an expression of political dissent. It would be absurd to read *R.A.V.*'s requirement of content-neutrality in speech regulation to protect the "expressive content" of physically violent and destructive crimes.

> *"To award a crime the status of protected speech would lead to horrific results."*

Speech May Be Used as Evidence

The First Amendment protects conventional forms of bigoted expression such as spoken statements, writings, and membership in organizations that espouse bigotry. Penalty-enhancement statutes do *not* criminalize such speech and association. They affect expression indirectly and only insofar as they consider it as *evidence* of bigoted motive. Yet Gellman insists that there is no difference between using speech as *evidence of* an element of the offense and using speech as an *element of* the offense itself. Although bigoted motive is sometimes indicated by bigoted speech, the two categories are readily distinguishable. On the one hand, a defendant could violate a penalty-enhancement statute "while remaining entirely mute" if his actions by themselves prove the element of bigoted motive, according to the New York Criminal Court. Thus even if a defendant said nothing during an attack on an Hispanic victim, the defendant could nonetheless be convicted under a penalty-enhancement statute if he had a history of going to

> *"Bigoted speech . . . may be introduced as evidence that an assailant singled out a victim in a discriminatory manner."*

Hispanic neighborhoods and attacking only Hispanic victims. On the other hand, evidence that bigoted words were uttered during a crime does not necessarily prove a bigoted motive. Harsh words of all kinds, including bigoted epithets, may fly before, during, and after a physical confrontation caused by factors other than bigotry. Thus, for example, an anti-Semitic statement made by a defendant during a violent attack on a Jewish victim would not necessarily establish a violation of a penalty-enhancement statute.

Although bigoted speech itself may not be criminalized, it may be introduced as evidence that an assailant singled out a victim in a discriminatory manner. The Supreme Court has approved such evidentiary use of speech in both civil and criminal proceedings. In the civil context, a plaintiff in a gender-discrimination suit brought under Title VII of the Civil Rights Act of 1964 "must show that the employer actually relied on her gender in making its decision," according to the Supreme Court. The employer's "stereotyped remarks can certainly be *evidence* that gender played a part," although sexist remarks in the workplace "do not inevitably prove" that gender discrimination affected an employment decision. In the criminal context, the Supreme Court in 1992 stated that "the Constitution does not erect a *per se* barrier to the admission of evidence concerning one's beliefs and associations at sentencing." Admission of such evidence is permissible as long as the information is relevant to the issues being decided. For example, in *Barclay v. Florida*, the Court held that a sentencing judge properly considered the defendant's membership in the "Black Liberation Army" in finding that "racial hatred" prompted the defendant's murder of a white victim. Despite the fact that freedom of association and membership in political organizations is a basic First Amendment right, the Supreme Court approved the trial court's consideration of that membership in sentencing the defendant to death.

More generally, defendants' statements are routinely introduced into evidence. It would clearly violate the First Amendment to punish person X merely for saying, "I wish Y were dead." If X were on trial for the murder of Y, however, it would be absurd to contend that the First Amendment prohibits using X's statement to help prove the element of premeditation.

Penalty-Enhancement Statutes Do Not Punish Motive

Gellman defines the three mental states basic to criminal law as follows:

> "[I]ntent". . . refers to the actor's mental state as it determines culpability based on volition, "purpose" connotes what the actor plans as a result of the conduct, and "motive" is the term for the actor's underlying, propelling reasons for acting, which may have no direct relationship to the type of conduct chosen.

She argues that although intent and purpose can be elements of offenses, motive cannot. Penalty-enhancement statutes are invalid, Gellman claims, because a defendant's motive is both irrelevant to substantive criminal law and protected by the First Amendment. Both the *Wyant* and *Mitchell* courts accepted this claim. This argument, however, fails on three grounds: first, Gellman's doctrinal structure distinguishing intent, motive, and purpose is inherently arbitrary; second, even in Gellman's own terms, penalty-enhancement statutes punish "purpose" rather than "motive"; and third, punishment of motive is a common and constitutional practice.

Gellman adopts Wayne LaFave's and Austin Scott's axiom that unlike purpose and intent, "motive is not relevant on the substantive side of the criminal law." This descriptive rule appears to rely upon a distinction between a criminal's punishable choice of means—his *intentional* resort to illegal conduct—and his unpunishable choice of ends—his *motive*. This simple distinction is complicated by the fact that *purpose*, which alludes more to ends than to means, is often part of the definition of an offense. To shore up this weakness in the descriptive theory, Gellman and the *Wyant* court rely on LaFave's and Scott's distinction between an ultimate end, or motive, and medial ends, or interim goals pursued for the purpose of attaining the ultimate end. For example, if a defendant chooses to break into a house in order to get money to repay a debt, he has chosen the means of burglary (his intent) to realize the intermediate end of taking money (his purpose). Taking money is not only his intermediate *end*, but also his *means* of repaying his debt (his motive). In such a situation, "it is appropriate to characterize the purpose of taking money as the intent and the desire to pay his debts as the motive," according to LaFave and Scott. Thus, although purpose bears an end-like relationship to intent, it also bears a means-like relation to motive. Gellman contends that because of its means-like nature, purpose can be an element of a substantive criminal law. Motive, by contrast, is the criminal's ultimate end; it is not a means to anything. Because it is entirely concerned with ultimate ends, motive cannot be punished, or so the labored argument asserts.

> *"Punishment of motive is a common and constitutional practice."*

Distinguishing Motive from Purpose

The distinction between motive and purpose, however, is a specious one. In the hypothetical involving the burglar, LaFave and Scott call the burglar's desire to repay his debts his "motive" because it is his "ultimate end." But the characterization of debt repayment as the *ultimate* end is arbitrary and conclusory. The burglar's repayment of debts can just as easily be cast as the means to some other, "more ultimate" end: for example, to avoid repossession of his car or to free up his spending money to buy drugs. Each of these "ends" is, in turn, the means to yet another end: perhaps to maintain a getaway vehicle for future crimes or to satisfy his drug addiction. And any competent lawyer can recharacterize each of these "ends" as the means to yet another end, *ad infinitum.* In other words, the concept of "ultimate end" is analytically meaningless, because any end can be seen as a means to another end; no clear line separates "purpose" and "motive."

Even if such a distinction could be sustained, it would be more accurate under the LaFave-Gellman model to characterize penalty-enhancement laws as a means of punishing intermediate ends (that is, purposes) than ultimate ends (that is, motives). The facts of *Mitchell* provide an illuminating example: in that case, a group of black youths who had just seen the film *Mississippi Burning* were angrily discussing a scene in which a white man brutalizes a praying black boy. Mitchell asked his friends, "Do you all feel hyped up to move on some white people?" and led them to attack a passing white boy. In LaFave's terms, Mitchell chose to incite violence in order to harm a white person so as to gain revenge for the abuse of blacks at the hands of whites. Thus instigating a beating was his intent (or means); harming a white victim was his purpose (or intermediate end), and his motive was revenge. Thus, under the intermediate/ultimate ends analysis, racial selection was Mitchell's "purpose," not his motive.

> *"No clear line separates 'purpose' and 'motive.'"*

A variety of examples lend further support to the argument that Gellman is mistaken in classifying discriminatory victim selection as motive rather than purpose. In *Barclay v. Florida*, the defendant killed a white victim as part of a plan to start a racial war. In Sacramento County, California, a thirty-seven-year-old white man "took a 15-year-old kid and rammed his head into a pole a couple of times. This man said he did it because he did not like Asians," according to Deputy Sheriff Michael Tsuchida. In each of these cases, race was central to the attacker's choice of victim. But in each case, harming a victim on the basis of race was only an intermediate end; the choice of victim served as the means to another end. In *Barclay*, that end was the instigation of revolution; . . . in the Sacramento incident, it was the expression of racial hatred.

Even within the malleable LaFave-Gellman typology, imposing enhanced sentences for crimes committed "because of race" [as the Wisconsin law does] can be seen as punishing the actor's purpose, not his motive. Revenge, revolution, and simple hatred are all possible motives, but penalty-enhancement statutes do not distinguish among them. Thus the ADL statute and its progeny do not target the "thought" of bigotry; instead, they punish the "purpose"—the intermediate end—of choosing a victim based on his or her race, religion, or other group characteristic. Gellman herself acknowledges that the criminal law may punish purpose, and the First Amendment thus poses no obstacle to penalty-enhancement statutes' efforts to punish crimes committed because of the race, religion, or similar characteristics of their victims.

Punishment of Motive Is a Common Practice

Gellman insists that penalty-enhancement statutes are invalid because the common law does not consider motive. However, even if we were to assume that Gellman's distinctions among the mental states were tenable and that these statutes punish motive, her conclusion is still unpersuasive. For regardless of what the common law's treatment of motive might be, federal statutory law considers motive in a multitude of ways.

For example, discriminatory motive is actually part of the *definition* of the tort of conspiracy to interfere with civil rights. A plaintiff has a cause of action when "two or more persons . . . conspire or go in disguise on the highway or on the premises of another, for the purpose of depriving, either directly or indirectly, any person or class of persons of the equal protection of the laws, or of equal privileges and immunities under the laws . . . ," according to federal law. The Supreme Court has interpreted this statute to require "some racial, or perhaps otherwise class-based, invidiously discriminatory animus behind the conspirators' action." In other words, "invidiously discriminatory motivation" is an express element of the tort.

Like penalty-enhancement statutes, anti-discrimination laws also prohibit certain conduct when it is performed "because of" a person's race, religion, gender, or disability. Thus, although hiring and firing decisions are normally left to the discretion of the employer, Title VII prohibits an employer from discharging, refusing to hire, or otherwise discriminating against an individual "because of that individual's race, color, religion, sex, or national origin." The Americans with Disabilities Act (ADA) and the Age Discrimination in Employment Act (ADEA) similarly prohibit employers from discriminating against individuals on grounds of disability or age. Statutes such as these prohibit otherwise legal acts when an employer's treatment of others is based on a discriminatory *motive.*

> *"Imposing enhanced sentences for crimes committed 'because of race' can be seen as punishing the actor's purpose, not his motive."*

Hate Crimes and Discrimination

Unlike penalty-enhancement statutes, which add penalties to otherwise illegal acts based on the actor's motive, anti-discrimination employment laws penalize otherwise *legal* discretionary decisions. For example, a given employment decision carries no legal sanction when the decisionmaker's reason is economic necessity, a personal disagreement, or sheer caprice. But when the decisionmaker's *reason* for the predicate act is a person's race, gender, or disability, the "predicate" legal consequence (no consequence) is "enhanced" to civil liability. Title VII penalizes otherwise *legal* treatment of another person when such treatment is invidiously motivated by race. In this context it is inconsistent to maintain that a penalty-enhancement statute may not further punish an actor's otherwise *illegal* treatment of another person when similarly motivated by race.

> *"Anti-discrimination laws also prohibit certain conduct when it is performed 'because of' a person's race, religion, gender, or disability."*

In voiding their respective states' penalty-enhancement statutes, both the *Wyant* and the *Mitchell* courts rejected the analogy to anti-discrimination laws. Both courts maintained that whereas anti-discrimination laws target the illegal *act* of discrimination, penalty-enhancement laws target bigoted motive, which is protected speech. However, both courts ignored the fact that protecting the racially discriminatory selection of an assault victim makes sense only if the racially discriminatory firing of an employee is protected as well. Title VII jurisprudence, however, shows the latter to be untrue. Alternatively, if racial discrimination in the hiring of an employee constitutes a separate, proscribable *act*, then how can the same be untrue for discriminatory selection of an assault victim? Both employment discrimination and discriminatory assault take their illegal character from the discriminatory thoughts motivating the act.

Finally, the Supreme Court has explicitly upheld the constitutionality of the punishment of bigoted motive. In *Barclay*, a Florida statute authorized capital punishment for murders which were "especially heinous, atrocious, or cruel." The Supreme Court approved the lower court's reliance on findings of "elements of racial hatred" in its determination that the defendant's murder of a white person met the statutory requirement.

Gellman's descriptive claim that the criminal law does not punish motive is plainly mistaken. But even if her assertion were true, that fact alone would not present any normative rationale, on either policy or constitutional grounds, for proscribing the punishment of motive. Gellman and the courts which have followed her model rely heavily on the subtle and likely inviable conceptual distinction between "purpose" and "motive," but they offer no explanation as to *why* one should be punishable but not the other. If inquiry into mental states such as purpose and intent does not offend the First Amendment by creating "thought crimes," why does inquiry into motive do so?

In sum, the First Amendment does not prohibit peering into a defendant's mind. Civil, criminal, common, and statutory law all make clear that certain thoughts and ideas are open to scrutiny. The real issue lies in distinguishing protected thoughts from unprotected thoughts. The *Wyant* and *Mitchell* courts, along with Gellman, would draw a bright line around motive in order to protect "pure thought." This rule is unsatisfactory, however, because first, even within the criminal law, the definitional distinctions are all but impossible to maintain. Second, forbidding scrutiny of motive conflicts with the large body of law that already punishes motive. Third, from the perspective of the First Amendment, such distinctions are arbitrary; no coherent theory of freedom of speech could award total protection to motive and none to intent or purpose. Therefore, a more principled and sensible method of restricting governmental inquiry into thought is to acknowledge the constitutionality of punishment of motive, but to draw a clear distinction between motive and "pure thought."

Special Penalties Should Not Apply to Hate Crimes

by James B. Jacobs

About the author: *James B. Jacobs is a professor of law at New York University School of Law in New York City.*

On May 29, 1989, a white man, David Wyant, occupied a campsite next to Jerry White, an African-American. White complained to the park authorities that Wyant was playing his music too loudly during "quiet hours." White and his companion later heard three comments directed at them from the Wyants' campsite: 1) "We didn't have this problem until those niggers moved in next to us"; 2) "The black motherfucker over there; I will take this gun and kill him"; 3) "In fact, I will go over and beat his black ass now."

Low-Level Harassment vs. Hardcore Racism

On the basis of these statements, without any accompanying conduct or evidence that there actually was a gun, Wyant was convicted of "ethnic intimidation" and sentenced to eighteen months' incarceration.

State (of Ohio) v. Wyant (1992) is the kind of case that ought to be carefully considered by proponents of hate crime legislation. The imagery that animates the passage of such legislation posits hardcore racists and anti-Semites waging a systematic campaign against blacks and Jews. By contrast, most of the cases that are labeled hate crimes result from impulsive behavior or situational disputes, often involving juveniles. One could easily think of the *Wyant* case as a fight about noise at a campground that activated the defendant's racial prejudice. Such prejudice is certainly not pretty but, unlike hardcore neo-Nazism, is widespread and often bubbles to the surface in the arguments, altercations, and conflicts that punctuate life in a multi-racial and multi-ethnic society. This kind of prejudice certainly needs attention, but not the kind of attention that is provided by elevating an occasional low-level, harassment-type crime into a serious offense.

Excerpted from "Should Hate Be a Crime?" by James B. Jacobs. Reprinted with permission of the author and *The Public Interest*, no. 113, Fall 1993, pp. 3–14; © 1993 by National Affairs, Inc.

The Problem of Motive

Wyant also reveals a more serious flaw in hate crime legislation. Criminal law has long struggled to define the criminal intent (*mens rea*) that transforms a harm into a crime. Defining criminal motivation is even trickier, because it requires getting to the *source* of the defendant's intent. For this reason criminal law generally has steered clear of motivation.

Motivation is particularly problematic in hate crime cases because the presumed motive, "prejudice," defies precise definition. According to the *International Encyclopedia of the Social Sciences*:

> Prejudice is not a unitary phenomenon. . . . [I]t will take varying forms in different individuals. Socially and psychologically, attitudes differ depending upon whether they are the result of deep-seated personality characteristics, sometimes of the pathological nature, of a traumatic experience, or whether they simply represent conformity to an established norm.

Indeed, some people speak of prejudice as being unconscious as well as conscious. Consider the view of Charles R. Lawrence III, an influential professor of law at Stanford University:

> Americans share a common historical and cultural heritage in which racism played and still plays a dominant role. Because of this shared experience, we also inevitably share many ideas, attitudes and beliefs that attach significance to an individual's race and induce negative feelings and opinions about non-whites. To the extent that this cultural belief system has influenced all of us, we are all racists. At the same time, most of us are unaware of our racism. . . . In other words, a large part of the behavior that produces racial discrimination is influenced by unconscious racial motivation.

If prejudice is this pervasive, subtle, and complex, the criminal justice system will certainly have a hard time sorting out which interracial crimes are motivated by prejudice and which are not. Moreover, recent efforts by law enforcement agencies and courts to define hate crimes more precisely do not inspire confidence. For example, the U.S. Department of Justice guidelines, which set out the government's criteria for labeling a hate crime, define ethnic prejudice as a "preformed negative opinion or attitude toward a group of persons of the same race or national origin who share common or similar traits, languages, customs, and traditions." If the prejudice required is no more than "a preformed negative opinion," most interracial crimes could be prosecuted as hate crimes.

> *"Most of the cases that are labeled hate crimes result from impulsive behavior or situational disputes, often involving juveniles."*

The Difficulty of Proving Prejudice

Prosecutors in hate crime cases must prove not only that the defendant was prejudiced, but that prejudice motivated his crime. But must prejudice be the sole or primary motivation, or simply a contributing motivation? If prejudice must be the sole or the primary motivation, it will be very difficult to prove a hate crime, since criminal behavior, like all behavior, is almost always motivated by many factors.

If, however, prejudice must be merely a contributing factor, practically any interracial crime could be prosecuted as a hate crime. Contemplate, for example, the percentage of interracial muggings, robberies, and assaults in bars that might be said to be "in part" attributable to a preformed negative opinion about the victim's racial group. Thus far, courts and legislatures have opted for an inclusive interpretation, so that in most jurisdictions the prosecution has to prove only that the criminal conduct was "in whole or in part" attributable to prejudice.

> *"Motivation is particularly problematic in hate crime cases because the presumed motive, 'prejudice,' defies precise definition."*

In labeling hate crimes there is immense potential for confusion and arbitrariness. In New York City, the police are instructed not to apply the hate crime label to an offense that started off as something else (e.g., a fight over a parking space) and then escalated into name calling. But they are also instructed: "If after applying the [eleven] criteria listed and asking the appropriate questions, substantial doubt exists as to whether or not the incident is bias motivated or not, the incident should be classified as bias motivated for investigative and reporting purposes."

It is uncertain where things will go from here. Police commissioners and politicians obviously will not wish to have their cities labeled the "hate crime capital." Yet they are also under constant pressure from advocacy groups to recognize racism, anti-Semitism, and homophobia, and they are vulnerable to criticism when they do not denounce, label, investigate, and prosecute various offenses as hate crimes. So there will probably be a tendency to err on the side of inclusion.

The First Amendment

In *R.A.V. v. City of St. Paul* (1992), the Supreme Court, in an opinion by Justice Antonin Scalia, held unconstitutional on First Amendment grounds a St. Paul, Minnesota, hate ordinance that outlawed symbolic speech (including cross burning and swastikas) which insults or provokes violence on the basis of race, color, creed, religion, or gender.

Although *R.A.V.* dealt with an ordinance that prohibited offensive "fighting words," the decision also cast a cloud over laws that enhance sentences for ordinary crimes (e.g., harassment, assault, rape) motivated by particular prejudices. Critics of such laws charge that enhancing the sentence of an offender for conduct motivated by politically disfavored opinion, thought, or belief also violates the First Amendment. Adopting that view, the Wisconsin Supreme Court held the state's hate crime enhancement statute to be unconstitutional: "the Wisconsin legislature cannot prohibit bigoted thought with which it disagrees."

In *Todd Mitchell v. State of Wisconsin* (1993), however, the U.S. Supreme Court overruled the Wisconsin Supreme Court. Chief Justice William H. Rehnquist's opinion for a unanimous Court noted that, "whereas the ordinance struck down in *R.A.V.* was explicitly directed at expression, the statute in this case is aimed at conduct unprotected by the First Amendment." The Court also rejected as "simply too speculative" the defendant's argument that the statute would have a chilling effect on speech, causing citizens to fear making prejudiced or racist statements or engaging in politically disfavored activities (reading, memberships, etc.) lest their words or deeds be used against them at some future criminal trial.

In response to the defendant's claim, the Court explained that "the First Amendment does not prohibit the evidentiary use of speech to establish the elements of a crime or to prove motive or intent." Thus, according to the Court, the admissibility of speech, speech-related, or associational activity can be properly managed under long-established evidentiary rules of relevancy and reliability.

That may turn out to be wishful thinking. In *Mitchell*, there was testimony of a close relationship between racist speech and criminal conduct—the defendant said to his friends: "Do you feel hyped up to move on some white people?" and "You all want to fuck somebody up? There goes a white boy; go get him." Clearly, this racist speech immediately preceding the brutal assault was relevant to proving that Mitchell had selected his victim because of racial prejudice. But how will the criminal justice system deal with beliefs, words, or associations that are not as closely connected to the criminal conduct?

In interracial cases, should the police routinely investigate the defendant's prejudices: what publications he subscribes to, what organizations he's a member of, what jokes he tells, what stereotypes he holds? Suppose, in *Mitchell*, that several days or weeks earlier the defendant had told friends or co-workers that he wanted to retaliate against whites for the injustice portrayed in the movie *Mississippi Burning*. Since prejudice would be an element of the offense, the defendant's conversations and activities regarding prejudice would definitely be relevant and, in my judgment, admissible. I am also led to this conclusion by cases like *People v. Aishman* (1993), where the fact that one of the defendants wore two tattoos, one a swastika and another reading "Thank God I'm White," was held admissible in considering whether the defendant selected his Mexican-American victim because of ethnicity. While admitting such evidence may not be unconstitutional, it certainly is not

> *"In labeling hate crimes there is immense potential for confusion and arbitrariness."*

consistent with the spirit of a strong First Amendment. It bristles with potential for defendants to be convicted or sentenced more harshly because of their "bad" beliefs and attitudes.

Defending Against Charges of Prejudice

In an effort to defend against a hate crime charge, some defendants may try to prove their lack of prejudice by introducing evidence of non-racist speech, memberships, and activities. How could a judge rule such evidence irrelevant? If the defendant is permitted to adduce such evidence, however, the prosecutor will almost certainly be allowed to introduce rebuttal evidence of the defendant's racism.

> *"In interracial cases, should the police routinely investigate the defendant's prejudices?"*

Thus, there is the all too likely possibility that hate crime trials will degenerate into inquisitions on the defendant's beliefs, attitudes, and personality. In *Wyant*, the attempt to determine the defendant's motivation led to the following cross-examination:

Q. And you lived next door to [Mrs. Ware, a 65-year-old black neighbor of the defendant's] for nine years and you don't even know her first name?

A. No.

Q. Never had dinner with her?

A. No.

Q. Never gone out and had a beer with her?

A. No.

Q. Never went to a movie?

A. No.

Q. Never invited her to a picnic at your house?

A. No.

Q. Never invited her to Alum Creek?

A. No, she never invited me nowhere, no.

Q. You don't associate with her, do you?

A. I talk with her when I can, whenever I see her out.

Q. All these black people that you have described that are your friends, I want you to give me one person, just one who was really a good friend of yours.

Examinations like this one are unlikely to ease racial tension. Rather, they seem more likely to turn hate crime trials into character tests of the most pernicious kind and to widen social divisions.

Even if judges find a way to limit cross-examinations and the admissibility of speech and thought evidence, the defendant's arguably racist words and thoughts will still be ventilated at pre-trial and trial hearings on the admissibility of evidence. Even if the jury does not hear the evidence, the media can and will seize on the defendant's beliefs as newsworthy. With prejudice the key factor distinguishing hate crime from ordinary crime, the inevitable result will be the further politicization of the criminal justice process. That can only have a negative effect on racial and other intergroup relations in American society.

Hate Crime Politics

On the one hand, to denounce hate crimes is to affirm the goal of a fair and tolerant society. On the other, to highlight the prejudicial and racial aspects of as many crimes as possible, transforming the crime problem into a prejudice problem, is to present an unduly bleak picture of the state of inter-group relations and rub salt into the wounds of festering angers and prejudices. Rather than defining violence as a social problem that unites all Americans in a search for a solution, this new approach defines the problem as a composite of different types of intergroup hate, and so may divide the political community.

In the last several years, New York City has experienced a new kind of political controversy: whether a particular crime merits denunciation as a hate crime by the criminal justice system, mayor, police commissioner, and media. These high visibility controversies put the politicians and police brass in a no-win situation. If they do not utter the words "hate crime," they are excoriated by the victim's group for bias and insensitivity. If they do apply the hate crime label, they are similarly criticized by the perpetrator's group for bias, hasty judgment, and double standards. . . .

> *"There is the all too likely possibility that hate crime trials will degenerate into inquisitions on the defendant's beliefs."*

The very existence of the hate crime label raises the political and social stakes in intergroup crimes. Groups are beginning to keep score cards. Applying or failing to apply the hate crime label triggers heated political battles. The result is not greater racial and ethnic harmony, but exacerbated social conflict. . . .

The basic civil rights paradigm posits whites as the prototypical discriminators or offenders; it does not contemplate discrimination by minorities against whites or against one another. Blacks and Hispanics, however, are disproportionately involved in violent crimes. Most of these are intragroup, but many are against whites and members of other minority groups.

While violence by whites against blacks occurs all too frequently, blacks also commit many crimes against whites. Thus, unlike other civil rights legislation and jurisprudence, hate crime laws will not necessarily work to advance the interests of all black Americans (although they might arguably advance the interests of nearly all gays and lesbians, who rarely engage in "heterosexual bashing"). Indeed, at some point in the future, some supporters of hate crime laws may be dismayed to find that these laws are frequently used against black offenders. Anticipating this outcome, several student law review writers have urged that hate crime laws should apply only (or more easily) to white defendants. To my knowledge, these proposals have not been seriously considered by state legislatures. . . .

Enhancing Deterrence

The horrendous crimes that provide the imagery and emotion for the passage of hate crime legislation are already so heavily punished under American law that any talk of "sentence enhancement" must be primarily symbolic. In fact, we have all the criminal and sentencing law we need to respond severely and punitively to criminal conduct inspired, in whole or in part, by prejudice.

I do not mean to say that the availability of enhanced punishments for hate crimes can never have any practical implications. When new powers are given to police and prosecutors, they will be used and from time to time make a difference. This is more likely to happen in low-level crimes which, because of overloaded dockets and jails, would otherwise fall through the cracks but for the added emphasis that a hate crime label might provide.

In speculating about the possible deterrent effect of hate crime laws, we need also take into account some facts about the offenders who commit these crimes. According to data from New York City and Los Angeles, the majority are teenagers. In New York City in 1990, over 50 percent of hate crime arrestees were under the age of nineteen, and over 20 percent were under sixteen. Ironically, hate crime laws do not apply to juveniles who are charged with "delinquency" rather than with specific code offenses. Moreover, when juveniles are convicted they are "committed" to juvenile institutions for indefinite terms, not "sentenced"; thus, sentencing enhancement statutes are not applicable. Even if they were, the youthful offenders who are arrested for such crimes are often alienated, impulsive, and generally hostile, hardly the kind of individuals likely to be deterred by sentencing enhancements.

> *"Applying or failing to apply the hate crime label triggers heated political battles."*

Even if the new wave of hate crime laws does not deter any hate crimes, some advocates believe these laws are justified because hate crimes are "worse" than other crimes in the same generic offense category and so deserve greater punishment. I agree that certain extremely violent, racist crimes warrant the most intense condemnation, but I would not be prepared to say that these crimes are without moral equals. Is it invariably worse to be raped by someone who hates you because of your race, rather than for your gender, appearance, social class, or for no reason at all? Is a racially bigoted rapist deserving of more condemnation than a "merely" hostile and anti-social rapist? . . .

The most horrible crimes—murder, rape, kidnapping, arson—are so devastating that it seems to deprecate the victim's pain and anguish to conclude, as the hate crime laws do, that there is more trauma if the perpetrator is a bigot as well as a brute. If distinctions must be made, wouldn't a more neutral statute make more sense; i.e., a rape warrants enhanced punishment if it involves terror, torture, or substantial gratuitous violence beyond the rape itself? Sentencing law already provides this option in many states.

Those who lobby for more hate crime laws claim that a crime motivated by prejudice ought to be punished more severely than other crimes because the effects ripple out beyond the individual victim; all members of the victim's group are made less secure and, depending upon which groups are involved, there may be retaliation or group conflict. Once again, I believe that this conclusion is applicable to

> *"Is a racially bigoted rapist deserving of more condemnation than a 'merely' hostile and anti-social rapist?"*

some hate crimes, but I do not believe that every hate crime (e.g., an act of shoving on the subway) generates serious social instability. Moreover, all sorts of crimes have serious social repercussions: carjackings, shootings and stabbings in schools and housing projects, "wildings" in parks, shootouts by rival gangs and drug dealers, and murderous attacks in subways. Over the last several decades, fear of crime has been a prime reason that hundreds of thousands, perhaps millions, of people have moved from cities to suburbs or from one neighborhood to another. Thus, it is surely an exaggeration to say that hate crimes are unique in their impact on people beyond the immediate victims.

The Wrong Tool

While many civil rights advocates view the passage of hate crime laws as a step toward the reduction of hate crimes and prejudice generally, I am skeptical. To fragment criminal law into specialized laws recognizing a moral hierarchy of motives and offender/victim configurations will have little, if any, crime-control benefit, while carrying serious risks for race relations and social harmony. The attempt to extend the civil rights paradigm to crimes committed by one private party against another is well-meaning but misguided. Prejudice and hate will not be stamped out by enhancing criminal penalties, and considerable damage may result from enforcing these laws. The new hate crime laws both reflect and contribute to the politicization of the crime problem and the criminal justice process, especially around issues of race, and thereby exacerbate social divisions and social conflict.

Reducing prejudice and hate must be a high priority for American society, but more criminal law is the wrong tool. We should exhaust all other strategies of social education and institution-building before pinning our hopes on the criminal law, which has, at best, a very unimpressive record in ameliorating social problems.

Hate-Crime Laws Endanger Free Speech and Equal Protection

by Nat Hentoff

About the author: *Nat Hentoff is a columnist for the* Village Voice *and the* Nation *and is the author of* Free Speech for Me—but Not for Thee: How the American Left and Right Relentlessly Censor Each Other.

I expect that there will be a plaque mounted at the City Hall of Kenosha, Wisconsin. It will celebrate the origin in that city of a Supreme Court hate-crimes decision that will allow police and the courts throughout the country to add extra prison years to the sentence of anyone found guilty of a crime allegedly motivated by hatred of certain groups.

The Case of *Wisconsin v. Mitchell*

It was in Kenosha that Todd Mitchell, black, and some of his friends, also black, came out of a movie, *Mississippi Burning,* that made them very angry at whites. They then saw a white teenager coming toward them across the street. As Chief Justice William H. Rehnquist later told of what happened next, Todd Mitchell said to his friends: "You all want to fuck somebody up? There goes a white boy! Go get him!"

In excerpting Rehnquist's June 11, 1993, decision in the case, the *New York Times* spared its readers the phrase, "You all want to fuck somebody up?" The chief justice does not flinch from the word "fuck," but the renowned delicacy of the *Times* required its censoring of the chief justice.

Anyway, the white teenager was beaten so severely that he was in a coma for four days. Todd Mitchell was convicted of complicity in aggravated battery (he didn't participate in the beating itself). That crime could have put him away for two years. But Wisconsin has a hate-crimes law that punishes you at least twice for the same crime if you selected the victim because of his or her race, reli-

Nat Hentoff, "Letting Loose the Hate-Crimes Police," *The Village Voice*, July 13, 1993. Reprinted with permission.

gion, color, disability, sexual orientation, national origin, or ancestry.

Under that statute, Todd Mitchell was eligible for five more years in prison—in addition to the two for the aggravated battery itself. The judge was more or less merciful, and sent Mitchell away for four years altogether (two plus two for the bias). The Wisconsin Supreme Court overturned that part of the conviction—along with the hate-crimes statute [in 1992].

Of course, the Wisconsin Supreme Court said, the crime itself can and should be punished. But once there is *additional* punishment because of the "hate" involved in the selection of the victim, the state is violating the First Amendment because it is punishing the defendant's thoughts and beliefs. No one has a right to physically attack someone else. But everyone has a right to his or her beliefs, however bigoted. Send Mitchell away for the criminal act, but do not add prison time for his thoughts.

This is the case, *Todd Mitchell* v. *Wisconsin,* that went up to the Supreme Court of the United States. Also on the way to the Court was a similar case, *State* v. *Wyant,* out of Ohio. The supreme court of that state had struck down a hate-crimes law that lengthened prison sentences for crimes committed "by reason of" race, color, religion, or national origin.

> *"Todd Mitchell said to his friends: . . . 'There goes a white boy! Go get him!'"*

Said Ohio's highest court:

> The question before us is not whether the government can regulate the conduct itself. . . . The issue is whether the government can punish the conduct more severely based on the thought that motivates the behavior. . . .
>
> By enacting [the hate-crimes statute] the state has infringed on the basic liberties of thought and speech. Once the proscribed act is committed, the government criminalizes the underlying thought by enhancing the penalty based on viewpoint. *If the legislature can enhance a penalty for crimes committed by reason of racial bigotry, why not "by reason" of opposition to abortion, war, the elderly (or any other political or moral viewpoint)?* (Emphasis added.)

But what about the laws punishing employers and landlords who discriminate against blacks, gays, lesbians, the disabled? Aren't they penalized because of their bigotry?

In those cases, the Ohio Supreme Court pointed out, "it is the *act* of discrimination that is targeted, not the motive. . . . Indeed, no discriminatory motive is necessary to prove that an employer violated Title VII of the Civil Rights Act [of 1964]."

If, for example, in a city with the demographics of New York, a workplace has few or no blacks or Hispanics, the motive of the employer doesn't have to be proved. The objective situation is enough to find him or her guilty of discrimination.

Or, as the Ohio court noted, "an employer may like blacks personally, but if employment practices statistically show that blacks are given far fewer promotions than whites, the employer is liable for sanctions under federal law."

And if anyone is found to discriminate in employment or housing or in any other situation, the punishment isn't inflicted *twice*—as in hate-crimes laws.

Is One Victim More Important than Another?

While the Wisconsin and Ohio cases were moving up to the Supreme Court, the press around the country was divided about hate-crimes statutes. The *New York Times* was enthusiastically in favor of adding prison time for bias crimes. So was the *Village Voice* (except for this columnist, whose name was on one of the few briefs to the Supreme Court arguing against these laws).

Among the newspapers opposed to punishing a crime twice because of the perpetrator's bigoted thoughts, the *Washington Post* was consistently perceptive.

In a December 16, 1992, editorial, the *Post* focused on Todd Mitchell getting his prison sentence doubled for his racist language:

> Does this make sense? Wouldn't it have been just as outrageous if the assailants had beaten a fourteen-year-old black boy? Why should one victim be more precious than the other in the eyes of the law? Surely, it is as reprehensible to kill one's mother as it is to kill someone else's because you object to her race, religion, color, disability, sexual orientation, national origin, or ancestry—the categories protected by the Wisconsin statute.

> Aside from the justice of making these distinctions, the constitutionality of such statutes is also questionable. The government has no right to punish prejudiced belief, the reading of hate literature, membership in racist organizations, or even the obnoxious expression of biased views.

> Yet all these acts, whether contemporaneous with the crime or years earlier, can be taken into account—under a sentence-strengthening law—to demonstrate animus, legitimizing all sorts of poking into political and other beliefs on the theory that these might be seen as evidence of bias.

On June 11, 1993, when the Supreme Court of the United States, in *Todd Mitchell v. Wisconsin*, unanimously decided that it is okay for the states and the federal government to poke around into people's thoughts to see if they should serve longer prison terms, a cop in Kenosha, the scene of the assault, reacted.

> *"Send Mitchell away for the criminal act, but do not add prison time for his thoughts."*

Having read the decision by the Rehnquist Court, James P. Farley, a commander in the Kenosha police department, told the *New York Times*: "I'm very fearful of the concept of thought police. . . . It makes me nervous."

But very few people in the nation appear to be nervous at the prospect of state investigators gathering dossiers on what a defendant might have said or read years ago that could now give him a long stretch in the slammer.

The Effect on Minorities

Every major civil rights organization vigorously supported additional prison time for bigoted *thoughts*. And so they told the Supreme Court. Among them was the National Association for the Advancement of Colored People (NAACP) Legal Defense Fund, which is among the best litigators in the country on habeas corpus and voting-rights cases. But in recent years, the Legal Defense Fund (LDF), like all the other civil rights groups, has been willing to trade off certain First Amendment rights for what seem to be gains in civil rights protections.

> *"Wouldn't it have been just as outrageous if the assailants had beaten a fourteen-year-old black boy?"*

In supporting hate-crimes laws—as I told a lawyer I know at LDF—civil rights groups, now applauding the Rehnquist Court's decision in *Mitchell*, are going to see more blacks in prison for longer terms as a result of that shallow ruling.

Think about it. For most police bias officers, for most judges and juries in most parts of the country, black-on-white crimes are going to be much more intensely punished than white-on-black crimes, even including assaults by skinheads. This is indeed a profoundly racist country, and hate-crimes laws are going to do much more injury to blacks than to any of the other classes given special "protection" by these statutes.

Also, as Michael S. Greve of the Center for Individual Rights in Washington noted in the April 21, 1993, *Wall Street Journal*:

> Todd Mitchell would have escaped the longer sentence if he and his friends had beaten a black grandmother half to death. In this single fact lies the message of hate-crimes laws to those most in need of protection: the victims of violence in the inner cities. They can rest assured that bigotry will not be tolerated, [but] as for their physical safety, they're on their own.

The Danger to Liberty

Both on constitutional and just plain commonsense grounds these statutes are so stupid and dangerous that I've found it hard to understand why usually intelligent people—including old friends of mine—rejoice at the *Todd Mitchell* v. *Wisconsin* outcome.

But then I remembered what Justice Louis Brandeis once said: "The greatest dangers to liberty lurk in insidious encroachment by men [and women] of zeal—well-meaning but without understanding."

On December 28, 1992, the *Washington Post*, in another editorial, tried again to bring some perspective into the debate:

141

Crimes like gang beatings, muggings, assaults, and purse snatchings should be prosecuted for what they are, not elevated to the level of an entirely different crime. . . .

Insults, especially those based on race, religion, or any other kind of bigotry, are nasty and infuriating, but they are not criminal. . . . The crime is bad enough, and the criminal deserves to be punished for his deed. But not for his words, or even his firmly held beliefs that some people are inferior to others. The First Amendment protects even obnoxious words and beliefs, and the government cannot penalize some forms of speech while promising to protect others.

But the righteous supporters of hate-crimes laws don't want to hear any of that. Like the applauders of speech codes—which the Court's *Mitchell* decision will strengthen—they have no patience with the notion that speech should be free of police investigations. Some of them say they're tired of people invoking the goddamn First Amendment.

There was an old-timer, a guy who fought against bigotry in the trenches for years and sometimes had to get out of town before the hate words he was called turned into a rope. He became a judge and said in a 1972 case: "Above all else, the First Amendment means that the government has no power to restrict expression because of its message, its ideas, its subject matter, or its content."

The name of the old-timer was Thurgood Marshall. He was never politically correct.

Some Hate-Crime Laws Punish Bigoted Thoughts

by Jeffrey Rosen

About the author: *Jeffrey Rosen is the legal affairs editor for the* New Republic, *a liberal weekly.*

In every Supreme Court term, there is at least one case that tests, and vividly exposes, the character of the justices. In 1992 it was abortion; in 1993 it was hate crimes. The outcome of *Wisconsin v. Mitchell*—which upheld a law that requires harsher sentences for criminals who "intentionally select" their victims "because of race, religion" and the like—was never really in doubt. But instead of being sensitive to the intricate First Amendment concerns that the case raised, William H. Rehnquist [chief justice of the court] dismissed them contemptuously. His unanimous opinion reads like a lazy summary of the government's brief: polemical, self-assured and profoundly superficial. The fact that none of the justices wrote a separate concurrence suggests that none of them is concerned about policing the boundary between speech and conduct with analytical precision.

Carefully Drafted Laws Are Constitutional

Civil libertarians are familiar with the powerful policy arguments against hate crimes laws, which increase the punishment for behavior that is already criminal. But the constitutional arguments are far more complicated. A less cavalier opinion could have endorsed something like the American Civil Liberties Union's (ACLU) position: carefully drafted sentence enhancement laws, like Wisconsin's, may be constitutional. But sloppily drafted laws, like the one proposed by Representative Charles Schumer, which would ratchet up the sentences for crimes "in which the defendant's conduct was motivated by hatred, bias or prejudice," are unconstitutional. A comparison of the Wisconsin law, which the ACLU supports, and the Schumer bill, which it properly opposes, shows the importance of the distinctions that Rehnquist ignored.

Jeffrey Rosen, "Bad Thoughts," *The New Republic*, July 5, 1993. Reprinted by permission of *The New Republic*; © 1993, The New Republic, Inc.

The most important distinction is that the Wisconsin law does not *formally* require judges in hate crimes cases to determine whether the offender was motivated by bigoted thoughts. The Wisconsin law's language is identical to the wording of many federal civil rights statutes, such as the section of the U.S. Code that imposes penalties on any person who, by "threat of force," interferes with the constitutional rights of another person "because of his race, color, religion or national origin." And you can be prosecuted under the Wisconsin law—and the civil rights laws—even if you never utter a hateful word. One way of proving that a criminal selected his victims on the basis of race, for example, would be to introduce evidence that he attacked black people on different occasions and in different cities.

Discerning Racial Attitudes

In the *Mitchell* case, the defendant's racial attitudes are hard to discern and are ultimately irrelevant. A group of black teenagers in Kenosha, Wisconsin, were discussing *Mississippi Burning* in 1989. "Do you all feel hyped up to get some white people?" asked Todd Mitchell, nineteen. "You want to fuck somebody up? There goes a white boy; go get him." As Mitchell stood in a parking lot, eight of his friends ran across the street to beat and rob Gregory Riddick, a fourteen-year-old white boy. Aside from the words he used to point out Riddick—and Rehnquist failed to note this—Mitchell did not

> *"Carefully drafted sentence enhancement laws . . . may be constitutional."*

participate in the beating. Rehnquist also ignored testimony that Mitchell yelled, "You should leave that boy alone," as soon as his friends began to charge; and that he then called the police and said he was sorry for what he had done. But under the Wisconsin law, it does not matter whether Mitchell was motivated by racism, or by peer pressure, or by a desire to steal Riddick's tennis shoes. Whatever his motive, he is liable for selecting his victim on the basis of race.

Rehnquist's opinion clashes, in important ways, with the 1992 cross burning case, *RAV v. City of St. Paul, Minnesota.* By ignoring the key language in *RAV*—"special hostility toward the particular biases thus singled out . . . is precisely what the First Amendment forbids"—Rehnquist misses the most convincing way of distinguishing the two cases. Unlike the Schumer bill, and unlike most hate speech laws, the Wisconsin scheme is not, on its face, an attempt to suppress politically incorrect ideas. As Clarence Thomas emphasized at the oral argument, you can be convicted under the Wisconsin law for intraracial as well as interracial violence. A black separatist who assaults a group of black attorneys for selling out would be no less liable than a white Klansman who assaults an African American out of racism.

Nadine Strossen of the ACLU points to a final difference between the Wisconsin law and the Schumer bill. In Wisconsin the defendant's discriminatory intentions must be proved beyond a reasonable doubt. The Schumer bill, by contrast, contains no such requirement; and evidence of the defendant's bigoted thoughts—such as the fact that a neighbor heard he had a copy of *Mein Kampf* on the bookshelf—can be admitted even if it is only tangentially related to the underlying crime. For the same reason, the ACLU has properly opposed Florida's law providing for an enhanced penalty if the crime "evidences prejudice."

Good vs. Bad Motivations

If Rehnquist had focused narrowly on the formal neutrality of the Wisconsin law, in short, he could have upheld it in a way that distinguished it from laws that explicitly target bigotry. Instead, he was expansive. He invited legislatures to punish what he called "good" motivations more severely than "bad" ones; and in the process, he exacerbated First Amendment concerns rather than minimizing them. As Susan Gellman of the Ohio Public Defender's Office notes, if a state can increase the punishment for motivations it finds especially abhorrent, such as racism, then it can also decrease the punishment for motivations it finds less abhorrent, such as homophobia or opposition to abortion.

Rehnquist dismissed the First Amendment concerns in two laconic paragraphs. Treason, he noted, can depend on proving the defendant's bad motive; and in a 1947 case, the Court allowed the government to introduce evidence of conversations that had taken place long before an indictment for treason because they cast light on the defendant's Nazi sympathies. Rehnquist's enthusiasm for a cold war treason opinion is startlingly insensitive. It slights what the Court had called, in an earlier case, "the concern uppermost in the framers' minds, that mere mental attitudes or expression should not be treason." And by going out of his way to compare hate crimes to treason, Rehnquist wrongly encourages the focus on politically unpopular views.

In the same spirit, Rehnquist belittles the real danger that the Wisconsin law—which increases the punishment for virtually every offense in the Wisconsin criminal code, from trespassing to adultery—can be applied in unconstitutional ways. "It is difficult," he writes sarcastically, "to conceive of a situation" where a minor misdemeanor, such as negligent operation of a motor vehicle, would be racially motivated. But other unconstitutional applications are not so difficult to conceive. The Wisconsin law threatens up to five years in jail for anyone who has sex with a married person "because of race," for example, bringing a ban on adultery perilously close to a ban on miscegenation. It creates a brand-new crime of group libel by increasing the punishment for race-based defamation. It would also require stiffer penalties for

> *"Unlike most hate speech laws, the Wisconsin scheme is not, on its face, an attempt to suppress politically incorrect ideas."*

pro-choice protesters who trespass on the front lawn of a church "because of religion." Even the ACLU emphasizes that these cases raise "serious constitutional problems."

Constitutional Laws and Unconstitutional Applications

Rehnquist also fails to acknowledge the powerful incentives to turn hate crimes trials into ideological witch-hunts, even when the language of the statutes is formally neutral. In Mitchell's case, the only evidence of his racial attitudes was the discussion about *Mississippi Burning*, which was not strictly necessary to prove that he selected his victim on the basis of race. But in other cases, defendants are encouraged to argue that their apparently racist conduct was not motivated by bigotry. A white man indicted under Ohio's similarly worded hate crimes law, for example, tried to prove he

> *"[William H. Rehnquist] invited legislatures to punish what he called 'good' motivations more severely than 'bad' ones."*

was not a bigot by emphasizing his "associations" with black friends and neighbors. This prompted the following remarkable cross-examination [in *State (of Ohio) v. Wyant*]: "And you lived next door to [Mrs. Ware, a sixty-five-year-old black neighbor] and you don't even know her first name?" "No." "Never had dinner with her?" "No." "Never invited her to a picnic at your house?" "No." "I want you to name just one [black] person who was a really good friend of yours. . . ."

By slighting the danger that technically constitutional laws can be applied in unconstitutional ways, Rehnquist encourages legislatures to be similarly insensitive. As a result, the Anti-Defamation League (ADL), whose model hate crimes statute has been followed in twenty-six states, no longer has an incentive to distinguish constitutional laws from clearly unconstitutional ones. "Before the *Mitchell* decision, we were planning to encourage states to follow the Wisconsin language. But the decision is so broad that I'm not sure we have to anymore," says Michael Lieberman, associate director of the ADL.

Why was no justice moved to write separately in this case? The charitable explanation is that all nine of them were so afraid of antagonizing their impatient and vindictive chief that they swallowed their doubts. The less charitable explanation is that no one cared enough about the delicate First Amendment issues to notice the distinctions that Rehnquist disparaged.

Hate-Crime Laws Are Difficult to Apply

by Barbara Dority

About the author: *Barbara Dority is president of Humanists of Washington and writes a regular column for the* Humanist, *a bimonthly magazine.*

Is hatred a moral crime against humanity? Of course it is. Is there any doubt that bigotry and hatred are at the root of incalculable human suffering, death, and injustice, and always have been? Of course not. Can we reduce this dreadful scourge by legally defining hatred itself as a crime and prescribing additional penalties for crimes committed because of it?

Washington's Hate-Crime Debate

Many well-intentioned people think we can. To this end, various state and federal measures, commonly known as anti-hate-crime or felony malicious-harassment laws, are being adopted.

Washington state adopted such a measure in 1993. Due to the intervention of the Washington chapter of the American Civil Liberties Union, the state's malicious-harassment law is far less restrictive than most. That notwithstanding, in King County Superior Court in March 1994, the jury trial of two persons charged with felony malicious harassment resulted in a hung jury.

And no wonder. Twelve good and true citizens were asked to determine whether or not two young men who, with about eight other teenagers, placed an eight-foot cross in the yard of an African-American family and set it on fire were "substantially motivated by, and intending to convey, hatred of black people."

At best, determining the motivation of a crime is a dubious undertaking. The defendants' attorney stated that he is convinced that his clients knew they were engaging in an insensitive prank but were not aware of its implications and did not intend to intimidate the family. It was confirmed that one of the defendants was a close friend of the family's son.

The defense attorney told the press: "We do such a poor job of teaching

"The Criminalization of Hatred" by Barbara Dority, *The Humanist*, vol. 54, no. 3 (May/June 1994), pp. 38–39, is reprinted with the permission of the publisher, American Humanist Association, © 1994.

history—especially black history—in this country that it isn't that surprising that some white suburban kids wouldn't realize the significance of what happened here." To thoughtful people, this statement is the most significant and tragic implication of this incident. It reminds us once again that the only way we can bring about a genuine reduction of hatred and bigotry is through education. Unfortunately, this long and arduous process has little appeal to those looking for quick-fix solutions to profoundly complicated social problems.

Even if it were possible to determine the mindset in which a crime is committed, is it appropriate in a free society for the government to punish people for their inner motivations, feelings, and beliefs, however venomous those beliefs and feelings may be? Feelings and motivations, whether considered good or bad, are private and mercurial; laws are not. It doesn't take much imagination to foresee all manner of abuses of this approach. George Orwell's *1984* springs unbidden to mind.

The Components of a Hate Crime

Most state "hate-crime" laws contain at least three of the following four components (originally written and promoted by the Anti-Defamation League of B'nai B'rith [ADL]):

Institutional Vandalism: This is a totally new crime, which increases the criminal penalties for vandalism if it is aimed at houses of worship, cemeteries, schools, and community centers. Some states have deleted entirely the existing crime of desecration and replaced it with the crime of institutional vandalism. The statute requires knowledge of the character of the property but does not require proof of motive for vandalism. Supporters readily admit that the law should not require proof of motivation "in order to make convictions easier to obtain."

Intimidation/Malicious Harassment: This charge provides for stepped-up criminal penalties for acts of intimidation, harassment, and vandalism (crimes already part of the criminal code) where persons or groups are victimized by a perpetrator who is substantially motivated by hatred of the victim's actual or perceived (any or all of the following): race; color; sex;

> *"At best, determining the motivation of a crime is a dubious undertaking."*

religion; age; ancestry; political affiliation; national origin; service in the armed forces; physical, sensory, or mental disability or handicap; HIV infection; or sexual orientation.

Miscellaneous Specific Prohibitions: Among these are specific prohibitions against cross-burning at any time or place, including on one's own property. Some states have expanded these specific prohibitions to include "other religious symbols, on public or private property, with or without authorization." Some include added punishments for "disturbing any religious assembly" and for theft of "any object used in connection with religious worship." Some prohibit the wearing of masks or hoods or other devices that conceal a person's identity. Although there are exemptions for holiday and theatrical productions, the overbreadth of this prohibition is still cause for concern. Obviously, several of these statutes punish symbolic speech, as did the prohibition on flag-burning struck down by the Supreme Court [in 1989].

Civil Action: These provisions provide for recovery from the perpetrator of punitive damages and attorneys' fees by the victim or any member of the victim's immediate family. They also mandate parental liability for minor children's actions—a type of recovery specifically prohibited under most states' common law tort actions. (A criminal conviction of the perpetrator is *not* a precedent condition for bringing this type of suit.)

Supporters of these measures believe that increased penalties will "make it more worthwhile for prosecutors to pursue convictions." The ADL advises legislative bodies that the enhanced penalties must be "sufficiently severe to have their desired deterrent impact" and that "state legislatures should increase the penalties for the broadest possible range of criminal conduct." The ADL further states that these statutes "do not

> *"Is it appropriate in a free society . . . to punish people for their inner motivations, feelings, and beliefs?"*

suppress free expression, since they do not affect the right of anyone to hold or express any viewpoint, publicly or privately, unless that person also engages in criminal activity *motivated by his or her viewpoint"* (emphasis added).

A Hodgepodge of New Laws

A brief look at existing legislation in various states reveals a hodgepodge of new legal terms and a host of inconsistent definitions.

Under New Hampshire law, simple assault and harassment are now fourth-degree crimes if they are "bias-motivated." A person convicted of a first-, second-, or third-degree crime may receive an extended prison term if the crime is "bias-motivated."

The Ohio statute heightens the offenses of menacing, aggravated menacing, criminal damaging or endangering, and telephone harassment if these crimes are committed "by reason of race, color, religion, or national origin of a person or group of persons."

Under Delaware law, the definition of the new hate offense is broadened even further, requiring only that the crime be committed "at least partially with ill will, hatred, or bias."

The U.S. House Judiciary Committee has approved legislation increasing by one-third the sentences of those convicted of federal crimes motivated by prejudice.

Application of Hate-Crime Laws

The many difficulties of applying these laws are already becoming evident. For example, in Florida, a white police officer was called to a domestic disturbance at the home of a black couple. The officer alleges that the male resident became "verbally aggressive" and said, "I'll shoot you, white cracker." In addition to charges of threatening assault, the man has been charged with violation of Florida's Hate Crimes Act and could face a prison sentence three times [greater than] that for threatening assault. A debate has developed as to whether the term *cracker* is a pejorative label and a synonym for *redneck* or *poor white trash* or a label of pride for some natives of the southeastern United States. And on the outcome of such esoteric debate hangs years of prison confinement for the accused. Is this really the kind of America we want?

A number of other state statutes are in the process of being challenged by defendants convicted under them on various grounds: that they are vague, overbroad, or discriminatory or impermissibly infringe upon the First Amendment right of free expression.

In June 1992, the U.S. Supreme Court ruled that St. Paul, Minnesota's, hate-crimes law prohibiting cross-burning was unconstitutional government regulation of free speech. The Court commented that the law singles out only certain kinds of hatred. As such, it also violated Fourteenth Amendment guarantees of due process and equal protection of the laws for all citizens. Thus, the subsequent proposals outlined above have been widened to include many additional types of hatred. But is this enough? What if a crime is found to have been motivated by hatred of the victim's material success or superior physical or mental abilities?

> *"The many difficulties of applying these laws are already becoming evident."*

What about the vast number of crimes undeniably motivated by vindictiveness and hatred inspired in the perpetrator due to a virtually limitless list of personal wounds and offenses inflicted by the victim?

There are sufficient legal grounds for prosecuting acts that are criminal in and of themselves: assault, arson, property damage, threatening assault, stalking, criminal menacing, and many more. A government given the power to outlaw certain expressions of hatred can also punish and control certain expressions of other human emotions.

As a humanist, a liberal, and a die-hard idealist, nothing would gratify me more than the eradication of hatred from the face of the earth. But in a free society, the cure for hatred cannot be found through the police powers of the state to restrict its awful expressions. The cure lies in the minds of a free people who possess, without aid from government, the liberty to reject it.

Chapter 4

Are Certain Groups Responsible for Promoting Hate and Violence?

CURRENT CONTROVERSIES

Chapter Preface

On the morning of April 19, 1995, a two-ton bomb constructed from fertilizer and fuel oil destroyed the Alfred P. Murrah Federal Building in Oklahoma City, Oklahoma, killing 168 people. Arrested and accused of the bombing were two army veterans, Timothy McVeigh and Terry Nichols. Allegedly motivated by extreme antigovernment views, the two were linked in news reports with the Michigan Militia, a loosely organized group that advocates the formation of citizen militias to guard against government abuses of power and that engages in paramilitary survival and firearms training. In June 1995 the Klanwatch Project reported that there are over 200 such militia groups in the United States, many with "deep roots in right-wing extremist movements" and "ties to neo-Nazi and other white supremacist organizations."

According to Klanwatch's monthly *Intelligence Report*, McVeigh and Nichols are "a deadly product of the racist right and the extremist militia movement." In the project's opinion, the extremist antigovernment rhetoric espoused by the militias directly incited the bombing of the federal building. "The Oklahoma City bombing was an act of domestic terrorism connected to the more extreme antigovernment militias where white supremacists have made significant inroads," asserts Klanwatch director Danny Welch. The militia's opposition to gun control laws and distrust of federal authority in general are dangerous outgrowths of the views of neo-Nazi, white supremacist, and other far-right groups, Klanwatch maintains.

But William F. Jasper, senior editor of the *New American*, accuses interest groups such as Klanwatch of engaging in hyperbole to discredit conservative views. "As far as most [liberals] are concerned, the Oklahoma bombing is the result of a massive conspiracy of the 'right-wing lunatic fringe,'" he argues. Liberals lump into this so-called fringe "those who oppose gun control, big government, [and] taxes; . . . Republicans and conservatives; . . . pro-life activists; 'right wing' radio talk show hosts; . . . and those who believe in 'conspiracy theories,'" along with neo-Nazis and white supremacists, according to Jasper. He counters that the majority of people who support the militia movement are law-abiding Americans who hold conservative values and that attacks by liberals on the militias are an attempt to use the Oklahoma bombing for political advantage. "The broad-brush smearing of honorable organizations and whole segments of society who had nothing to do with this violent act must be opposed and scorned as the most contemptible calumny and political opportunism," he states.

The viewpoints in the following chapter debate the role of militias and other groups in promoting hate crimes and violence.

White Aryan Resistance Promotes Hate Crimes

by Jack Levin and Jack McDevitt

About the authors: *Jack Levin is a professor of sociology and criminology at Northeastern University in Boston, Massachusetts. Jack McDevitt is associate director of the Center for Applied Research at Northeastern and has served as a consultant on hate crimes for the Federal Bureau of Investigation.*

Life hadn't been easy for twenty-seven-year-old Mulugeta Seraw, but his future looked bright. The dark-skinned young man with a foreign accent and a ready smile lived and worked in the city of Portland, Oregon. Having emigrated from Ethiopia seven years earlier, Seraw was a part-time student while working as an Avis shuttle-bus driver at the airport. He was far from wealthy but hoped eventually to save enough money to finish college and improve his standard of living. As an ambitious newcomer, Seraw was every bit the embodiment of the American Dream.

The Killing of Mulugeta Seraw

Early on a Sunday morning, November 13, 1988, Seraw and his two compan-ions, also of Ethiopian descent, were returning home from a nearby party. Be-fore turning in, they stopped their car in the middle of the street to chat awhile, totally unaware that they were being watched by three local skinheads. The three members of a group known as East Side White Pride were returning from an evening of recruiting, drinking, and partying. Wearing military jackets, steel-toed boots, and sporting shaved heads, the racist skinheads—Kenneth Mieske, Steven Strasser, and Kyle Brewster—stood on a corner about a hundred feet from Seraw and his friends. Brewster said, "Hey, I see a nigger. Let's go over there and mess with him."

The skinheads immediately hopped in their car and drove down the block to the car of the three Ethiopians. Mieske got out of the car first and exchanged angry words with Seraw and his companions. Strasser and Brewster joined in and there was a scuffle.

Then Mieske went further. Moving up behind Seraw, he repeatedly struck him in the back of the head with a baseball bat, while Strasser and Brewster kicked all three black men. When it was over, Seraw and his companions were taken to Emmanuel Hospital and Health Center. Two of the Ethiopians were treated and released; Seraw was pronounced dead on arrival. He had died as a result of a fractured skull.

In May 1989, Mieske pleaded guilty to murdering Seraw and admitted that his motivation was racist. He was given a life sentence. The other two skinheads, Strasser and Brewster, were convicted of first-degree manslaughter, for which they are presently serving prison sentences up to twenty years in length.

The Lawsuit Against the Metzgers

Despite the convictions, the courtroom battle was far from over. In October 1990, Oregon's Multnomah County courthouse became the scene of a civil action—a wrongful death suit—brought on behalf of the Seraw family by Morris Dees, chief trial counsel of the Southern Poverty Law Center in Montgomery, Alabama, the Anti-Defamation League of B'nai B'rith, and attorney Elden M. Rosenthal.

The lawsuit was aimed not only at two of the skinheads who had attacked Seraw and his Ethiopian companions in 1988, but also at Tom and John Metzger and their White Aryan Resistance (WAR) organization, headquartered in Fallbrook, California. Tom runs WAR—hosts its long-running cable-access TV program, oversees its newspaper, and is heard on its Washington, D.C., hotline. To make a living, he repairs TV sets. In the 1960s, Metzger was a member of the John Birch Society. During the 1970s, he served as California grand dragon of the Knights of the Ku Klux Klan (KKK). In 1980,

> *"Mieske pleaded guilty to murdering Seraw and admitted that his motivation was racist."*

he won the Democratic nomination to the House of Representatives and later ran unsuccessfully for the Senate. Tom Metzger's son John, leader of the Aryan Youth Movement (formerly the White Student Union), is responsible for recruiting young people to the cause.

The Metzgers, both Tom and John, were accused of being liable for Seraw's murder. The suit claimed that, in their roles as heads of WAR, the two men had encouraged and instigated the skinheads, who "conspired to inflict serious bodily harm" on Seraw.

Writing in *The Nation*, Elinor Langer suggests that the influence of the Metzgers and the organization WAR on racial violence in the streets of Portland actually began in March 1988. An Asian-American man, the white woman to whom he was married, and their young daughter were leaving a local restaurant when they were accosted by three skinheads shouting racial slurs and insults. The publicity surrounding this incident caught the attention of the Metzgers at their

Fallbrook, California, headquarters. During the summer of 1988, John Metzger began writing to Portland skinheads, including Mieske, Brewster, and Strasser, urging them to join his cause. By the fall, WAR organizers had arrived.

Self-Defense in the Minds of Skinheads

Not unlike entire nations, organized hate groups have broadened the meaning of the term "defense" to include aggressive behavior toward innocent people. In a recent issue of his *WAR* newspaper, for example, Tom Metzger asserts: "We have every right to use force in self-defense, in retaliation, and *in preemptive strikes against those who openly threaten our freedom.*"

Thus, no pretext of a precipitating event is even required. Blacks need not move into an all-white neighborhood; Jews need not join a "Protestants-only" club. The very *presence* of members of a particular group—no matter where and in what numbers—may be considered enough to call for a group response.

In civil court, Ken Mieske argued self-defense: his lethal attack on Mulugeta Seraw had been part of a spontaneous street fight; he had merely reacted to the Ethiopian man's attempt to strangle one of his skinhead companions. Representing the Seraw family, however, Attorney Dees was able to show that Mieske's notion of defense was absurdly inclusive and out of touch with reality. The Metzgers, through agents they had sent to recruit Portland's skinheads, had aided and encouraged the violent behavior that led to Seraw's death. In their campaign of hate, the Metzgers had conspired to do violence to blacks and had been reckless in sending representatives, including a former vice president of John Metzger's Aryan Youth Movement, Dave Mazzella, to Portland as their agent.

Mazzella's testimony left little to the imagination. Testifying for the plaintiffs, he candidly confessed that he had in fact been sent by WAR for the purpose of recruiting and training Portland skinheads. Tom Metzger had taught him how to assault blacks by provoking them first, attacking them with baseball bats, and then claiming self-defense. According to Mazzella, he would send "report cards" to the Metzgers consisting of newspaper accounts of

> *"The suit claimed that . . . [the Metzgers] had encouraged and instigated the skinheads."*

his beatings. In addition, he had distributed copies of John Metzger's Aryan Youth Movement newspaper as a tool for recruiting skinheads in Portland. In one issue, an article entitled "Clash and Bash" introduced the "sport" of bashing, whereby "hunting parties of white youth seek out non-whites and break their bones."

Metzger Supported and Encouraged Skinhead Violence

In court, Tom Metzger attempted to distance himself from the murder. He had never met Mazzella, and, in any event, he claimed he was only exercising his freedom of speech. But Seraw's side produced damaging evidence to implicate the Metzgers in a more direct manner. First, they showed records of numerous telephone calls between Metzger in Fallbrook and Mazzella in Portland. Then, they produced a photograph in which Tom Metzger was holding an assault rifle as he gave paramilitary training to a group of skinheads.

On October 22, 1990, after deliberating for little more than five hours, the jury reached a decision on an eleven to one vote. Tom Metzger was ordered to pay $5 million, his son John was ordered to pay $1 million, their White Aryan Resistance organization was directed to pay $3 million—all in damages to the family of Mulugeta Seraw. In addition, skinheads Kenneth Mieske and Kyle Brewster were ordered to pay $500,000 each. Another $2,500,000 in damages was also awarded.

> *"Tom Metzger had taught him how to assault blacks by provoking them first . . . and then claiming self-defense."*

It took only hours for Tom Metzger to publicize his defiant response to the verdict against him. In a recorded telephone message on his hate-filled hotline, the head of WAR issued a warning to his "new" targets everywhere. In an emotional statement of purpose, he proclaimed that "we will put blood on the streets like you've never seen and advocate more violence than both World Wars put together. . . . We have a new set of targets to play with. So if you're white and work for the system, watch your step. Whether you be a system cop, a controlled judge, or a crooked lawyer, your ass is grass."

The vicious murder of twenty-seven-year-old Mulugeta Seraw could easily serve as a textbook illustration of the operations of organized hate groups today. First, we learn that *Metzger's White Aryan Resistance supports and encourages the violence committed by skinhead groups.* Though only about 15 percent of all hate crimes are perpetrated by organized groups such as WAR, their impact is actually much more pervasive. Thousands of racist skinheads rely on such organizations for slogans, mottoes, and guidance. In 1969, Charles Manson apparently did not physically assault actress Sharon Tate and her four companions. He wasn't even at the Tate residence when the massacre occurred—but he ordered the murders. Similarly, Hitler may not have been present at the scene of the Nazi atrocities, but they were orchestrated by him. In the same way, there may be thousands of alienated youngsters looking for a role model who will encourage them to express their profound resentment. Such impressionable youths may not actually join some hate group. They may not be willing to shave their heads and don the uniforms of skinheads, but they are nevertheless *inspired* by the presence of such groups and *intrigued* by the use of their symbols of power. In some cases, they receive their marching orders from the leaders of organized hate.

The marginal teenagers who spray paint racist graffiti on buildings are usually not members of WAR, but they are attracted by its slogans. In the murder of Mulugeta Seraw, the White Aryan Resistance attracted youngsters looking for a thrill and used them as instruments to carry out its group mission of ridding the United States, if not the world, of its "subhuman" residents. In this scenario, we see the potential strength of an organized hate group. It is able to mobilize more than one source of motivation for action. Its leadership may be motivated by missionary zeal. Many of its members may believe that their violence is defensive, aimed at protecting the "American way of life" or their Aryan heritage. Its "field soldiers" may consist of skinheads, or other disgruntled youths, with minimal political consciousness, who are looking for a thrill and, at the same time, a way of seeing themselves as special. They are typically working-class youngsters who have not been successful at school or on the job. They usually don't get along with their parents or other family members. Among fellow skinheads, however, they feel both accepted and important.

Some skinhead groups lack either formal structure or ties to organized hate groups. Their alliance is maintained by little more than common haircuts, shared racism, political alienation, and more-or-less spontaneous outbursts of violence which they direct against blacks or Latinos in their communities. At the other end of the continuum, however, there are thousands of skinheads who have organized for action. They give themselves a name ("Romantic Violence," "American Front Skinheads," "Reich Skins," "Confederate Hammer Skins," or the like), select a leader, hold regular meetings, distribute racist propaganda, and attend rallies sponsored by organized hate groups like the KKK. While there is no single national organization of skinheads, networks of skinhead gangs have been known to exist. For example, the Confederate Hammer Skins, Western Hammer Skins, American Front, National White Resistance, and Old Glory Skins are presently linked together in a loose confederation. Even among skinheads associated with organized hate groups, however, members typically move in and out of different groups and switch their allegiances. . . .

Hate Is Becoming Mainstream

Another important lesson to be learned from the Seraw murder is that *the leaders of organized hate groups have tended to become mainstream rather than fringe, at least in the image they attempt to project.* Tom and John Metzger wear ties, not sheets. Some of the most influential members of WAR are former KKK members who recognize the futility of looking deviant, perhaps even anti-American. They wear suits and ties. Some get face-lifts or don hairpieces. Several have run for public office. Even in their support of bizarre-looking skinhead youths, they themselves are

> *"Metzger's White Aryan Resistance supports and encourages the violence committed by skinhead groups."*

more concerned with projecting a respectable public image. They realize that younger people often reject the robes and ritual in favor of paramilitary dress. Concerned with the reaction of both the public and the police, some skinhead groups have recently taken a cue from their mentors by wearing their hair long and getting rid of their black leather jackets. The new groups talk in code words and phrases about the issues that concern middle America. They preach that the *heritage* (meaning: race) of white Christians is being eroded by *foreign* (meaning: Jewish/communist) influence; they lament the rise of *government interference* (meaning: Jews in high places who force racial integration down the throats of white Americans) in the lives of *average citizens* (meaning: white Christians); and they condemn *welfare cheating* (meaning: blacks), which they see as being of overwhelming proportions and on the rise.

Even some Klan leaders have changed their tune, at least in the way it is played for recruiting purposes. The leader of the Knights of the Ku Klux in North Carolina barred the participation of violent neo-Nazis from its meetings. The head of the Klan in Florida urged its members to become a group "known for hating evil, instead of being a group known for hating Negroes." And the national leader of the Knights of the Ku Klux Klan has repeatedly suggested that his group does not hate anyone, but "loves the white race."

> *"The leaders of organized hate groups have tended to become mainstream rather than fringe . . . in the image they attempt to project."*

A third important message derived from the Portland murder is that *organized hate groups are technologically sophisticated.* Metzger's WAR uses computer networking, answering machines that leave hate messages, and public-access cable television. He and his colleagues are seen on nationally syndicated programs like "Geraldo," "Oprah," "PrimeTime Live," and "20/20."

Since 1984, Metzger's White Aryan Resistance has operated a computerized bulletin board that can be accessed by anyone with a personal computer and a modem. WAR uses its computer bulletin board, among other things, to spread propaganda, announce its future meetings, and provide the addresses of various hate organizations around the country.

Metzger's WAR telephone message line offers white supremacist news and philosophy. It chastises government officials for their economic policies ("All you worthless bastards in the House and Senate, what are you up to now? What's your beloved Pentagon pork barrel going to do for you now that the phony cold war is being flushed down the toilet? What other ways are you planning to destroy white working people in the U.S.?"); for their policies toward immigrants ("Stop bringing in all these Asians and make room for national parks. Boxcar a few million Mexicans and Central Americans south of the border and watch the streets get cleaner overnight"); and for their treatment of Jews ("Why do you allow the Jew Mossad secret police full freedom to spy on Americans from the seventh floor of the Jew anti-defecation league right there in front of you? You chicken-shits worship the Jews so much you must have holes in the knees of all your pants"). . . .

Hate on Television

According to the Anti-Defamation League, the number of cable television programs devoted to preaching hate is on the rise. Featuring interviews with skinheads, hate group leaders, and other hate activists, there are [as of 1991] fifty-seven such programs being broadcast on public-access channels in twenty-four of the country's top television markets. Most have been found in California, thirty-one of them entitled "Race and Reason" and produced by Tom Metzger's White Aryan Resistance. But programs preaching racial and religious hatred have also turned up in other top markets such as Boston, New Haven, Phoenix, Denver, Tampa, Atlanta, Chicago, St. Paul, Cincinnati, Albuquerque, Pittsburgh, Houston, Richmond, and Seattle.

Concerned citizens in these communities often wonder how the media activities of hate groups like the White Aryan Resistance are financed. Actually, they typically operate on a small budget provided by membership dues and private contributions. The exact amount and sources of their funding are closely kept secrets intended to protect the confidentiality of donors and to create a false impression of widespread support. Moreover, because of public-access laws and technological advances, a minimal budget is probably all that is needed to express bigotry on a widespread basis. Cable-access television provides an effective soapbox at virtually no expense. For the cost of a personal computer, a VCR, and an answering machine, an organization can easily create regional, if not national, exposure for itself.

According to the Southern Poverty Law Center's Klanwatch Project in Montgomery, the number of organized hate groups has grown significantly, perhaps as a result of hard economic times during the last few years. More specifically, Klanwatch estimates there has recently been a 27 percent increase in the number of white supremacist groups, mainly in Georgia, Florida, Southern California, northeastern states, and around Chicago. But numbers alone do not tell the full story. In total, there may be less than 20,000 and almost certainly no more than 50,000 members of white supremacist groups across the country. It is not only their revolutionary activism, however, but the growing sophistication of these organized hate groups in reaching the young people of America, through their finesse and ostensible respectability, that represents the real cause for alarm. It should also be noted that hundreds of thousands of Americans agree to some extent, if not wholeheartedly, with the principles of white supremacy, even if they would never join a hate group.

> *"Metzger's WAR uses computer networking, answering machines that leave hate messages, and public-access cable television."*

The Old Klan vs. New Hate Groups

Most Americans are at least somewhat acquainted with the objectives of white hate groups like the Ku Klux Klan and the neo-Nazis. Those who are familiar with American history know that the Klan has risen and fallen time and time again in response to challenges to the advantaged position of the white majority. During a short period of post–Civil War Reconstruction, for example, many whites were challenged by newly freed slaves who sought some measure of political power and began to compete for jobs with white, working-class Southerners. The Klan, responding with a campaign of terror and violence, lynched many blacks. Klan-initiated violence increased again during the 1920s, as native-born Americans sought "protection" from an unprecedented influx of immigration from eastern and southern Europe. Those old enough to remember the 1950s and 1960s might recall uniformed members of George Lincoln Rockwell's American Nazi Party giving the Nazi salute and shouting "Heil Hitler," or Klansmen in their sheets and hoods marching in opposition to racial desegregation in schools and public facilities.

> *"No longer can we point an accusatory finger only at hooded Klansmen or at uniformed Nazis."*

By contrast, the newer organized hate groups of the 1980s and 1990s don't always come so easily to mind for their bizarre uniforms or rituals. As noted, followers of Metzger's White Aryan Resistance have shed their sheets and burning crosses in favor of more conventional attire. They often disavow the Klan and the Nazi movement in favor of a brand of "American patriotism" that plays better among the working people of Peoria (not to mention Rochester, Akron, Burbank, and so forth). . . .

White Supremacists and Hate Crimes

White supremacist groups represent a fringe element among those who commit hate crimes. In statistical terms alone, the membership of all organized hate groups combined constitutes a tiny fraction of American citizens, most of whom wouldn't consider burning a cross or wearing a swastika. Even so, the influence of white supremacist groups like Posse Comitatus, White Aryan Resistance, Aryan Nations, and the Klan may be considerably greater than their numbers suggest. It takes only a small band of dedicated extremists to make trouble for a large number of apathetic middle-of-the-roaders. Even in this age of activism, there are many solid citizens who have neither the time nor the inclination for political action.

It is of even greater concern that the bigotry espoused by white supremacists has moved into the mainstream of American society, even if in more subtle terms. No longer can we point an accusatory finger only at hooded Klansmen or at uniformed Nazis. On the contrary, we must now turn to examine our young, our own schools, and perhaps even ourselves.

The Church of the Creator Incites White Supremacist Violence

by Sarah Henry

About the author: *Sarah Henry is a freelance writer and a former staff writer for the Center for Investigative Reporting in San Francisco, California.*

Rick McCarty carries a tan briefcase and wears a navy blazer, starched white shirt, pressed trousers and a vibrant red tie with a fishhook pattern—a fashionable motif, no doubt, in the small Gulf Coast town of Niceville, Florida. McCarty is dining in a neighborhood eatery not far from his suburban tract home. In keeping with the seaside theme, the restaurant's walls are adorned with fake fish.

Marketing Prejudice

McCarty alternately stabs at a salad smothered in ranch dressing and responds to questions about his latest business venture. A large man with a prominent stomach—sweaty-palmed, jittery, and prone to nervous tics—he twists his neck from side to side before he talks. He peppers his speech with terms like "operating capital," product "positioning" and the "bottom line to what we do."

McCarty, a former Bhagwan Shree Rajneesh devotee and a self-described psychotherapist, claims to have a doctorate in philosophy from an East Coast university he refuses to name. However, this October (1993) day he appears most comfortable speaking in the jargon of a marketing mogul.

What he's selling, McCarty says excitedly, is "like Coca-Cola. As far as positioning, [it's] number one." But the product is nowhere near as innocuous as a soft drink.

McCarty is the proud peddler of prejudice. He is the current leader of the white supremacist Church of the Creator (COTC), "the only racist religion known to mankind right now," as the businessman is wont to boast. McCarty's official title is Pontifex Maximus (Latin for "high priest"), although in keeping with his preference for corporate culture, he favors the lower-keyed title of executive director, because, he says, it makes "the whole thing a bit more acceptable and recognizable."

Sarah Henry, "Marketing Hate," *Los Angeles Times Magazine*, December 12, 1993. Reprinted with permission.

Chapter 4

The Church of the Creator

The COTC espouses a race-based religion known as Creativity, which worships nature—not a higher God—and is "dedicated to the survival, expansion and advancement of the White Race." It is virulently anti-Semitic, racist and, unlike most white supremacist groups, anti-Christian as well.

The group has a striking emblem: a red crown, a white halo and a large black W. When asked what it signifies, McCarty fumbles through a highlighted notebook for the answer, mumbling "I've got it all written down, I'm tired and my mind's not working." (The crown, it turns out, stands for the COTC's "kingly position." The halo indicates that the white race is "sacred above all others." And the large W? It represents the white race, of course.)

Church of the Creator dogma, as outlined in such books as *The White Man's Bible*, written in 1981 by COTC founder Ben Klassen, dictates that a racial holy war, or RAHOWA in COTC parlance, must ensue to rid the world of "parasitical Jews" and the so-called "mud races" (people of color). A "Jewish conspiracy," according to the COTC, controls the federal government, international banking and the media.

> *"Church of the Creator dogma . . . dictates that a racial holy war . . . must ensue [against] the so-called 'mud races.'"*

McCarty took over the COTC in January 1993 and readily concedes that his mission is to make it profitable. Asked if anything is unique about running a business that preaches hatred of Jews and other minorities, he responds: "It's all the same thing. It doesn't really matter. It's just a different commodity. We've had people say that a religion is not a business, but I don't know any that aren't."

Long a bit player in the already marginal world of white supremacists, the Church of the Creator has recruited heavily since the late '80's—and with some success. McCarty brags of a following in the thousands, including members in all fifty states and thirty-seven countries, with strong chapters in Germany, South Africa and Sweden. And he says the COTC prints between 20,000 and 40,000 copies a month of *Racial Loyalty*, its tabloid.

White-supremacist watchdogs say McCarty's numbers are inflated; they estimate the church's following in the hundreds instead of thousands. But the COTC has been especially successful in reaching the most active, impressionable and violent disciples of the hate movement today: young, racist skinheads. In recent years, more than thirty COTC skinhead chapters have popped up in states such as New York, California and Wisconsin.

The Racist Message and Violence

Numbers, however, don't tell the whole story. Indeed, the group's real strength may lie not in signing up supporters but in the particular power of its message. "They're dangerous in that they influence young kids," explains Danny Welch, director of Klanwatch, a project of the Southern Poverty Law Center [in Montgomery, Alabama]. "The number one reason why we go after the COTC," he adds, "is because they instill violence in people through their rhetoric." The COTC membership is so violent that the group has leapfrogged to the top of the list of organizations that Klanwatch tracks—superseding. the Ku Klux Klan in the South, the California-based White Aryan Resistance and the Aryan Nations, headquartered in Idaho.

The most obvious sign of the group's higher profile is the growing list of criminal acts committed by its followers. The group has a national prison-based "brotherhood" of about 180, many of whom are doing time for racially motivated crimes, according to Klanwatch. COTC members have been linked to terrorist conspiracies and violence—including murder—against minorities both in the United States and abroad.

In July 1993, a Florida jury convicted George Loeb, a COTC minister, of murdering Harold Mansfield, an African American who had served in the Persian Gulf War. Loeb, who does not hide his hatred for blacks, shot Mansfield after a parking-lot altercation. And at least five of the COTC's Canadian members have been arrested on charges ranging from kidnaping to assault for crimes against immigrants, anti-racists and rival white supremacists.

In July 1993, one of three skinheads suspected of firebombing the National Association for the Advancement of Colored People (NAACP) office in Tacoma, Washington, confessed that he was a COTC minister, or area organizer. The heavily armed trio planned to carry out a string of attacks on Jewish buildings and black rap stars. Also in July, two Orange County residents associated with the COTC—Geremy von Rineman, twenty-two, and his then-girlfriend Jill Marie Scarborough—were arrested on weapons charges in conjunction with a federal undercover sting. As part of the operation, Joe Allen, working on behalf of the Federal Bureau of Investigation (FBI), had infiltrated the Church of the Creator.

Ironically, the COTC's emergence as a big-league player in global racist circles coincides with potentially self-destructive growing pains. The group has been embroiled in leadership struggles and faces financial uncertainty as well as the mounting scrutiny of federal law-enforcement officials and hate-group watchdogs.

> *"The most obvious sign of the group's higher profile is the growing list of criminal acts committed by its followers."*

Just who are the followers that worship at the Church of the Creator and why are they preparing for a racial holy war? And does the COTC have the staying power of veteran racist groups like the Klan and White Aryan Resistance? Or will the world's only white-power religion become a victim of its own success?

Chapter 4

One Man's Racial Holy War

Jeremiah (Jeremy) Knesal of Auburn, Washington, has a long juvenile record with a racist bent. Knesal, nineteen and awaiting sentencing in a Northern California prison, is a recent COTC convert who took its prophecy of a racial holy war very much to heart. In fact, he tried to start one. But after his side trip to a J.C. Penney store in a failed attempt to steal jeans, T-shirts and underwear, the race war that was just beginning was all over.

It was a summer day in Salinas, California, a small farm community south of San Francisco, and Knesal got busted for shoplifting. A routine police search of Knesal's car turned that dime-a-dozen arrest into a large-scale investigation involving the FBI, the U.S. Attorney's Office and the Bureau of Alcohol, Tobacco and Firearms. Inside his 1987 green Volvo were three metal pipe bombs, four loaded rifles, ammunition, racist literature, military-style clothing and wigs. The car also contained a certificate from the Church of the Creator: Knesal was "a member in good standing."

> *"Knesal . . . is a recent COTC convert who took its prophecy of a racial holy war very much to heart."*

It didn't take long for Knesal to spill the beans. He told an FBI agent, who says Knesal was "very proud" to be a COTC reverend and state director, that he had bombed the NAACP building in Tacoma a week earlier. He also admitted targeting a Seattle gay bar, according to FBI Agent John Zent, where an explosion had occurred a few days later. (No one was hurt in either blast.) Court documents reveal that Knesal, along with two other white supremacists not connected to the COTC, intended to start a race war in a battleground ranging from Oregon to the U.S.–Canadian border. The trio planned to murder black rap artists Ice-T and Ice Cube and to bomb synagogues and military installations.

Knesal snitched on Wayne Wooten, eighteen, also of Auburn, who along with Jeremy was arrested on explosives and firearms charges in Salinas, and he implicated a third man—the alleged ringleader, ex-convict Mark Kowaalski, twenty-four, who was later picked up in Seattle. In October, Kowaalski pleaded guilty to the Tacoma NAACP bombing. On December 1, 1993, Wooten pleaded guilty to one felony count and Knesal to four counts. Knesal faces a maximum sentence of thirty-five years in prison and more than $1 million in fines.

When he was arrested, Knesal perfectly fit the profile of a recent COTC recruit. He favored the skinhead look: shaved head, Doc Martens boots and racist tattoos, which, according to Zent, "cover his body from the neck on down to his ankles and out to his wrists." He was affiliated with more than one racist group, and he was kicked out of two high schools for distributing hate literature.

A Confused and Troubled Teen

A worthy warrior in the race war, Knesal is also a confused and troubled teen. He has a prior conviction for malicious harassment of a Latino. But his father,

Gordon Knesal, describes him as a "great kid" who always treated Gordon's fiancée, Adriana Pittaluga, a Latina, with kindness and respect. "He listened to her more than he would listen to me," says the elder Knesal, a Seattle resident. "I adore the kid," chimes in Pittaluga, who has two children of her own. "When I talk with him [from prison] he tells me he misses me and the kids so much and he doesn't stop crying." Knesal had other good—and close—relationships with minorities: his mother remarried an African American man with whom Jeremy went fishing and hunting. One of his best friends was another African American who taught him how to be a cowboy.

Gordon Knesal, who got custody of his son Jeremy at age two, has searched for a reason for his child's behavior. He says the only motivation the teen-ager might have for hating people of color was that he was beaten up by several black men while skateboarding a few years ago. But Jeremy's racist inclinations were not tolerated at home, says his father, who reprimanded him on several occasions. "I tried everything," says Gordon, his voice sounding both weary and sad, "I couldn't get through."

The COTC is especially attractive to young people like Knesal, experts say, because the group's dogma offers a reason for their failures. "We see a lot of kids in schools hurting; people can't get jobs, they're worried about crime, unlimited numbers of immigrants, this gives cause to a lot of people," says Klanwatch's Welch. "And someone is listening. I think white Americans do feel left out."

Today's racist organizations are often less structured and more decentralized than traditional hate groups. Now, the elder statesmen of hate provide a basic framework of beliefs for a younger generation of racists, who are being encouraged to start a worldwide white revolution on their own. Jeremy Knesal may have felt like a mover and shaker within the COTC, but he had only been a member for about two months and he was unknown to McCarty before he acted on the church's gospel.

The Strategy of Recruiting Teens

Welcoming the young has proved to be a savvy strategy of the COTC. "It's hard to get a lot of old-line Klansmen to hand out newspapers, but you can get together four or five skinheads, and they'll put out 2,000 pieces of literature in a neighborhood," says Klanwatch chief investigator Joe Roy. Teen-agers are also effective at fulfilling racism's ultimate goals. As COTC founder Ben Klassen wrote in 1988, the movement wants to get "rid of" Jews and nonwhite races through "murder, treachery, lying, deceit, mass killing, whatever it takes to win." Unlike seasoned hatemongers, skinheads are impatient for change. "Kids get frustrated, they don't want to wait; they are hands-on people," Roy says.

The COTC's largest "hands-on" youth followings have been in Milwaukee, Wisconsin, and Toronto, Canada. At its peak in 1992, the Milwaukee chapter had about eighty active members and an aggressive leader, Mark Wilson (also known as Reverend Brandon O'Rourke—many COTC devotees use pseudonyms in an attempt to foil police). Several of Wilson's followers are White Berets, members of the COTC's security forces. According to McCarty, the White Berets are an "elite unit" who "protect [COTC] members and their property from harm."

> *"Welcoming the young has proved to be a savvy strategy of the COTC."*

Asked whether the White Berets are armed, he laughs and responds: "in ways." The COTC contingent in Milwaukee has run a "white survivor hot line" and hosted overseas supporters at paramilitary training courses that feature pictures of blacks and Jews as targets, according to a British informant. Hate-group monitors also suspect that the chapter runs guns from Wisconsin across the Canadian border.

The Canadian group, about one hundred strong, is led by George Burdi, who calls himself the Reverend Eric Hawthorne, a twenty-three-year-old bodybuilder and college dropout with a penchant for quoting [the philosopher Friedrich] Nietzsche. In a telephone interview, Burdi says concern over immigration, multiculturalism, unemployment and the environment are all strong drawing cards. "There's a tremendous amount of support" for the COTC message, says Burdi, adding that he's looking for "a higher quality of person that's talented, educated, middle- and upper-class who [is] as concerned about what's going on as we are.". . .

McCarty concedes that there is "probably a lot of violence" within the group, that many of its members own guns and other weapons and that some could be dangerous. "They're not a majority," he says. And, "They have their times when they're nice to have around, of course." Pressed on whether the COTC's rhetoric encourages violence among the young, McCarty replies with a laugh: "Saying yes to a question like that would probably get you sued later on. So I'd have to answer no to that."

The Militia Movement Promotes Violence

by Daniel Junas

About the author: *Daniel Junas is the author of* The Religious Right in Washington State, *published by the American Civil Liberties Union of Washington.*

Winter is harsh in western Montana. Short days, bitter cold and heavy snows enforce the isolation of the small towns and lonely ranches scattered among the broad river valleys and high peaks of the Northern Rockies. But in February 1994—the dead of winter—a wave of fear and paranoia strong enough to persuade Montanans to brave the elements swept through the region. Hundreds of people poured into meetings in small towns to hear tales of mysterious black helicopters sighted throughout the United States and foreign military equipment moving via rail and flatbed truck across the country, in preparation for an invasion by a hostile federal government aided by United Nations (U.N.) troops seeking to impose a New World Order.

Militia Mania

In Hamilton (pop. 1,700), at the base of the Bitterroot Mountains dividing Idaho and Montana, 250 people showed up; 200 more gathered in Eureka (pop. 1,000), ten miles from the Canadian border. And 800 people met in Kalispell, at the foot of Glacier National Park. Meeting organizers encouraged their audiences to form citizens' militias to protect themselves from the impending military threat.

Most often, John Trochmann, a wiry, white-haired man in his fifties, led the meetings. Trochmann lives near the Idaho border in Noxon (pop. 270), a town well suited for strategic defense. A one-lane bridge over the Clark Fork River is the only means of access, and a wall of mountains behind the town makes it a natural fortress against invasion. From this bastion, Trochmann, his brother David, and his nephew Randy run the Militia of Montana (MOM), a publicity-seeking outfit that has organized "militia support groups" and pumped out an array of written and taped tales of a sinister global conspiracy controlling the

Daniel Junas, "Angry White Guys with Guns: The Rise of the Militias." This article was adapted from *CovertAction Quarterly*, #52 (Spring 1995), 1500 Massachusetts Ave., #732, Washington, DC 20005; (202) 331-9763. The issue containing the full text of this article, with footnotes, is available from CAQ for $8 in the U.S. and $12 elsewhere.

U.S. government. MOM also provides "how to" materials for organizing citizens' militias to meet this dark threat.

It is difficult to judge from attendance at public meetings how many militias and militia members there might be in Montana, or if, as is widely rumored, they are conducting military training and exercises. The same applies across the country; there is little hard information on how many are involved or what they are actually doing.

> *"The appearance of armed militias raises the level of tension in a region already at war over environmental and land use issues."*

But the Trochmanns are clearly not alone in raising fears about the federal government nor in sounding the call to arms. By January 1995, movement watchers had identified militia activity in at least 40 states, with a conservatively estimated hard-core membership of at least 10,000—and growing.

The appearance of armed militias raises the level of tension in a region already at war over environmental and land use issues.

A threat explicitly tied to militias occurred in November 1994, at a public hearing in Everett, Washington. Two men approached Ellen Gray, a National Audubon Society [environmental conservation] activist. According to Gray, one of them, later identified as Darryl Lord, placed a hangman's noose on a nearby chair, saying, "This is a message for you." He also distributed cards with a picture of a hangman's noose that said "Treason = Death" on one side, and "Eco fascists go home" on the other. The other man told Gray, "If we can't get you at the ballot box, we'll get you with a bullet. We have a militia of 10,000." In a written statement, Lord later denied making the threat, although he admitted bringing the hangman's noose to the meeting.

Militias, Patriots, and Angry White Guys

As important as environmental issues are in the West, they are only part of what is driving the militia movement. The militias have close ties to the older and more broadly based Patriot movement, from which they emerged, and which supplies their worldview. According to Chip Berlet, an analyst at Political Research Associates in Cambridge, Massachusetts, who has been tracking the far right for over two decades, this movement consists of loosely linked organizations and individuals who perceive a global conspiracy in which key political and economic events are manipulated by a small group of elite insiders.

On the far-right flank of the Patriot movement are white supremacists and anti-Semites, who believe that the world is controlled by a cabal of Jewish bankers. This position is represented by, among others, the Liberty Lobby and its weekly newspaper, the *Spotlight*. At the other end of this relatively narrow spectrum is the John Birch Society, which has repeatedly repudiated anti-Semitism, but hews to its own paranoid vision. For the Birchers, it is not the

Rothschilds but such institutions as the Council on Foreign Relations, the Trilateral Commission, and the U.N. which secretly call the shots.

This far-right milieu is home to a variety of movements, including Identity Christians, Constitutionalists, tax protesters, and remnants of the semi-secret Posse Comitatus. Members of the Christian right who subscribe to the conspiratorial worldview presented in Pat Robertson's 1991 book, *The New World Order*, also fall within the movement's parameters. Berlet estimates that as many as five million Americans consider themselves Patriots.

While the Patriot movement has long existed on the margins of U.S. society, it has grown markedly in recent years. Three factors have sparked that growth.

One is the end of the Cold War. For over forty years, the "international communist conspiracy" held plot-minded Americans in thrall. But with the collapse of the Soviet empire, their search for enemies turned toward the federal government, long an object of simmering resentment.

> *"While the Patriot movement has long existed on the margins of U.S. society, it has grown markedly in recent years."*

The other factors are economic and social. While the Patriot movement provides a pool of potential recruits for the militias, it in turn draws its members from a large and growing number of U.S. citizens disaffected from and alienated by a government that seems indifferent, if not hostile, to their interests. This predominantly white, male, and middle- and working-class sector has been buffeted by global economic restructuring, with its attendant job losses, declining real wages and social dislocations. While under economic stress, this sector has also seen its traditional privileges and status challenged by 1960s-style social movements, such as feminism, minority rights, and environmentalism.

Someone must be to blame. But in the current political context, serious progressive analysis is virtually invisible, while the Patriot movement provides plenty of answers. Unfortunately, they are dangerously wrong-headed ones.

Ruby Ridge and Waco

Two recent events inflamed Patriot passions and precipitated the formation of the militias. The first was the Federal Bureau of Investigation's (FBI) 1992 confrontation with white supremacist Randy Weaver at Ruby Ridge, Idaho, in which federal agents killed Weaver's son and wife. The second was the federal government's destruction of David Koresh and his followers at the Branch Davidian compound in Waco, Texas, in April 1993. Key promoters of the militia movement repeatedly invoke Ruby Ridge and Waco as spurs to the formation of militias to defend the citizenry against a hostile federal government.

The sense of foreboding and resentment of the federal government was compounded by the 1993 passage of the Brady Bill (imposing a waiting period and background check for the purchase of a handgun) followed by the Crime Bill (banning the sale of certain types of assault rifles). For some members of the Patriot movement, these laws are the federal government's first step in disarming the citizenry, to be followed by the much dreaded United Nations invasion and the imposition of the New World Order.

> *"The Ku Klux Klan began as a militia movement, and the militia idea has continued to circulate in white supremacist circles."*

But while raising apocalyptic fears among Patriots, gun control legislation also angered more mainstream gun owners. Some have become newly receptive to conspiracy theorists and militia recruiters, who justify taking such a radical step with the Second Amendment:

> A well-regulated Militia, being necessary to the security of a free State, the right of the people to keep and bear Arms, shall not be infringed.

Right-wing organizers have long used the amendment to justify the creation of armed formations. The Ku Klux Klan began as a militia movement, and the militia idea has continued to circulate in white supremacist circles. It has also spread within the Christian right. In the early 1990s, the Coalition on Revival, an influential national Christian right networking organization, circulated a twenty-four-plank action plan. It advocated the formation of "a countywide 'well-regulated militia' according to the U.S. Constitution under the control of the county sheriff and Board of Supervisors."

Varying Ideologies and Memberships

Like the larger Patriot movement, the militias vary in membership and ideology. In the East, they appear closer to the John Birch Society. In New Hampshire, for example, the fifteen-member Constitution Defense Militia reportedly embraces garden variety U.N. conspiracy fantasies and lobbies against gun control measures. In the Midwest, some militias have close ties to the Christian right, particularly the radical wing of the anti-abortion movement. In Wisconsin, Matthew Trewhella, leader of Missionaries to the Preborn, has organized paramilitary training sessions for his churchmembers.

And in Indianapolis, Linda Thompson, the self-appointed "Acting Adjutant General of the Unorganized Militia of the U.S.A.," called for an armed march on Washington in September 1994 to demand an investigation of the Waco siege. Although she canceled the march when no one responded, she remains an important militia promoter. While Thompson limits her tirades to U.S. law enforcement and the New World Order, her tactics have prompted the Birch Society to warn its members "to stay clear of her schemes."

Despite slight variations in their motivations, the militias fit within the margins of the Patriot movement. And a recurring theme for all of them is a sense of deep frustration and resentment against the federal government.

Nowhere has that resentment been felt more deeply than in the Rocky Mountain West, a hotbed of such attitudes since the frontier era. The John Birch Society currently has a larger proportional membership in this region than in any other. Similarly, the Rocky Mountain West is where anti-government presidential candidate Ross Perot ran strongest.

And nowhere in the West is anti-government sentiment stronger than along the spine of wild mountains that divide the Idaho panhandle from Montana. In the last two decades, this pristine setting has become a stomping ground for believers in Christian Identity, a religious doctrine that holds that whites are the true Israelites and that blacks and other people of color are subhuman "mud people."

In the mid-1970s, Richard Butler, a neo-Nazi from California who is carrying out a self-described war against the "Zionist Occupational Government," or "ZOG," relocated to the Idaho panhandle town of Hayden Lake to establish his Aryan Nations compound. He saw the Pacific Northwest, with its relatively low minority population, as the region where God's kingdom could be established. Butler also believed that a racially pure nation needs an army.

Butler is aging, and his organization is mired in factional disputes. But he has helped generate a milieu in which militias can thrive. In May 1992, one of his neighbors and supporters, Eva Vail Lamb, formed the Idaho Organized Militia. During the same year, Lamb was also a key organizer for presidential candidate Bo Gritz (rhymes with "whites"), another key player in the militia movement.

Bo Gritz and the Origins of the Militias

A former Green Beret, retired Lieutenant Colonel Gritz is a would-be Rambo, having led several private missions to Southeast Asia to search for mythical U.S. prisoners of war (POWs). He also has a lengthy Patriot pedigree. With well-documented ties to white supremacist leaders, he has asserted that the Federal Reserve is controlled by eight Jewish families. In 1988, he accepted the vice-presidential nomination of the Populist Party, an electoral amalgam of neo-Nazis, the Ku Klux Klan, and other racist and anti-Semitic organizations. His running mate was ex-Klansman David Duke. Gritz later disavowed any relationship with Duke, but in 1992, Gritz was back as the Populist Party's candidate for president.

> *"[Bo Gritz] has emerged as a mentor for the militias."*

He has emerged as a mentor for the militias. During the 1992 campaign, he encouraged his supporters to form militias, and played a key role in one of the events that eventually sparked the militia movement, the federal assault on the Weaver family compound at Ruby Ridge, Idaho.

In the mid-1980s, Randy Weaver, a machinist from Waterloo, Iowa, moved to Ruby Ridge in Boundary County, the northernmost county in the panhandle. A white supremacist who subscribed to anti-government conspiracy theories, he attended Richard Butler's Aryan Nations congresses at least three times. And acting on the long-held far-right notion that the county ought to be the supreme level of government, he even ran for sheriff of Boundary County.

But in 1991, after being arrested on gun charges, Weaver failed to show up for trial and holed up in his mountain home. In August 1992, a belated federal marshals' effort to arrest him led to a siege in which FBI snipers

> *"[Militia of Montana] has recruited 'militia support groups' throughout the nation into its intelligence network."*

killed Weaver's wife and son, and Weaver associate Kevin Harris killed a federal marshal. Gritz appeared on the scene and interposed himself as a negotiator between the FBI and Weaver. He eventually convinced Weaver to surrender and end the eleven-day standoff. The episode gave Gritz national publicity and made him a hero on the right.

He moved quickly to exploit both his newfound fame and the outrage generated by the Weaver killings. In February 1993, Gritz initiated his highly profitable SPIKE training—Specially Prepared Individuals for Key Events. The ten-part traveling program draws on Gritz's Special Forces background and teaches a rigorous course on survival and paramilitary techniques. Gritz—who has already instructed hundreds of Christian Patriots in Oregon, Washington, Idaho, California, and elsewhere—recommends the training as essential preparation for militia members.

Militia of Montana

The Randy Weaver shoot-out also led directly to the formation of the Trochmanns' Militia of Montana (MOM). In September 1992, during the Ruby Ridge standoff, John Trochmann helped found United Citizens for Justice (UCJ), a support group for his friend Weaver. Another steering committee member was Chris Temple, who writes regularly for the *Jubilee*, a leading Christian Identity publication. Temple also worked as a western Montana organizer for Gritz's presidential campaign. One of the earliest mailing lists used to promote MOM came from UCJ.

But despite Trochmann's links to their adherents, white supremacist and Christian Identity rhetoric is conspicuously absent from MOM literature. Instead, Trochmann purveys the popular U.N./New World Order conspiracy theory with an anti-corporate twist. The cabal, he claims, intends to reduce the world's population to two billion by the year 2000.

At public events, he cites news accounts, government documents and reports from his informal intelligence network. Trochmann also reports on the mysterious black helicopters and ties them to the U.N. takeover plot. In one of his lectures, distributed on a MOM videotape, he uses as evidence a map—found on the back of a Kix cereal box—which divides the United States into ten regions, reflecting, he implies, an actual plan to divide and conquer the nation.

The Trochmanns give talks around the country and are part of a very effective alternative media network which uses direct mail, faxes, videos, talk radio, TV, and even computers linked to the Internet to sustain its apocalyptic, paranoid worldview.

The Trochmanns use all these venues to promote MOM materials, including an organizing manual, "Militia Support Group," which provides a model military structure for the militias and lays out MOM's aims:

> The time has come to renew our commitment to high moral values and wrench the control of the government from the hands of the secular humanists and the self-indulging special interest groups including private corporations.

It also reveals that MOM has recruited "militia support groups" throughout the nation into its intelligence network, which provides MOM with a steady stream of information to feed into its conspiracy theories. . . .

Smoke on the Horizon

Incendiary rhetoric, commonplace in the Patriot/militia movement, makes an armed confrontation between the government and militia members seem increasingly likely. If past behavior is any guide, federal law enforcement agencies are all too ready to fight fire with fire.

Obviously, militias do not pose a military threat to the federal government. But they do threaten democracy. Armed militias fueled by paranoid conspiracy theories could make the democratic process unworkable, and in some rural areas of the West, it is already under siege.

As ominously, the militias represent a smoldering right-wing populism—with real and imagined grievances stoked by a politics of resentment and scapegoating—just a demagogue away from kindling an American fascist movement.

> *"The militias represent a smoldering right-wing populism . . . just a demagogue away from kindling an American fascist movement."*

The militia movement now is like a brushfire on a hot summer day atop a high and dry mountain ridge on the Idaho panhandle. As anyone in the panhandle can tell you, those brushfires have a way of getting out of control.

The Political Right Promotes Racism

by Chip Berlet

About the author: *Chip Berlet is an analyst at Political Research Associates, a left-wing advocacy group in Cambridge, Massachusetts.*

As the United States slides toward the Twenty-first Century, the major movements offering a critique of the bipartisan status quo are to be found not on the left of the political spectrum but on the right. The resurgent Right is made up of several different strands, but together, ultraconservative organizations and dogmatic religious and political movements pose a grave threat to democracy in America.

The Rise of Right-Wing Movements

The Religious Right has come to dominate the Republican Party in at least ten of the fifty states. As part of its aggressive grass-roots campaign, the Religious Right is targeting electoral races from school boards to state legislatures, as well as campaigns for the U.S. Senate and House of Representatives. It is a social movement that uses a pious and traditionalist constituency as its mass base to pursue the political goal of imposing a narrow theological agenda on secular society.

Along with the Religious Right, two other significant right-wing political movements threaten democracy: Regressive Populism, typified by diverse groups ranging from members of the John Birch Society to followers of Ross Perot, and Racial Nationalism, promoted by Pat Buchanan and his shadow, David Duke of Louisiana, and increasingly influential in conservative political circles closer to the mainstream.

Finally, there is the militant, overtly racist Far Right that includes the White Supremacists, Ku Klux Klan, skinheads, neo-Nazis, and armed right-wing revolutionaries. Although numerically smaller, the Far Right is a serious political factor in some rural areas, and its propaganda promoting violence reaches into major metropolitan centers where it encourages alienated young people to commit hate crimes against people of color, Jews, and gays and lesbians, among

Excerpted from "The Right Rides High" by Chip Berlet, *The Progressive*, October 1994. Reprinted by permission from *The Progressive*, 409 E. Main St., Madison, WI 53703.

other targets. The electoral efforts of Buchanan and Duke serve as a bridge between mainstream conservatives and these Far Right movements.

All four of the right-wing movements are antidemocratic in nature, promoting in various combinations and to varying degrees authoritarianism, xenophobia, conspiracy theories, nativism, racism, sexism, homophobia, demagoguery, and scapegoating. There are constant differences and debates within the Right, as well as considerable overlap along the edges. The relationships are complex: The Birchers feud with Perot on trade issues, even though their other basic themes are similar, and the Religious Right has much in common with Regressive Populism, though the demographics of their respective voting blocs appear to be remarkably distinct.

Despite the differences, however, one goal has united the various sectors of the antidemocratic Right in a series of amorphous coalitions since the 1960s: to roll back the limited gains achieved in the United States by the civil-rights, antiwar, feminist, environmental, and gay-rights movements.

The Beliefs of the Religious Right

Each wing of the Right has a slightly different vision of the ideal nation:

The Religious Right's ideal is a theocracy in which Christian men interpret God's will as law in a hierarchy where women are helpmates, children are property of their parents, and the Earth must submit to the dominion of those to whom God has granted power. People are basically sinful, and must be restrained by harsh punitive laws. Social problems are caused by Satanic conspiracies aided and abetted by liberals, homosexuals, feminists, and secular humanists. These forces must be exposed and neutralized.

Newspaper columnist Cal Thomas, a longstanding activist in the Religious Right, recently suggested that churches and synagogues take over the welfare system "because these institutions would also deal with the hearts and souls of men and women." The churches "could reach root causes of poverty"—a lack of personal responsibility, Thomas wrote. "If government is always there to bail out people who have children out of wedlock, if there is no disincentive for doing for one's self, then large numbers of people will feel no need to get themselves together and behave responsibly."

> *"All four of the right-wing movements are antidemocratic in nature, promoting . . . racism . . . and scapegoating."*

For Regressive Populism, the ideal is economic Darwinism, with no regulations restraining entrepreneurial capitalism. The benevolent despot rules by organically expressing the will of the people. Social problems are caused by corrupt and lazy government officials who are bleeding the common people dry in a conspiracy fostered by secret elites, which must be exposed and neutralized.

Linda Thompson, a latter-day Joan of Arc for the New Patriot movement, represents the most militant wing of Regressive Populism. She has appointed herself "Acting Adjutant General" of the united militias that have formed armed cells across the United States. Operating out of the American Justice Federation of Indianapolis, Thompson's group warns of secret plots by "corrupt leaders" involving "Concentration Camps, Implantable Bio Chips, Mind Control, Laser Weapons," and "neuro-linguistic programming" on behalf of bankers who "control the economy" and created the illegal income tax.

The Beliefs of the Far Right

The Racial Nationalists' ideal oscillates between brutish authoritarianism and vulgar fascism in service of white male supremacy. Unilateral militarism abroad and repression at home are utilized to force compliance. Social problems are caused by uncivilized people of color, lower-class foreigners, and dual-loyalist Jews, who must all be exposed and neutralized.

> *"The Religious Right's ideal is a theocracy in which Christian men interpret God's will as law."*

Samuel Francis, the prototypical Racial Nationalist, writes columns warning against attempts to "wipe out traditional white, American, Christian, and Western Culture," which he blames on multiculturalism. Francis's solution: "Americans who want to conserve their civilization need to get rid of elites who want to wreck it, but they also need to kick out the vagrant savages who have wandered across the border, now claim our country as their own, and impose their cultures upon us. If there are any Americans left in San Jose [California], they might start taking back their country by taking back their own city. . . . You don't find statues to Quetzalcoatl in Vermont."

For the Far Right, the ideal is white revolution to overthrow the corrupt regime and restore an idealized natural biological order. Social problems are caused by crafty Jews manipulating inferior people of color. They must be exposed and neutralized.

The Truth at Last is a racist Far Right tabloid that features such headlines as Jews Demand Black Leaders Ostracize Farrakhan, Clinton Continues Massive Appointments of Minorities, and Adopting Blacks into White Families Does Not Raise Their IQ, which concluded that "only the preservation of the white race can save civilization. . . . Racial intermarriage produces a breed of lower-IQ mongrel people."

All of these antidemocratic tendencies are trying to build grass-roots mass movements to support their agendas. . . .

Pat Robertson's Authoritarianism

Of the hundreds of Religious Right groups, the most influential is the Christian Coalition led by televangelist and corporate mogul Pat Robertson. Because of Robertson's smooth style and easy access to power, most mainstream journalists routinely ignore his authoritarianism, bigotry, and paranoid dabbling in conspiracy theories. Robertson's gallery of conspirators parallels the roster of the John Birch Society, including the Freemasons, the Bavarian Illuminati, the Council on Foreign Relations, and the Trilateral Commission.

In Robertson's book *The New World Order*, he trumps the Birchers (their founder called Dwight Eisenhower a communist agent) by alluding to an anti-Christian conspiracy that supposedly began in ancient Babylon—a theory that evokes historic anti-Jewish bigotry and resembles the notions of the fascist demagogue Lyndon LaRouche, who is routinely dismissed by the corporate media as a crackpot. Robertson's homophobia is profound. He is also a religious bigot who has repeatedly said that Hindus and Muslims are not morally qualified to hold government posts. "If anybody understood what Hindus really believe," says Robertson, "there would be no doubt that they have no business administering government policies in a country that favors freedom and equality."

Robertson's embrace of authoritarian theocracy is equally robust: "There will never be world peace until God's house and God's people are given their rightful place of leadership at the top of the world. How can there be peace when drunkards, drug dealers, communists, atheists, New Age worshipers of Satan, secular humanists, oppressive dictators, greedy money changers, revolutionary assassins, adulterers, and homosexuals are on top?". . .

Scapegoating on the Right

The pull of the antidemocratic Right and its reliance on scapegoating, especially of people of color, is a major factor in the increased support among centrist politicians for draconian crime bills, restrictive immigration laws, and punitive welfare regulations. The Republican Party's use of the race card, from Richard Nixon's Southern Strategy to the Willie Horton ads of George Bush's 1988 campaign, is made more acceptable by the overt racism of the Far Right. Racist stereotypes are used opportunistically to reach an angry white constituency of middle- and working-class people who have legitimate grievances caused by the failure of the bipartisan status quo to resolve issues of economic and social justice.

> *"All of these antidemocratic tendencies are trying to build grass-roots mass movements to support their agendas."*

Scapegoating evokes a misdirected response to genuine unresolved grievances. The Right has mobilized a mass base by focusing the legitimate anger of parents over inadequate resources for the public schools on the scapegoat of gay and lesbian curriculum, sex education, and AIDS-awareness programs; by focusing confusion over changing sex roles and the unfinished equalization of power between men and women on the scapegoat of the feminist movement and abortion rights; by focusing the desperation of unemployment and underemployment on the scapegoat of affirmative-action programs and other attempts to rectify racial injustice; by focusing resentment about taxes and the economy on the scapegoat of dark-skinned immigrants; by focusing anger over thoughtless and intrusive government policies on environmental activists; and by focusing anxiety about a failing criminal-justice system on the scapegoat of early-release, pro-

> *"[Pat] Robertson's homophobia is profound. He is also a religious bigot."*

bation, and parole programs for prisoners who are disproportionately people of color.

Such scapegoating has been applied intensively in rural areas, and there are signs of an emerging social movement of "new patriots" who are grafting together the conspiracy theories of the John Birch Society with the ardor and armor of the paramilitary Right.

These Far Right forces are beginning to influence state and local politics in the Pacific Northwest and Rocky Mountain states through amorphous sovereignty campaigns, county autonomy and "posse" movements, and some portions of the anti-environmentalist "wise use" effort. The same regions have seen contests within the Republican Party on the state level between mainstream Republicans and the Religious Right. The political spectrum in some states now ranges from repressive corporate liberalism on the "left" through authoritarian theocracy to nascent fascism.

Paul Weyrich's Culture War

Spanning the breadth of the antidemocratic Right is the banner of the Culture War. According to current conspiratorial myth, liberal treachery in service of godless secular humanism has been "dumbing down" schoolchildren with the help of the National Education Association to prepare the country for totalitarian rule under a "One World Government" and "New World Order."

The idea of the Culture War was promoted by strategist Paul Weyrich of the Free Congress Foundation. In 1987 Weyrich commissioned a study, *Cultural Conservatism: Toward a New National Agenda*, which argued that cultural issues provided antiliberalism with a more unifying concept than economic conservatism. *Cultural Conservatism: Theory and Practice* followed in 1991.

Earlier, Weyrich had sponsored the 1982 book *The Homosexual Agenda* and the 1987 *Gays, AIDS, and You*, which helped spawn successive and successful waves of homophobia. The Free Congress Foundation, founded and funded with money from the Coors Beer family fortune, is the key strategic think tank backing Robertson's Christian Coalition, which is building a grass-roots movement to wage the Culture War.

For Robertson, the Culture War opposes sinister forces wittingly or unwittingly doing the bidding of Satan. This struggle for the soul of America takes on metaphysical dimensions combining historic elements of the Crusades and the Inquisition. The Christian Coalition could conceivably evolve into a more mainstream conservative political movement, or—especially if the economy deteriorates—it could build a mass base for fascism similar to the clerical fascist movements of mid-century Europe.

John C. Green is a political scientist and director of the Ray C. Bliss Institute at the University of Akron in Ohio. With a small group of colleagues, Green has studied the influence of Christian evangelicals on recent elections, and has found that contrary to popular opinion, the nasty and divisive rhetoric of Pat Buchanan, Pat Robertson, and Marilyn Quayle at the 1992 Republican convention was not as significant a factor in the defeat of Bush as were unemployment and the general state of the economy. On balance, he believes, the Republicans gained more votes than they lost in 1992 by embracing the Religious Right. "Christian evangelicals played a significant role in mobilizing voters and casting votes for the Bush-Quayle ticket," says Green.

Green and his colleagues, James L. Guth and Kevin Hill, wrote a study entitled *Faith and Election: The Christian Right in Congressional Campaigns 1978–1988.* They found that the Religious Right was most active—and apparently successful—when three factors converged: (1) the demand for Christian Right activism by discontented constituencies; (2) religious organizations who supplied resources for such activism; and (3) appropriate choices in the deployment of such resources by movement leaders. The authors see the Christian Right's recent emphasis on grass-roots organizing as a strategic choice, and conclude that "the conjunction of motivations, resources, and opportunities reveals the political character of the Christian Right: much of its activity was a calculated response to real grievances by increasingly self-conscious and empowered traditionalists.". . .

> *"The Republican Party's use of the race card . . . is made more acceptable by the overt racism of the Far Right."*

The Right-Wing Infrastructure

Since the 1960s, the secular, corporate, and religious branches of the Right have spent hundreds of millions of dollars to build a solid national right-wing infrastructure that provides training, conducts research, publishes studies, produces educational resources, engages in networking and coalition building, promotes a sense of solidarity and possible victory, shapes issues, provides legal advice, suggests tactics, and tests and defines specific rhetoric and slogans. Today, the vast majority of "experts" featured on television and radio talk shows, and many syndicated print columnists, have been groomed by the right-wing infrastructure, and some of these figures were first recruited and trained while they were still in college.

Refining rhetoric is key for the Right because many of its ideas are based on narrow and nasty Biblical interpretations or are of benefit to only the wealthiest sector of society. The Religious Right seeks to breach the wall of separation between church and state by constructing persuasive secular arguments for enacting legislation and enforcing policies that take rights away from individuals perceived as sinful. Matters of money are interpreted to persuade the sinking middle class to cheer when the rich get richer and the poor get poorer. Toward these ends, questionable statistics, pseudoscientific studies, and biased reports flood the national debate through the sluice gates of the right-wing think tanks.

Thus, the Right has persuaded many voters that condoms don't work but trickle-down theories do. The success of the Right in capturing the national debate over such issues as taxes, government spending, abortion, sexuality, child-rearing, welfare, immigration, and crime is due, in part, to its national infrastructure, which refines and tests rhetoric by conducting marketing studies, including those based on financial response to direct-mail letters and televangelist pitches. . . .

The Response from the Left?

If the left of the current political spectrum is liberal corporatism and the right is neofascism, then the center is likely to be conservative authoritarianism. The value of the Culture War as the new principle of unity on the Right is that, like anticommunism, it actively involves a grass-roots constituency that perceives itself as fighting to defend home and family against a sinister threatening force.

Most Democratic Party strategists misunderstand the political power of the various antidemocratic right-wing social movements, and some go so far as to cheer the Religious Right's disruptive assault on the Republican Party. Democrats and their liberal allies rely on short-sighted campaign rhetoric that promotes a centrist analysis demonizing the "Radical Right" as "extremists" without addressing the legitimate anger, fear, and alienation of people who have been mobilized by the Right because they see no other options for change.

That there is no organized Left to offer an alternative vision to regimented soulless liberal corporatism is one of the tragic ironies of our time. The largest social movements with at least some core allegiance to a progressive agenda remain the environmental and feminist movements, with other pockets of resistance among persons uniting to fight racism, homophobia. and other social ills. Organized labor, once the mass base for many progressive movements, continues to dwindle in significance as a national force. It was unable to block the North American Free Trade Agreement, and it has been unwilling to muster a respectable campaign to support nationalized health care. None of these progressive forces, even when combined, amount to a fraction of the size of the forces being mobilized on the Right. . . .

> *"On balance . . . the Republicans gained more votes than they lost in 1992 by embracing the Religious Right."*

Unless progressives unite to fight the rightward drift, we will be stuck with a choice between the nonparticipatory system crafted by the corporate elites who dominate the Republican and Democratic parties and the stampeding social movements of the Right, motivated by cynical leaders willing to blame the real problems in our society on such scapegoats as welfare mothers, immigrants, gays and lesbians, and people of color.

The only way to stop the antidemocratic Right is to contest every inch of terrain. Politics is not a pendulum that automatically swings back and forth, left and right. The "center" is determined by various vectors of forces in an endless multidimensional tug of war involving ropes leading out in many directions. Whether or not our country moves toward democracy, equality, social justice, and freedom depends on how many hands grab those ropes and pull together.

Militias Do Not Promote Violence

by William F. Jasper

About the author: *William F. Jasper is senior editor of the* New American, *published by the John Birch Society.*

The Establishment media cartel has discovered a new demon. Over the past several months, Phil Donahue, Tom Brokaw, CNN, *Time* magazine, the *New York Times*, the *Christian Science Monitor*, the *Chicago Tribune*, and other politically correct paragons of the fourth estate have been reporting breathlessly on a dangerous and growing threat to the republic: Armed Militias.

Bigots and Bubbas

In a December 12, 1994, article that is fairly typical of coverage nationwide, the *Philadelphia Daily News* presented militia members as paranoid gun nuts who "believe their government is brutally out of control, unlawfully seeking to seize their firearms." And, said the *Daily News*, they are convinced that "the only way for patriots to protect themselves against this tyranny is to pick up their guns—preferably assault rifles—and learn how to shoot Marines."

The article by *Philadelphia Daily News* staff writer Don Russell presented a decidedly alarming picture of heavily armed bigots and kooks run amok:

> The way some from this growing fringe see it, it's an evil, totalitarian New World Order out there, full of lying politicians, UFOs, greedy international corporations, secretive government agencies, Zionist bankers, gun-grabbing liberals, foreign troops on American soil, mysterious supermarket bar codes and dizzying conspiracies.

> Under other circumstances, it might be easy to write this off as paranoid, bigoted cult lunacy. Some militia leaders have past connections with the KKK [Ku Klux Klan], Aryan Nation, Posse Comitatus and other white supremacist groups.

Over-the-Hill GI Joes

. . . You get the picture: rabid, right-wing, religious extremists with guns, swastikas, hoods, and burning crosses. But, hey, don't accuse the media "liberals"

Excerpted from "The Rise of Citizen Militias" by William F. Jasper, *The New American*, February 6, 1995. Reprinted with permission.

of stereotype overkill; they know how to provide "balance" in reporting. They'll grant that not *everybody* associated with the growing militia movement is a certified, goose-stepping Hitlerite. There are less menacing types as well: over-the-hill and overweight bubbas living out Walter Mittyish "GI Joe" fantasies. *The Daily News'* Russell presents this "side" of the militia image in a companion piece entitled "Not Exactly America's Finest." It begins:

> If citizen militias are the valiant patriots who are going to defend America from tyranny, God help us.
>
> Imagine 40 or 50 pot-bellied guys from the corner taproom wearing I. Goldberg surplus fatigues and Doc Marten boots playing hide-and-seek on a snowy field.
>
> Now give them semiautomatic weapons, which they may or may not know how to use, and you have a training session of the Southern Michigan Regional Militia. . . .

Not exactly a flattering portrait, or one likely to comfort communities where militias may be forming. But the theme—"Nazi Terminators Hook Up with the Gang That Couldn't Shoot Straight"—is one that has gotten a lot of media play recently, and is almost certain to be cranked up louder in the months ahead. In December 1994 *NBC Nightly News* featured a special segment on the militias. While militia members in camouflage fatigues ran through drills in the Michigan woods, NBC reporter Jim Cummins intoned, "This is the Michigan Militia, a self-proclaimed fighting force of ordinary citizens preparing to defend themselves—against the federal government." The NBC report warned that "civil liberties organizations say hate groups have infiltrated at least eight civilian militias" and that "police fear a deranged person could get the wrong message from a [militia] computer screen and start killing people.". . .

"Expert" Analysis

Featured prominently in virtually every militia story are the "experts" and publications of the Anti-Defamation League of B'nai B'rith (ADL) and the Southern Poverty Law Center (SPLC). In November 1994, the ADL released *Armed and Dangerous: Militias Take Aim at the Federal Government*, a state-by-state report on the thirteen states where the ADL says militia "extremists, numbering in the thousands," are preparing for "paramilitary resistance against the federal government." Many of these "embrace conspiracy fantasies involving the Council on Foreign Relations, the Trilateral Commission, and the Rockefeller Foundation," and advocate "the abolition of the Federal Reserve." Accordingly, the ADL report offers an "ADL Model Paramilitary Training Statute" to curb

> *"Don Russell presented a decidedly alarming picture of heavily armed bigots and kooks run amok."*

the dangers which it sees in the militias and says, "In states where such laws have yet to be adopted, ADL urges that they be given prompt consideration."

The Southern Poverty Law Center, headquartered in Montgomery, Alabama, is the creature of millionaire lawyer-activist Morris Dees, a financier of the McGovern and Carter campaigns and an implacable gun foe who boasted back in 1976, "Within five years we'll break the NRA [National Rifle Association]." Klanwatch, a project of SPLC, publishes the *Klanwatch Intelligence Report.* The cover story headline in the December 1994 issue of the newsletter loudly blared, "Racist Extremists Exploit Nationwide Militia Movement: White Supremacists Linked to Brigades in Nine States." Klanwatch Di-

> *"The theme—'Nazi Terminators Hook Up with the Gang That Couldn't Shoot Straight'—is one that has gotten a lot of media play."*

rector Danny Welch was quoted in the story as saying, "The foot soldiers in these [militia] groups are just the type of people that Klan and neo-Nazi leaders have recruited in recent years. . . . This is one of the most significant and, potentially, most dangerous developments in the white supremacy movement in a decade." In a box on the same front page, Klanwatch announced that in October 1994 it had formed "a militia task force to systematically monitor hate group activity within the movement" and that, "beginning in February 1995, the *Klanwatch Intelligence Report* will feature a special section called 'Militia Update.'"

On November 1, 1994, Morris Dees sent a letter on SPLC stationery to Attorney General Janet Reno urging her "to alert all federal law enforcement authorities to the growing danger posed by the unauthorized militias that have recently sprung up in at least eighteen states." Dees also sent a copy of the Reno letter, along with a fund-raising letter, to his supporters, appealing for funds so that the center might "monitor the activities of the new militias."

Dees and his race-baiting colleagues over at ADL know that this is the stuff that brings in big money from their liberal constituents and starts their fellow ideologues in the media salivating.

On the other hand, conservatives familiar with the ADL's and SPLC's penchants for seeing a fascist Klansman under every bedsheet may tend to reject *en toto* these groups' warnings as simply more of the smear jobs for which they have become notorious.

However, our own research—which includes interviews with dozens of militia leaders, members, sympathizers, and observers in fifteen states—indicates that the ADL/SPLC/media alarms are not completely without basis. Although our investigation leads us to believe that the vast majority of individuals involved in militia organizations do not remotely resemble either the menacing villains or the pathetic misfits portrayed by the media and the militia critics, those elements do indeed exist. In fact, we found that it is often the militia leaders themselves who are most acutely aware of this problem, and who are working conscientiously to weed out the real extremists, racists, and hatemongers.

The Second Amendment and the Militia

Before looking at that issue in more detail, however, we must make a detour through another matter. Besides labeling the militia movement as racist-fascist, the critics have also muddied the waters with a confusing welter of misinformation about the legal, historical, and constitutional standing and meaning of the Second Amendment of the Bill of Rights as it relates to the militia and to the right of individuals to possess firearms. That amendment states:

> A well regulated Militia, being necessary to the security of a free State, the right of the people to keep and bear Arms, shall not be infringed.

. . . America's Founding Fathers were not only extremely literate, well-read men, but prolific writers as well. Their private and public writings and records form a vast corpus from which we can derive an accurate understanding of the original intent behind any words that might be called into doubt today. And, as Stephen P. Halbrook has indicated, any honest examination of the facts of history must acknowledge that on this important issue there was no debate; the framers of our Constitution were unanimous in the belief that private ownership of arms is an essential right of all free men.

While this diverse and immensely talented assemblage of intellects hotly debated numerous other points of political philosophy, economics, government, and law, on this question there is no evidence of the slightest controversy. Federalist and anti-Federalist alike stated their sentiments on the matter in unequivocal terms: . . .

> *"It is often the militia leaders themselves . . . who are working conscientiously to weed out the real extremists, racists, and hatemongers."*

Patrick Henry: "Guard with jealous attention the public liberty. Suspect every one who approaches that jewel. Unfortunately, nothing will preserve it but downright force. Whenever you give up that force, you are ruined. . . . The great object is that every man be armed. . . . everyone who is able may have a gun."

Tench Coxe, a prominent Federalist from Pennsylvania, was the equal of anti-Federalist Patrick Henry in defense of this right. In his influential essay, "An American Citizen," he declared:

> The powers of the sword are in the hands of the yeomanry of America from sixteen to sixty. The militia of these free commonwealths, entitled and accustomed to their arms, when compared with any possible army, must be tremendous and irresistible. Who are the militia? Are they not ourselves? . . . Congress have no power to disarm the militia. Their swords, and every other terrible implement of the soldier, are the birth-right of an American. . . . [T]he unlimited power of the sword is not in the hands of either the federal or state

governments, but, where I trust in God it will ever remain, in the hands of the people.

. . . Who are the militia? That was George Mason's exact question during debates at Virginia's own state constitutional convention [in 1776]. He answered his own rhetorical inquiry in these words: "They consist now of the whole people, except a few public officers." This was the common view of the Founders. Most of them had served in organized militias during the War for Independence and knew how essential these forces had been to the colonies' ultimate victory. They shared near unanimity also in the opinion that standing armies in times of peace posed a most serious threat to public liberty. Many of them also considered select militias as little less threatening than armies.

> *"The framers of our Constitution were unanimous in the belief that private ownership of arms is an essential right of all free men."*

Noah Webster averred that a standing army could become oppressive only when it is "superior to any force that exists among the people," since otherwise it "would be annihilated on the first exercise of acts of oppression" by the armed people as a whole. Furthermore, said Webster:

> Before a standing army can rule, the people must be disarmed; as they are in almost every kingdom of Europe. The supreme power in America cannot enforce unjust laws by the sword; because the whole body of the people are armed and constitute a force superior to any band of regular troops that can be, on any pretense, raised in the United States.

. . . You may have noticed something here: These men are talking about an armed citizenry, the militia, as a counterforce to the military and police powers of the government. How subversive! . . .

Serious Considerations

Even granting the historical and constitutional legitimacy of the militia, and the possible benefits of restoring that venerable institution to full vigor, some serious considerations remain that all patriots should ponder before embracing the militia movement as "the salvation of America," as some militia publications are wont to put it.

Under our U.S. Constitution, Congress has power (Article I, Section 8) over organizing, arming, disciplining, and calling forth the militia; and, once they have been called forth into federal service, they are under the command of the president. When not in federal service, the militia traditionally has been under the authority of the governor and/or the state legislature, county, and city.

However, in order to receive federal funding under the National Defense Act of 1916, most states have passed legislation subsuming their organized state militias under the National Guard and have withdrawn authority for local governments to organize militias. While the new Congress [elected in 1994] may look considerably better than the old, it shouldn't be forgotten that the new Republican leaders in the House and Senate have urged the president to step up U.S. involvement in the United Nations' (UN) war for the new world order in Bosnia. Would they support calling the militia into service in Bosnia, Rwanda, or elsewhere under Commander in Chief Bill Clinton? Might your governor or state legislature call out the militia to keep abortion clinics open so more babies can "safely" be killed? Are these far-out scenarios? Not when we consider what is already happening in this country.

It quickly becomes apparent that unless one has sound, moral public officials, the militiaman is potentially at the service of bad government. The necessity then is for a plan of action to educate citizens so that they will elect and influence good leaders. Some militia leaders do stress civic responsibility and urge their members to vote, contact their elected officials, and become knowledgeable about important public issues. Others, though, proclaim that it

> *"These men are talking about an armed citizenry, the militia, as a counterforce to the military and police powers of the government."*

is too late for these things and direct their followers instead to concentrate all of their time, money, and energy on stockpiling weapons, food, and survival gear and on training for Armageddon. Neutralizing messages like this, of course, can become self-fulfilling prophecies. If patriots give up on restoring constitutional government and drop out of the daily fight for God, family, and country in order to spend all of their time oiling their guns and preparing for bloody conflict, they are helping to guarantee that tyranny will soon be upon us. . . .

Beware Extremists

Militia organizations come in all shapes, sizes, and flavors. Some are strictly local affairs with no affiliation to state or national organizations; others are affiliated in a formal state or regional structure. Some are secret "underground" groups; others are very public and high profile, appearing regularly on radio and television and in the print media. Some make a point of going to local and state public officials and law enforcement personnel to educate and work with them on matters of concern to the militia; others view all authorities with hostility. Some regularly assemble for drills and exercises with arms on public or private lands; others forbid those activities as illegal and inappropriate for their members. . . .

As we mentioned at the beginning of this viewpoint, there are genuinely sinister elements in the militia "movement" that cannot simply be brushed aside as inventions of the controlled media and the radical-left lobbyists. Besides those . . . who attempt to translate widespread anti-Washington feelings, outrage over Waco, and anger over the Brady bill into dangerous insurrectionist schemes, there are also veteran racist and fascist figures who are trying to use and promote the growing militia movement. Tom Stetson, Louis Beam, Pete Peters, Adam Troy Mercer, and other longtime leaders in groups such as the Aryan Nations, the Order, the KKK, Christian Identity, and other virulently racist and violent organizations are making the rounds at militia gatherings, trying to recruit new followers and sow their gospels of hate. These and other dangerous demagogues are adept at grabbing the spotlight and encouraging violent confrontations and provocations. Militia leaders in several states have stated that they are very concerned about the efforts of these individuals and organizations to disrupt, infiltrate, and/or take over militia units, or to taint the militia by association. . . .

M. Samuel Sherwood, founder and director of the United States Militia Association (USMA) in Blackfoot, Idaho, believes that many (if not most) militia groups are "on very shaky legal ground." Most states have laws, he says, that prohibit private paramilitary groups, and "simply calling yourself a militia doesn't make you one" and thereby exempt you from those laws. "They may think what they are doing is legal and constitutional, but they will probably find out differently," he says. Sherwood is the author of *The Guarantee of the 2nd Amendment*, which has served as a handbook and organizing manual for much of the growing movement. He has helped set up USMA affiliates in twelve counties in Idaho and in ten other states. He has interested parties forming affiliates in thirty-five other states. As such, it might seem odd that he would be alarmed at the success of a movement he has played such a large role in launching. But Sherwood believes that many of those using his material misunderstand some very important points of principle and law.

> *"Unless one has sound, moral public officials, the militiaman is potentially at the service of bad government."*

Working Within the Law

Sherwood points out that under the U.S. Constitution and federal and state laws, all able-bodied citizens are already members of the "unorganized militia." However, when private citizens begin organizing into armed groups without state sanction, "they are just private armies which are in violation of the law" in most states. In Idaho, for instance, he points out, the law (Idaho 46-802) provides that "no body of men" other than the National Guard and the "organized militia" called into service by the state may assemble with arms. Texas law (Chapter 431.010a) provides:

> Except as provided by Subsection (b), a body of persons other than the regularly organized state military forces or the troops of the United States may not associate as a military company or organization or parade in public with firearms in a municipality of the state.

According to Sherwood, similar laws are on the books in many states and, sooner or later, are bound to be used against those groups calling themselves militias. Many individuals involved with these organizations also don't understand, he says, that their careless use of words like "armed resistance" and their public utterances about willfully flouting the laws may fall under the definition of sedition and may end up being used against them in federal court. . . .

Living in Perilous Times

While the legal standing of many of the militia organizations may be uncertain, there should be no uncertainty about this: Bill Clinton, Janet Reno, [Federal Bureau of Investigation director] Louis Freeh, and their federal minions can be counted on to fully exploit any and all incidents involving militias, and to be monitoring the actions and rhetoric of militia members. Together with the media, they will attempt to construct the spectre of a terrible armed threat amongst us. Unfortunately, there appear to be many in the ranks of the militia movement who will play right into their hands. And if that doesn't happen on its own, the militias provide the perfect medium for federal *agents provocateurs* to instigate outrageous offenses that can be used to justify even more draconian gun control laws and police-state repression.

We are indeed living in perilous times, times that demand of all patriots not only courage and steadfast determination, but also wisdom and perseverance. Those who are intent on transforming the United States into a socialist cog in a totalitarian new world order want, above all, to engender a spirit of despair, hopelessness, hatred, conflict, and anarchy. They want the law-abiding to give up on the constitutional system and to take rash courses of action and reaction that will label them as "rebels" and "enemies" of law and order. Those who fall into this trap are tragic fools. The right to keep and bear arms must be defended, yes. But free men can best preserve that right and every other by exercising the rights which they still have to speak, to write, to pray, to assemble, to vote, and to educate. We *must* stay the course and resist all temptations to despair or reckless folly.

> *"Most states have laws . . . that prohibit private paramilitary groups."*

The Religious Right Does Not Promote Anti-Semitism

by Midge Decter

About the author: *Midge Decter is a distinguished fellow at the Institute on Religion and Public Life in New York City.*

In June of 1994, the Anti-Defamation League (ADL), an established and highly respected organization dedicated to the protection and security of the American Jewish community, published a 193-page study entitled *The Religious Right: The Assault on Tolerance & Pluralism in America.* The study, prepared by David Cantor of the ADL research department, is intended to warn the country of the growth, in the words of Cantor's introduction, of an "exclusionist religious movement" seeking to "unite its version of Christianity with state power."

The ADL's View of the Religious Right

Essentially this movement as the ADL defines it is made up of fundamentalist and evangelical Protestants (though a number of its leaders happen in fact to be Catholics) and its program, according to the ADL, consists of various

> grass-roots campaigns to "return faith to our public schools," subsidize private religious education, roll back civil-rights protections, oppose all abortions, and ensure that "pro-family Christians" gain control of the Republican party.

Though the movement came to public attention in the 1980s, says the ADL, in the 1990s its leaders have grown ever more virulent and paranoiac in their rhetoric, referring to their opponents, for example, as "the enemy" and "satanic." And finally,

> this bitter push to replace the wall of separation [between church and state] with a citadel of Christianity . . . has been abetted, sometimes at the highest levels, by figures who have expressed conspiratorial, anti-Jewish, and extremist sentiments.

In short, rather than compete for the spiritual allegiance of their fellow Americans, as true pluralists have always done, the members of the religious Right wish instead to impose their own beliefs on everyone—and hence, the ADL claims, the movement ironically sets about to attack the very spirit of toleration that has for so long been the source of its own protection and strength.

So far as the ADL is concerned, at least as bad as the ideas of the religious Right are its methods. Somewhere around 1990, the study notes, the decision was taken by the move-

> *"So far as the ADL is concerned, at least as bad as the ideas of the religious Right are its methods."*

ment's leaders to engage in serious organizing and political activity at the grass roots, and by 1994 this decision has menacingly borne fruit:

> The national offices of the movement's major organizations provide resources, strategy, and political training, often by means of weekend civic-activism courses in local churches. . . . These sessions, though often premised on distorted and sectarian notions of the Constitution and American history, have equipped activists with an estimable nuts-and-bolts political know-how and dedication.

What, in the view of the ADL, lends even more weight to the threat posed by all this grass-roots activity is the close coordination among groups with ostensibly varying agendas, whether it be barring gays and lesbians from the military or opposing abortion or campaigning for school vouchers. The leaders of these groups keep in regular contact with one another, speak at one another's conferences, appear on one another's broadcasts, and contribute to one another's publications. In this way they manage to a significant degree to increase their collective strength and resources.

The Intentions of the ADL Revealed

Following this general description of the threat posed by the Christian Right are a dozen profiles of figures and organizations clearly intended to serve as more detailed documentation for the ADL's allegations. Some of these profiles are full-length, some no more than a paragraph or a single page; some of those discussed are people and groups it is legitimate to regard as important to the conservative Christian community, while others are to be found only at its outermost margin.

It is in these profiles that the methods and intentions of the ADL study are most clearly revealed. And, at least for anyone who has learned to value much of the work done by the ADL over the years, these methods and intentions are apt to be as disquieting as they are almost unrelievedly nasty.

For one thing, some of the profiles are profusely supplied with quotations, and yet rarely are we given any but the vaguest details about where they are taken from. Just about the only precise citations are from sources not exactly sympathetic to conservative Christian thought and purposes, such as the *Washington Post*, the *Los Angeles Times*, and *Newsweek*. In the case of what might be considered primary sources—for instance, the newsletter put out by the Christian Broadcasting Network called *Pat Robertson's Perspective*, a publication freely quoted in the lengthy profile of Robertson—we are asked to take the ADL's word not only for the accuracy of the many secondhand quotations themselves but for the irrelevance of the particular contexts in which they were spoken .

Aside from the generally cavalier attitude toward the use of sources, the study's acknowledgments page leaves the reader in little doubt about the general underlying tendency of its research. Among those thanked for their generous assistance in completing this study are the Institute for First Amendment Studies, Americans United for Separation of Church and State, People for the American Way, the Coalition for Human Dignity, Mainstream Voters Project, and Women's Project—in other words, groups which are often in the business of rousing public hostility against conservative Christian sensibilities and values.

The way Pat Robertson is treated here is a good example of how the study works. Though the ADL itself informs us that Robertson is among the staunchest supporters of Israel, including even Israel's claim to Jerusalem, and that he has contributed hundreds of thousands of dollars to help Russian-Jewish émigrés, it asks us to believe that he views the Jews "as akin to spiritual pawns." The evidence for this is that at a Christian Broadcasting Network prayer meeting in 1980, he declared (according to a report in *Reform Judaism*) that "Jews were 'spiritually deaf' and 'spiritually blind' but that in the climactic end times many would be converted."

> *"The [ADL] study's acknowledgments page leaves the reader in little doubt about the general underlying tendency of its research."*

Even assuming that these quotes are accurate, they are left hanging without any indication of the specific context in which they were spoken or the larger theological context from which Robertson's attitude toward Jews derives (a context, incidentally, that helps explain why he is so vehemently pro-Israel).

Supposedly Shocking Revelations

In other instances, the report simply misreads things Robertson has said. Thus, on more than one occasion, in complaining that Christian believers feel more and more oppressed in an increasingly secularized society, he has likened their lot in America to that of the Jews under the Nazis. This is morally offensive and intellectually ludicrous, and it is especially grating to Jewish ears (though a great many Jews have for decades now been easygoing about comparably hyperbolic rhetoric coming from blacks). Yet it hardly qualifies as "anti-Jewish sentiment."

Nor, to anyone not being determinedly tendentious, is the following quote from Robertson "reminiscent of traditional anti-Semitic thinking":

> Perhaps we can assume that the current wave of anti-Semitism is being allowed by God to force the large number of the chosen people residing in the Soviet Union out of what the Bible calls the land of the north.

Another unpleasant feature of *The Religious Right* is the breathy, triumphal tone in which it offers some supposedly shocking revelations of ideas and activities of the Right about which no secret has ever been made. Christian conservatives, for example, have never concealed their view that when the Constitution says there shall be no established church, it does not intend that there shall be no expression of religion in public life. And as the ADL should know, Christian conservatives are by no means alone in this view. Indeed, the question of whether there may or may not be any religious expression in schools and other government-supported institutions is now at the center of a growing and ever noisier public debate, as is the somewhat related issue of parental choice in education. To suggest that those who side with Christian conservatives on these issues are being manipulated, or are part of a malignant conspiracy themselves, is both ridiculous and defamatory.

> *"Why is this turn to the grass roots depicted by the ADL as something sinister?"*

It is true that the term "stealth candidates" has been used by a conservative Christian activist in referring to the fact that he and his associates had supported certain candidates from behind the scenes (a practice, it might be observed, not always abjured either by Jewish activists or left-wing ones). But it has certainly never been concealed from the world that this movement seeks to organize and offer assistance to local pressure groups wherever it can.

In any event, why is this turn to the grass roots depicted by the ADL as something sinister? Is it not what some of the very organizations thanked for their assistance in the preparation of *The Religious Right* have been doing for many years now without rousing the anxieties of the would-be defenders of pluralism?

Guilt by Association

Even more disturbing than any of this, however, is the study's use of that once thoroughly discredited trick, guilt by association.

Here, too, Pat Robertson is a target. Thus, we are told that at the age of twenty-six, he was introduced by his mother to a Philadelphia minister named Cornelius Vanderbreggen. "A short time later," according to the study, Robertson experienced a "charismatic spiritual rebirth." We are not told how much and what kind of influence Vanderbreggen had on Robertson. Vanderbreggen is brought in entirely for the sake of a footnote which informs us that he was someone who had a long history of anti-Israel propagandizing and also wrote for the *Spotlight*, weekly tabloid of Liberty Lobby, the nation's leading anti-Semitic propagandists." Yet as we have seen, the study itself acknowledges elsewhere that Robertson is pro-Israel. The only purpose served by this footnote is to insinuate that he is linked with anti-Israel and anti-Semitic forces.

But perhaps the most sustained example of guilt by association is the study's treatment of Paul Weyrich. The founder and president of the Free Congress Foundation, a training facility for conservative activists, Weyrich also heads a think tank as well as a lobbying group called Coalitions for America; in addition, he recently set up a cable television network called National Empowerment Television (NET). All his work is guided by the belief that, in his own words, there is "an unbreakable link between traditional Western, Judeo-Christian values and the secular success of Western societies" (hardly, need one add, an extremist view).

In attempting to cast a shadow on all this daylight activity, the ADL sets about to provide it with a dark and guilty underside. In 1981, the study charges, Free Congress published a pamphlet written by one Warren Richardson, who many years before had served as general counsel to the Liberty Lobby. Never mind that Weyrich has said, "I dislike the Liberty Lobby and have thrown them out of my office." The connection between Weyrich and the Liberty Lobby is nevertheless made.

It is made again in the case of Father Enrique Rueda, who, the ADL informs us, was asked by Weyrich to "research the social and political impact of the homosexual movement in America." The book that resulted, *The Homosexual Network: Private Lives and Public Policy*, described in a Free Congress Foundation release as an exposé of the homosexual movement in America, was then put out in 1982 by Devin Adair, a small publishing house in Connecticut. Devin Adair, notes the ADL, was also one of the

> *"[The ADL has] become guilty of the one bigotry that seems to be acceptable these days—bigotry against conservative Christians."*

leading publishers of Holocaust-denial material and advertised its books in the *Spotlight.* (Perhaps the ADL imagines that Father Rueda preferred not to have his book put out by, say, Random House and gave it to Devin Adair merely out of a desire to be published by a small and obscure house.)

Finally: in 1983, the Free Congress PAC contributed to the congressional campaign of Joseph Morecraft in Georgia. About this campaign or its opponent, the ADL tells us nothing. Instead, it simply quotes the liberal *Christian Century* as saying of Morecraft that he "has been trying to convince Georgia's Republican party to declare the Bible the source of all civil law." But the Free Congress PAC also contributed to the campaign of Jon Hinson of Mississippi, a homosexual. Would the ADL cite this as evidence of Weyrich's support for gay rights?

Why Single Out Conservative Christians?

No doubt people hostile to the Jews exist here and there among conservative Christians. But so do people hostile to the Jews exist among liberal Christians and among the fiercest of secularists as well. The question, then, is why an organization long regarded as expert in the study of anti-Semitism should have singled out the conservative Christians for opprobrium—especially when, as a group, they have been perhaps the most outspoken friends of Israel in this country.

Judging from the book itself, the answer has to do not with Christians and Jews but with secular politics. The religious Right is a force dedicated to implementing a series of ideas and measures that are anathema to most liberals. In attacking this agenda, and the people who support it, as a threat to pluralism, the ADL has chosen to join hands with all those on the liberal Left who are determined to delegitimize any challenge to the power they have long enjoyed over the basic institutions of American life and culture.

Thus has an organization which is devoted to fighting bigotry against Jews, and which now claims to be undertaking a defense of pluralism, defined the sensibilities and convictions of some 50 million Americans as beyond the pale. And thus has it become guilty of the one bigotry that seems to be acceptable these days—bigotry against conservative Christians.

Oppressive Government Causes Some People to Commit Violent Acts

by *The Spotlight*

About the author: *The* Spotlight *is the weekly publication of the conservative, populist Liberty Lobby in Washington, D.C.*

For years the *Spotlight*—and before the *Spotlight*, our publisher, Liberty Lobby—has been doing everything humanly possible to organize enough voters to stop the trend toward national disintegration with international government supplanting local government. For the twenty years of our existence (forty years for Liberty Lobby) we have consistently warned of the slide toward the New World Order and have been met with not just a lack of support, but opposition from the entire Establishment and its sycophantic news media.

The Government's Responsibility for Violence

We have warned that Americans will not stand by while a cabal of super rich global elitists turn the United States into a Third World province of their Global Plantation. Now, with the April 1995 terrorist attack in Oklahoma City [which destroyed the Murrah Federal Building and killed 168 people], the Establishment is forced unwillingly to recognize the fact that their policies have created a large body of people who feel they have been disfranchised to the point that some will resort to violence.

Naturally, since the government and the Establishment media cannot accept their own responsibility for the current state of affairs, they must attempt to fix the blame for not only the bombing, but for the growing disenchantment of the American people, on "right-wing extremists." They have attempted to equate the word "patriot" with "terrorist." But if there is one thing that is obvious to any rational observer, it is that the very last institution that can be said to be responsible for the violence abroad in the land is Liberty Lobby.

Liberty Lobby and the *Spotlight* have warned for years that violence breeds violence; that a government that preys on its own citizens is feared and hated by those citizens. They have sown the wind and they will reap the whirlwind. Instead of recognizing problems that exist brought on by a rush toward an international government, they ignored the growing unrest in the country, thinking their social engineering would induce the population to accept the precepts of the Trilateral Commission, Bilderberg group and the scroungy intellectuals and mouthpieces they hire.

But it won't be that way. Now the government, run by ruthless mattoids [insane people] who profit by war and who orchestrated the killing of literally millions in the useless wars in which they have involved America in this century, has declared war on all Americans who stand in the way of their world dictatorship. The murder of many patriots such as Gordon Kahl [in Arkansas in June 1983]; Arthur Kirk, John Singer, and John Lekan; Vicki and Sammy Weaver [at Ruby Ridge, Idaho, in August 1992]; and more than eighty members of the Branch Davidians [in Waco, Texas, in April 1993], and the imprisonment of literally thousands of political prisoners who have run afoul of their treacherous conspiracy, speaks for itself.

Growing Resentment Toward the Government

A recent poll indicated that 52 percent of the American people resent and/or fear the government and the same percentage feel animosity toward the Establishment media which Americans think—correctly—lies to protect the Washington regime. How far "out of it" is the Establishment media? Judge it by media pundit and self-styled expert on just about everything George Will who, on national television on Sunday, April 30, 1995, said: "No one ever talked about the militia movement before."

How's that for arrogance? But just because the mouthpieces of the internationalist elite do not deign to talk about facts will not extinguish those facts. Well-paid flacks like Will may disregard the feelings of the middle class—those who work for a living, pay the taxes and obey the laws of the nation. But if they would get smart and read the *Spotlight* they would know about the militia movement and quite a bit more.

A lot of people know the facts and they are disturbed by what is happening. Liberty Lobby and the *Spotlight* will continue to give the people of America the facts they need to know, despite the best efforts of the would-be tyrants. Thomas Jefferson said he had no fear that the people would not govern wisely if they knew the facts. The crime of America's rotten media is that they work to obscure, cover up or invent facts to try to change a reality they find unpleasant.

If the government continues its terrorist activities, then we fear that anti-government terrorist activities will escalate. And it is the innocent who will suffer. This is a crucial time in the life of the United States. Whether the would-be masters of the Global Plantation like it or not, patriots mean to restore government of the people, by the people and for the people. We sincerely hope that Washington—and the American voters—get the message.

Bibliography

Books

Michael Barkun

Religion and the Racist Right: The Origins of the Christian Identity Movement. Chapel Hill: University of North Carolina Press, 1994.

Morris Dees and
Steve Fiffer

Hate on Trial: The Case Against America's Most Dangerous Neo-Nazi. New York: Villard Books, 1993.

Mark S. Hamm

American Skinheads: The Criminology and Control of Hate Crimes. Westport, CT: Praeger, 1993.

Nat Hentoff

Free Speech for Me—but Not for Thee: How the American Left and Right Relentlessly Censor Each Other. New York: HarperCollins, 1992.

Gregory M. Herek and
Kevin T. Berrill

Hate Crimes: Confronting Violence Against Lesbians and Gay Men. Newbury Park, CA: Sage Publications, 1992.

Jack B. Moore

Skinheads Shaved for Battle: A Cultural History of American Skinheads. Bowling Green, OH: Bowling Green State University Popular Press, 1993.

Alphonso Pinkney

Lest We Forget: White Hate Crimes—Howard Beach and Other Racial Atrocities. Chicago: Third World Press, 1994.

Jonathan Rauch

Kindly Inquisitors: The New Attacks on Free Thought. Chicago: University of Chicago Press, 1993.

James Ridgeway

Blood in the Face: The Ku Klux Klan, Aryan Nations, Nazi Skinheads, and the Rise of a New White Culture. New York: Thunder's Mouth Press, 1990.

Rodney Smolla

Free Speech in an Open Society. New York: Knopf, 1992.

Samuel Walker

Hate Speech: The History of an American Controversy. Lincoln: University of Nebraska Press, 1994.

Periodicals

Jennifer Allen

"The Kids Are All White," *Rolling Stone*, June 30, 1994.

Jesse Birnbaum

"When Hate Makes a Fist," *Time*, April 26, 1993.

Allan W. Bock

"Ruby Ridge," *Reason*, October 1993.

Richard Corliss

"Look Who's Talking," *Time*, January 23, 1995.

Henry Louis Gates Jr.

"Let Them Talk," *New Republic*, September 20 & 27, 1993.

Hate Crimes

Susan Gellman	"Sticks and Stones Can Put You in Jail, but Can Words Increase Your Sentence?" *UCLA Law Review*, December 1991.
Philip Gourevitch	"The Crown Heights Riot and Its Aftermath," *Commentary*, January 1993.
Philip Gourevitch	"Dial Hate," *New York*, October 24, 1994.
William Norman Grigg	"Letter from Utah: The New Race War," *Chronicles*, April 1, 1994. Available from 934 N. Main St., Rockford, IL 61103.
Adam Hochschild	"Changing Colors," *Mother Jones*, May/June 1994.
James B. Jacobs	"Hate Crime Legislation," *Current*, September 1992.
Jeffrey Kaplan	"On the Far Far Right: Christian Identity," *Christian Century*, November 2, 1994.
Charles R. Lawrence III	"If He Hollers Let Him Go: Regulating Racist Speech on Campus," *Duke Law Journal*, June 1990.
Michael Lind	"Rev. Robertson's Grand International Conspiracy Theory," *New York Review of Books*, February 1995.
Scott McLemee	"Public Enemy," *In These Times*, May 15, 1995.
Newsweek	"Cracking Down on Hate," May 15, 1995.
Jonathan Rauch	"In Defense of Prejudice," *Harper's Magazine*, May 1995.
Laurence R. Stains	"Speech Impediment," *Rolling Stone*, August 5, 1993.
Nadine Strossen	"The Controversy over Politically Correct Speech," *USA Today*, November 1992.
David Van Biema	"When White Makes Right," *Time*, August 9, 1993.
Bruce Watson	"Today's Topic: How Much More Talk Radio Can You Take?" *Smithsonian*, July 1993.
Jon Weiner	"Talk Radio and the Left," *Dissent*, Spring 1995.
James Weinstein	"Hate Crime and Punishment: A Comment on *Wisconsin v. Mitchell*," *Oregon Law Review*, Summer 1994.
Jacob Weisberg	"Playing with Fire," *New York*, May 8, 1995.

Organizations to Contact

The editors have compiled the following list of organizations concerned with the issues debated in this book. The descriptions are derived from materials provided by the organizations. All have publications or information available for interested readers. The list was compiled on the date of publication of the present volume; names, addresses, and phone numbers may change. Be aware that many organizations take several weeks or longer to respond to inquiries, so allow as much time as possible.

American-Arab Anti-Discrimination Committee
4201 Connecticut Ave. NW, Suite 500
Washington, DC 20008
(202) 244-2990

This organization fights anti-Arab stereotyping in the media and discrimination and hate crimes against Arab-Americans. It publishes a series of issue papers and a number of books, including the *1991 Report on Anti-Arab Hate Crimes.*

Anglo-Saxon Christian-Patriots
c/o E.S. (Gene) Hall
1948 Fabersham Ct.
Snellville, GA 30278
(404) 972-4445

This organization promotes the study of and adherence to the biblical proscription against race-mixing. It publishes and distributes a Bible-study book on racial separatism.

Anti-Defamation League (ADL)
823 United Nations Plaza
New York, NY 10017
(212) 490-2525

The ADL works to stop the defamation of Jews and to ensure fair treatment for all U.S. citizens. It advocates state and federal governments' adoption of penalty-enhancement laws and antiparamilitary training statutes to fight hate crimes. It publishes the quarterly *Facts* magazine and distributes reports such as *Hate Crimes Laws: A Comprehensive Guide.*

Artists for a Hate-Free America (AHFA)
PO Box 40146
Portland, OR 97240
(503) 274-9623

AHFA is a nonprofit organization that recruits artists and entertainers to educate audiences about issues concerning bigotry, violence, and censorship. It publishes the *Artists for a Hate-Free America Update.*

Canadian Centre on Racism and Prejudice

CP 505, Succ Desjardins
Montreal, PQ H5B 1B6
CANADA
(514) 727-2936

Affiliated with the Center for Democratic Renewal in Atlanta, Georgia, the Canadian center monitors the activities of white supremacist groups and the development of the far right in Canada. It publishes the bimonthly newsletter *Bulletin.*

Center for Democratic Renewal

PO Box 50469
Atlanta, GA 30302-0469
(404) 221-6614

Formerly known as the National Anti-Klan Network, this nonprofit organization monitors hate group and white supremacist activity in America and opposes bias-motivated violence. It publishes the bimonthly *Monitor* magazine. Its Los Angeles affiliate, People Against Racist Terror (PART), publishes the semimonthly magazine *Turning the Tide.* PART can be reached at PO Box 1990, Burbank, CA 91507-1990; (310) 288-5003.

Center for the Applied Study of Prejudice and Ethnoviolence/The Prejudice Institute

Stephens Hall Annex
Towson State University
Towson, MD 21204-7097
(410) 830-2435

The center studies responses to violence and intimidation motivated by prejudice. It publishes the quarterly newsletter *Forum* as well as numerous books and reports, including *Hate Speech, Ethnoviolence, and the First Amendment on Campus.*

Center for Women Policy Studies (CWPS)

2000 P St. NW, Suite 508
Washington, DC 20036
(202) 872-1770

CWPS supports policy research and advocacy programs on issues such as women's reproductive rights, women's health, and preventing violence against women. It publishes many books and reports, including *Violence Against Women as Bias-Motivated Hate Crime: Defining the Issues.*

Crusade Against Corruption

PO Box 4063
Marietta, GA 30061

This organization advocates measures such as the complete separation of races, outlawing interracial marriages, and banning nonwhite, non-Christian immigration in order to promote a totally white, Christian United States. It publishes numerous pamphlets and a monthly *Crusade Against Corruption* newsletter.

Euro-American Alliance
PO Box 2-1776
Milwaukee, WI 53221
(414) 423-0565

This organization opposes racial mixing and advocates self-segregation for whites. It publishes a number of pamphlets, including *Who Hates Whom?* and *Who We Really Are*.

Feminist Majority
1600 Wilson Blvd., Suite 801
Arlington, VA 22209
(703) 522-2214

This nonprofit research and advocacy organization promotes legislation that combats bias-motivated violence against women. It publishes the quarterly newsletter *Feminist Majority Report*, and its Feminist Majority Foundation publishes reports on clinic violence.

Gay & Lesbian Advocates and Defenders (GLAD)
PO Box 218
Boston, MA 02112
(617) 426-1350

GLAD is a nonprofit civil rights law firm that specializes in gay and lesbian public interest law. It also operates the AIDS Law Project, which represents people who have been affected by HIV-related discrimination. It publishes annual *Anti-Gay/Lesbian Violence* reports and periodic fact sheets.

League for Human Rights of B'nai B'rith Canada
15 Hove St.
Downsview, ON M3H 4Y8
CANADA
(416) 633-6227

Affiliated with the U.S. Anti-Defamation League, this organization works to end the defamation of Jews and to ensure fair treatment for all Canadian citizens. It publishes the annual *Review of Anti-Semitism in Canada*.

Liberty Lobby
300 Independence Ave. SE
Washington, DC 20003
(202) 546-5611

This organization lobbies Congress in support of populist and nationalist positions on a wide variety of issues. It opposes the influence of foreign and domestic special-interest groups on the American government. It publishes the weekly newspaper the *Spotlight*.

National Criminal Justice Reference Service (NCJRS)
U.S. Department of Justice
Box 6000
Rockville, MD 20850
(800) 851-3420

For a nominal fee, the NCJRS provides topical searches and reading lists on many areas of criminal justice, including bias-related violence.

National Gay and Lesbian Task Force (NGLTF)
2320 17th St. NW
Washington, DC 20009
(202) 332-6483

The NGLTF is a civil rights organization that fights bigotry and violence against gays and lesbians. It sponsors conferences and organizes local groups to promote civil rights legislation for gays and lesbians. It publishes the quarterly newsletter *Task Force Report* and distributes reports, fact sheets, and bibliographies on antigay violence.

National Urban League
1111 14th St. NW, 6th Fl.
Washington, DC 20035
(202) 898-1604

A community service agency, the Urban League provides services for minorities who experience discrimination in employment, housing, welfare, and other areas. It publishes the annual *State of Black America* and a discussion paper series that includes *Racially Motivated Violence.*

Northwest Coalition Against Malicious Harassment (NWCAMH)
PO Box 16776
Seattle, WA 98116
(206) 233-9136

This nonprofit organization collects data on incidents of bias-motivated crime and opposes the growth of white supremacist groups in the northwest United States. It sponsors annual conferences and publishes numerous pamphlets as well as the monthly *Northwest Beacon* newsletter.

Resisting Defamation
2530 Berryessa Rd., #616
San Jose, CA 95132
(408) 995-6545

This organization fights stereotypes and discrimination against European Americans. It provides free seminars and publishes a syllabus entitled *Sensitivity Toward European Americans.*

Sojourners
2401 15th St. NW
Washington, DC 20009
(202) 328-8842

Sojourners is an ecumenical Christian organization committed to racial justice and reconciliation between races. It publishes *America's Original Sin: A Study Guide on White Racism* as well as the monthly *Sojourners* magazine.

Southern Poverty Law Center/Klanwatch Project
PO Box 2087
Montgomery, AL 36102
(205) 264-0286

The center litigates civil cases to protect the rights of poor people, particularly when those rights are threatened by white supremacist groups. The affiliated Klanwatch Project and the Militia Task Force collect data on white supremacist groups and militias and promote the adoption and enforcement by states of antiparamilitary training laws. The center publishes numerous books and reports as well as the monthly *Klanwatch Intelligence Report*.

U.S. Commission on Civil Rights
1121 Vermont Ave. NW
Washington, DC 20425
(202) 376-8177

A fact-finding body, the commission reports directly to Congress and the president on the effectiveness of equal opportunity programs and laws. A catalog of its numerous publications, which include reports on white supremacist activities throughout the country, can be obtained from its Publication Management Division.

White Aryan Resistance
PO Box 65
Fallbrook, CA 92088
(800) 923-1813

This organization promotes white superiority and political action on behalf of white workers. It publishes the monthly *WAR* newspaper, produces the *Race and Reason* television show, distributes "white power" music recordings, and maintains a racial news and information hotline.

Index